monsoonbooks

STIR-FRIED AND NOT SHAKEN

Singapore's favourite cookbook author, TV chef and food writer Terry Tan was born during the Japanese Occupation when Singapore was not Singapore but Syonanto. By the time he'd learnt to spell Syonanto it was back to being Singapore. Confusion reigned until Terry found how to make sense of the world through words and food. Schooled in the art of Nonya cooking and trained in broadcast journalism, Terry is the author of over twenty cookbooks, former Editor-in-Chief and, at time of press, Editor-at-Large of *Wine & Dine* magazine. He has also been a schoolteacher, chef, broadcaster, journalist, copywriter and food consultant.

After forty years in Singapore, Terry relocated to London, where he continues to represent Singapore as its unofficial food ambassador. This trip down Singapore's memory lane is rich with the author's comic patter and wry observations. And flying fox curry.

STIR-FRIED AND NOT SHAKEN

TERRY TAN

monsoon

monsoonbooks

Published in 2008
by Monsoon Books Pte Ltd
52 Telok Blangah Road
#03-05 Telok Blangah House
Singapore 098829
www.monsoonbooks.com.sg

ISBN: 978-981-08-0705-4

Tan, Terry.
Stir-fried and not shaken / Terry Tan. – Singapore : Monsoon Books,
2008.
p. cm.
ISBN-13 : 978-981-08-0705-4 (pbk.)
1. Tan, Terry. 2. Cooks – Singapore – Biography. I. Title.
TX649
641.5092 -- dc22 OCN232074784

Printed in Singapore

12 11 10 09 08   1 2 3 4 5 6 7 8 9

Introduction

As you turn the pages of this book that has been gestating for more than twenty years, a passage of time that I spent mulling over my six decades and tickling my funny bone, I hope you find moments of mirth and poignancy that match those of your memory bank. I honestly do not know why I chuckle at the worst possible moments of life's many treadmills, but as the saying goes, laughter is the best medicine, and if you find something to laugh about in the morning, the rest of the day takes care of itself. A philosopher I am not, but it is far better to laugh than steep yourself in negative juices that only put more lines on your face. Heaven knows, the lines on my face resemble a map of the London Underground. Call them what you may—laughter lines, ageing crevices or plain dying skin—but they are at least a crinkly indication that there is still fire in the grate, even if there's snow on the roof. Forgive the occasional blurring of the years; trends are not necessarily dictated by calendar phases and my endorphins have dwindled somewhat. This book is dedicated to all who have lived through the same eras as I, as well as those who have not but still find my chronicles amusing enough to provoke a chuckle or two.

1940s

Japanese Occupation

I was born on 27th September 1942, not exactly a pleasant moment to arrive in a world turned upside down by the Japanese invasion of the little British colony of Singapore. Actually it was the Japanese fighter planes that were upside down and every which way as they bombed the bejesus out of our pleasant island. I never actually saw any aerial battles or bombing missions, but when I was old enough to understand that there was something terrible going on, I asked many questions of my mother: 'When is the next plane coming?' 'Are they going to bomb us?' 'Can I watch the bombing?'

The only answer I got was a clout on the ear from Mother who intimated that I would bring even more bad luck with my morbid sense of doom. I was only curious, as any toddler would be living amid the kind of violence that kids today can only watch on television or experience through computer games.

It all began on 8th December 1941, when the Japanese megalomania went into overdrive and they invaded Malaya with an amphibious assault on the northeast coast of the peninsula at Kota Bahru. The wily Japanese had already coerced the Thai government into letting them use Thai military bases to launch their attacks into Malaya, after having fought Thai troops for eight hours early in the morning. While the Imperial Japanese Army was well trained and focused into narrow-eyed concentration, the British and Allied Forces were wide-eyed with unawareness of the situation and not exactly primed for defence.

There were Allied fighter squadrons already based in Malaya but they had poorly built equipment and war planes, few spare parts, insufficient support staff and an incoherent command structure.

British offensive aircraft were decrepit or obsolete, and were quickly destroyed by Japanese fighter planes in the air and on the ground. By mid-January the Japanese had reached Johore.

On 7th February 1942 they landed on Pulau Ubin and strafed Changi from there.

My grandfather, who had a few coconut plantations in the area, later told us that the Japanese had ground his coconuts into milk. I dared to ask if that was why Grandmother used so much coconut milk in her cooking, which earned me a thwack on my head. The next day the Japanese sneaked in from the northwest, and furious hand-to-hand fighting took place. By the morning of 10th February, they had secured a foothold on the island.

There was some resistance from the Indian Army and several British Army battalions but it was a futile attempt. The Japanese had even used bicycle infantry overland through terrain that hampered heavy vehicles. They had really done their homework and it was humiliating to know that we had been overcome by an enemy on bicycles! Grandfather was heard to say he wouldn't have been surprised if they had used trishaws as well, as it was the Japanese who brought this mode of transport to Singapore in the early twentieth century. Can you imagine a trishaw being armed with an ack-ack gun? Eventually the Allied Forces and the British surrendered unconditionally on 15th February. The rest is history that most Singaporeans would rather forget.

Syonanto

If I could turn back the clock, it would have to be a made-in-Japan timepiece. Come to think of it, we were to become awash with made-in-Japan appliances for the next few decades. You couldn't turn on a fan, rice cooker or transistor radio that was not made in Japan. You see, I was actually born in a part of Japan that probably few can, or wish to, remember today. But I wasn't allowed to forget. Every time I applied for anything remotely resembling a job, I had to present my birth certificate as documentary evidence of my existence. This decaying, almost putrid piece of yellowed paper still reads: 'Date of birth: 27th September 1942, Syonanto.'

Once, in London, when I had to present this same certificate for a legal matter, I was asked if I'd been born in one of the Polynesian islands! Perhaps it was my full Chinese name of Tan Kim Tho that prompted this line of questioning. 'Was it something of a clan thing then?' the official asked, as if everyone born in Syonanto would have a name ending with the same consonant.

We can thank Buddha the Japanese did not name their new colony Ajinomoto. And if they had not been routed by the end of 1945, we would be eating shabu shabu, teppanyaki and sashimi instead of our beloved hawker fare. This would have been a fate worse than death, no? I had other problems too. My family had this peculiar penchant for inventing nicknames. My genealogy was really stir-fried—and not just shaken—to confusion. Maybe Mother was fed up to her betel-nut-stained teeth with dragging me and my two brothers around during numerous evacuations from bomb shelter to bomb shelter. During the formative years of my life, I really believed my name was Jepun Kia (Japanese waif).

When I was old enough to feel the prick of verbal chastisement, I bore the onerous belief that I had been found in a dustbin as an abandoned Japanese orphan. A bundle of joy I was not, for the slightest whimper from me would evoke a hissing retort from Mother. 'Quiet, you weeping devil, or I will give you back to the Japanese.'

She grumbled that it was bad enough having to carry me through such difficult times without me rewarding her with bad behaviour. So the threats came fast and thick. It wasn't just Mother who had this knack but other mothers too, as I have heard many a time even today. Why do we have such a punitive philosophy about bringing up children? Like if a child wandered into a dark room, he would be told the devil would catch him. If you didn't finish the rice on your plate, you would end up with a pock-marked wife. Or if I cut my fingernails at night, I would release devils, for underneath each nail lived some unmentionable spirit itching to get out. For years afterwards I didn't dare indulge in nocturnal manicures. Even today I am still not totally comfortable in a darkened room and cannot sleep without at least a night light. In every gloomy corner, it seemed, lurked some ghoul or other, especially dead Japanese soldiers.

As for the Japanese-waif threat, long afterwards I could not walk past a dustbin without feeling a squeamish sense of deja vu. In truth, Japanese soldiers during the post-war years—many stayed back right through to the 1950s—were not too pugnacious out of uniform. One small group had laid claim to a house next door to ours, and from our upstairs side balcony we could see them going about their peacetime activities.

Father even learnt to speak fairly good Japanese, but the only words I learnt in later years were *banzai* and *hara-kiri*. The former was a war cry meaning 'attack' and the latter was employed by the Japanese who preferred to commit suicide than be dishonoured. *Banzai* became a favourite word among my childhood friends whenever we played war games, but no one committed *hara-kiri*, to the best of my knowledge.

There was one disconcerting thing, however. A few Japanese were in the habit of walking around their forecourt wearing T-shaped loincloths, similar to those that sumo wrestlers wear. Some even took to bathing at public standpipes, of which there were several dotted along the road on which we lived. These were meant for the fire brigade but the Japanese, obsessed with cleanliness, would spend a long time sitting on small stools, sluicing themselves with buckets of water, cleansing their near-naked bodies in full view of the neighbourhood.

They were pretty nonchalant about it all but Mother made my three sisters look and act like boys. Their hair was shorn, they were made to wear trousers and ordered to behave like boys, or else it would be a fate worse than death. They were also warned never to go near any public standpipe or they would end up as handmaidens of the soldiers. In secret, my two sisters would whisper to each other about how well-endowed the soldiers were, as when their loincloths were soaked, their manhood would be clearly visible. If Mother had heard these whispers, she would have been horrified enough to lock my sisters in our attic.

It didn't happen, thank goodness, but it was a few years before my sisters were allowed to look like girls again. As young boys we were still terrified of the unknown; war stories told around the dinner table were scary, to say the least. Many people's houses had been bombed, and as many had lost their lives. Even though the war was over, we still looked over our shoulders, or rather, over our balcony.

There was some social interaction though, really to placate the soldiers so they wouldn't let their rampaging hormones spill over to my sisters. Mother occasionally cooked curries and *sambals* and offered them to the soldiers, and we were, in turn, introduced to sushi and endless pickles. If American GIs could not fight without their beloved Coke, the Japanese would rather have committed *hara-kiri* than go without their pickles. I don't think they liked *sambal belacan* as upon tasting some, they curled their lips in disgust. The departing Imperial Army did give us another memento that is still in my brother's possession. It was a war relic, a samurai sword no less, I swear, and it had bloodstains on the blade. We used to play with it until Mother put a stop to it.

And so the 1940s rolled on. Peace reigned and we were less twitchy after the soldiers were ordered by their superiors to return home. If they had stayed on, there would probably now be a sushi bar or two in our neighbourhood. There were plenty of reasons to celebrate after liberation, and bonfires were lit with some trepidation. There was a crackly reason for this.

During the occupation, the Japanese had printed, willy-nilly, their own currency with tropical designs of banana trees. These banana notes became utterly useless tender and we had baskets of them. I remember my parents' discomfort at incinerating hundreds and thousands of banana yen. Privately, Father had said they might come in useful one day if the Japanese were to return. But the British instructions were quite stringent: destroy them or we would be regarded as dissidents. My brothers and I managed to keep a few in secret and we made paper boats out of them for play. We would sink them in rain-swollen monsoon drains shouting '*Banzai*!' as each was swallowed by the murky water. This was our soggy contribution to the war effort.

Chin Peng, the Guerilla

Some unpleasant situations also arose after the war had ended. During the war, a bunch of guys had formed guerrilla units so they could fight back. They lived mostly in the Malayan jungle, frequently instigating skirmishes on Japanese camps. After the war, for some inexplicable reason, they refused to return to civilian life and became turncoats, chafing at the bit against British colonialism. Singapore was still part of the Malayan Peninsula and the threat to Singaporeans now came from a different quarter.

One such personage was the Secretary-General of the Malayan Communist Party, Mr Chin Peng. He was born in Sitiawan, Perak, in 1921 and his father ran a small bicycle shop. Rumour has it that he sold his bicycles to the Japanese when they mounted their two-wheeler units, but this has never been proven and was probably a vicious rumour to besmear Chin Peng. He joined the Party in 1940 and became the leader of the 5th regiment of the Malayan People's

Anti-Japanese Army. He liaised with British officers of Special Operations Executive Far East and was later awarded an OBE.

After the British defeated the Japanese forces in 1945, Chin Peng became frustrated with the Party's slow progress and eventually abandoned the 'united front' strategy in favour of armed struggle. The British declared a State of Emergency which would last until 1960. The Communists adopted Maoist techniques, deploying between 4,000 and 5,000 guerrilla fighters, supported by a network of food and intelligence gatherers, in order to undermine colonialism and establish liberated areas.

After failing to gain recognition after many years of political negotiations, and starved of supplies by the British counter-insurgency forces, he returned to the Thai border in 1955. They launched sporadic incursions but this Cold War ended in 1989 and Chin Peng was last heard of as recently as 2006 to be living in Southern Thailand. Selling bicycles no doubt, one wag commented.

During these years it was unsafe to visit Malaya, but one time Father took my second sister with him on one of his frequent visits to Endau, where he had interests in a sawmill. His jeep was attacked, probably by Chin Peng's henchmen, and flipped over. Father escaped unscathed but my sister suffered a deep gash to her left arm.

She still bears the scars today. As she was First Mother's daughter, and therefore our half-sister, there was little love lost between Mother and her. I shall not go into the many battles of will between them as it was all so long ago, and we do get along with our half-sister today who is in her eighties. My mother had a smug smile or two on her face when my half-sister came home in a bloody mess, and she used this as means to threaten us: if we ever dared to go on such a trip, we would end up in the same way or worse.

We didn't, else I wouldn't have been able to write this book.

My Father, the Monkey's Uncle ...

I guess it would have been marginally better to be likened to an anorexic ghost than a monkey. This strange twist of the tongue could be a lifetime's bane. My father's parents had named him Tan Ah Kau, the reasons for which had been lost in the mists of antiquity somewhere in Banjarmasin, South Kalimantan, Borneo. We knew nothing of our paternal antecedents as Father had stowed away as a young lad of ten or eleven in a trader's junk to come to Singapore to seek his fortune. By the time he had made his fortune in several enterprises, he was ready to take a wife or two.

Mother never ceased to moan about how unfortunate she was to be married to a man sight unseen, and to top things off she was his secondary wife. Till the day he shed his mortal coils, he was Lau Kau (Old Monkey) to her. But for the difference in tonal pronunciations, his name could have been Old Dog. But, no. In the Swatow dialect, *kau* means more monkey than mongrel. It never seemed to bother Father none, not even when the whole community in which we lived referred to him as Kau Peh (Monkey Uncle). The belief that we are descended from apes is not that improbable after all.

There was another reason for the monkey tag. On one of his trips, Father brought back a baby monkey as a house pet. It had orange hair and we kept it on a long leash until it became very tame. I called him Jeremy and would often show him off to my classmates. Jeremy became very attached to me and would cling to my neck, whimpering like a baby when frightened. I don't know what breed of monkey he was but he was really cute, especially when First Mother made him a little pink dress in satin. But whenever we dressed him in it, Jeremy would claw at it in protest.

I told First Mother that Jeremy was a boy monkey and probably objected to being dressed like a girl. Actually it was the satin that irritated him, and was crinkly and scratchy where First Mother had made ruffles. Sadly, one night during a storm Jeremy must have been frightened out of his wits as we'd forgotten to bring him in from his cage that we'd placed on our balcony. I found him cold and dead the next morning and we buried him in our back yard with full ceremony. I had him for about three years.

And thus we earned this primate progeny taunt, all of us bearing the brunt of cruel jibes by the neighbourhood children. We grew up trailing in the wake of childishly spiteful monkey remarks. First I had been called Jepun Kia (Japanese waif), then Kau Kia Tee (Little Monkey's Brother on account of Jeremy), neither of which I particularly thrived on.

I had a brief eight years with Father for he died before I reached my ninth year. It could have been ninety years for all the wonderful memories he bestowed on us during his brief sojourn on Earth.

...and His Testosterone

Several things about my father still live in my memory: he liked women, gold and castor oil. For his penchant for the first, he bore the brunt of my mother's and his principal wife's regular wrath. Whether it was by tradition or choice, Mother paid due respect to the latter, who was always referred to as First Mother. No, she was not the mother of a president but we and the grandchildren had to differentiate between them. The penchant for nicknames came to an 'udder' pinnacle, and for some imponderable reason Father addressed Mother as 'Mother Cow'.

I shudder to think what friends and schoolmates thought about our family menagerie. Still, Mother received the affection of the community as a Nonya lady of munificent culinary skills. As for his fondness for the ladies, we knew only of Father's indiscretions during his frequent absences, ostensibly to play mahjong. In truth—and I can bear this out with impunity—he was off having it off with some painted sing-song lady or off-duty cabaret girl. That Father made me privy to his philandering was probably due to paternal guilt.

There was a Teochew business association house near where we lived called Chwee Huay Lim. Father used to take me there sometimes. Businessmen would gather there to chew the fat about their enterprises. Actually, it was much more than business matters they chewed on. Amid the raucous blend of clacking mahjong tiles and animated chatter about rice and rubber prices were the tinkling voices of women who, to my childish mind, looked like painted dolls with red talons and vermilion lips. They seemed to do no more than lean heavily on old men's shoulders, and in between cracking melon seeds they would tickle the ears of whichever man they were clinging on to.

I cannot now recall which one of these 'aunties' was Father's favourite, probably because during these long mahjong sessions, Father would send requests to the cavernous kitchen wherein several sweaty cooks were forever stirring or frying in huge woks. Thus I was fed endless rounds of *char kway teow*, chicken macaroni soup, red bean soup, duck porridge, red bean paste cakes and many more dishes that I do not remember. What I do remember through the haze caused by dyspepsia is not worth remembering. Father displayed all the shrewdness of his primate characteristics, as each time I could never identify his particular painted trollop, even when I got home to Mother's threats to spill the beans. What I did spill was more of the regurgitated variety, due to a surfeit of red bean paste cakes.

However, I do have one vague memory of a lady who not only gleamed from her fingernails but from her mouth too. She was always the one lingering closest to Father. I remember the sun's rays bouncing off her two incisor teeth when she smiled—which was often, especially when Father fondled her lustrous hair. She wore gold on her wrists, neck, ankles and earlobes. I never actually saw Father giving her the jewellery but the conversations I overheard amongst the gold-bedecked ladies were peppered with references to Poh Heng and Meng Heng. They were not names of their children or gynaecologists, for sure. It was only much later, when I was in my teens, that I discovered them to be goldsmiths along North and South Bridge Roads.

There were brief interludes during mahjong breaks when Father and the other men would fish wads of notes from their pockets and press them into their ladies' perfumed palms. The delighted recipients would squeal, tinkle with merry laughter and disappear en masse for a few hours, only to return with even more jangling gold hanging from their cheongsam-clad bodies.

Of Trousers and Sarongs

The never-ending dilemma for the younger generation of my family was how to address our two matriarchs, especially in later years when they themselves had grandchildren. It would have been confusing to refer to both as Ah Ma, or Grandmother, in all the local dialects. So it came to pass that one would be Grandmother With Trousers, and the other would be Grandmother Without Trousers. The translation of this can be rather risqué: Cheng Kor Ah Ma and Bo Cheng Kor Ah Ma in Hokkien. First Mother always used to wear a pair of black cotton or silk trousers and a white *samfoo* top. My mother's regulation gear was, without fail, a sarong and *kebaya*, the typical dress of traditional Indonesian and Malay women.

These unflattering honorific titles stuck with both women all their lives but there is further reason for my mother's trouserless state. Nonya women of a certain age did not see the need for underwear as they rarely left the house. Such modest cover was deemed unnecessary in the home so Mother only had a few pairs of cotton shorts. I say this without any snide mirth, for it was true. She would only wear a pair of these shorts if she went out, which was usually to the wet market. This knickerless state was truly a Nonya tradition, at least in my family.

Actually, wearing a sarong was not exclusive to the female domain. Practically every off-work Malay man wore one as well, but not the ones with ornate batik designs. Men's sarongs were inevitably bold checks in muted colours (they still are) and when I was growing up it was popular to wear them to sleep in. Till this day I do not wear pyjamas to bed, and have in my wardrobe two checked sarongs that I wear during the warmer months, or when I visit my home in Penang. Sarongs are most versatile for you can whip one up and wrap it around your shoulders to ward off wind—with underwear on, of course—or let it down to cover your ankles. It is also useful as a mat for when you go to the beach, as a tablecloth, although perhaps not expedient, and even as a child's cradle suspended from a spring attached to a strong rope fixed to a ceiling. Many of the babies in my family were coddled this way, and it was believed to be extremely comforting as the sarong cradle simulates the closeness of the womb. Alas, by the 1960s sarongs rapidly became passé as they were not considered to be garments conducive to the fast-paced life of working women, Nonya or otherwise.

Adoption

After the war, many children had been made orphans and adoption was commonplace. At that time it was largely a process derived from compassion and less about legal parameters, compared with today's adoption laws. There was no bureaucracy involved and there were no watchdogs. If a child needed parents and if a couple wanted one, some money changed hands, the child was taken in by the new family and that was that.

Most of the time orphaned babies and even older children were taken in not by childless couples, but by those who felt sympathetic or wanted a larger family.

However, there were also more traditional and less humane reasons behind people wishing to adopt. Many migrant Chinese women, who'd left behind their mother country, were used to having what was then called *mui tsai* (Cantonese for 'slave girls'). These women were not necessarily middle class or of the social elite; they simply subscribed to the age-old practice of having such indentured handmaidens. (Janet Lim's book *Sold for Silver*, published by Monsoon Books, deals with this issue.)

For these unfortunate orphaned girls it was to be a life of toiling servitude—slavery if you like, whichever way you cut it. Some local Singaporean old-school ladies, though not migrants, were also persuaded by their mahjong cronies to get themselves one of these babies or, better yet, an older girl to be at their beck and call. This brought a social cachet that would be considered criminal today but it happened a lot. I truly believe this term 'handmaidens' came about because these little girls were made to endlessly pummel the backs of their mistresses to alleviate imagined aches and pains.

I saw this happen within the families of some of my relatives. Even in my own family, for my mother adopted two girls: a one-month-old baby from a fisherman's wife from Siglap; and a much older girl under circumstances I shall mention later. The baby's father had recently died leaving his sick and ailing wife with six children, ranging in age from one month to ten years old.

At first I thought Mother had adopted the baby out of pity, but lurking not far behind her seemingly humane decision was the fact that she was looking for someone to tend to her in her old age. This was explained to us in a way that seemed acceptable enough, given the fact that the baby would probably have otherwise had a wretched life. So she came, a sickly bundle of pink with her head covered in cradle cap. When she was old enough, we forced Mother to send her to school, a decision that Mother probably wouldn't have made without coercion. We could not condone this kind of slavery. She is now fifty-five and, I'm happy to say, a contented wife and mother of a pretty daughter. She never took our family surname but retained her own family name of Lim.

Other adopted girls—rarely boys as male progeny were too precious, however poor families might have been—were not so lucky. In later years I heard many horror stories about these slave girls who were treated abominably. They were no more than chattel, tending to the every need of their madams. They were not paid and lived Cinderella-like lives with no hope of a Prince Charming coming to their rescue. They cooked, cleaned and generally slaved from sunrise to sunset and were never sent to school. Some were even abused by the sons of the family but they had little recourse for complaint. When they got too old to be of use, these girls were simply shunted to one side or married off to the first desperate man looking for a wife.

As for my other adopted sister, she was about twelve when she was brought to our attention by her former neighbour. Her family home had been bombed by the Japanese and her parents killed. She was illiterate and homeless. Mother took her in out of pity and she was useful as another pair of hands.

When she was seventeen, probably due as much to raging hormones as seeing her future as bleak, she ran away from our home to become a prostitute. We did not know she'd taken up this profession until a neighbour chanced upon Ah Muay, as she had been named, somewhere in Jalan Besar.

'Ayoh, I saw her standing in a back alley in Desker Road and she was a *pai char bo* (bad woman or hooker). Such shame on your family,' gloated the neighbour, clearly in her element.

My mother was utterly mortified and we were never again allowed to mention her name or try to see her. Many years later I chanced upon Ah Muay on the beach at Tanah Merah. There she was, as large as life. By then she was in her late thirties, and was with a man who appeared to be either her partner, husband or lover.

I said hello and was quite keen to catch up with her after more than two decades. I discovered she had married, had several children and her husband was a taxi driver. When I asked if she was okay, she smiled and showed me her arm decked with many gold bangles. She did not have to say anything and I didn't probe further. I haven't seen her since.

My Sex Education

When Ah Muay was growing up, she was a kind older sister and was often up to her wanton tricks. She would flirt with all the neighbourhood boys and once told me that she felt strange urges and wanted to meet men. She had an overt sexuality that could be unsettling. My mother called her 'itchy', a term generally reserved for girls of a carnal bent.

Our neighbours were a Eurasian family and one of the sons, a boy called Jerry, used to make unsavoury remarks about Ah Muay whenever she passed by their home. Taunted thus for many months, she got her own back one day in full measure. Jerry was passing by our home on his way to school when she sneaked up behind him, pulled up her *samfoo* top and pressed his now-quivering face into her ample bosom. He ran home shrieking but never offended her again.

In an obtuse way, she gave me and my brothers the kind of sex education you could not obtain in any classroom or back alley, going into extremely graphic detail about her menstrual cycles or her 'itchiness' ad nauseam. She was my Masters and Johnson, if you like.

Talking of back alleys, my sex education was to continue during my secondary-school days. I attended Beatty Secondary School, off Serangoon Road, and my daily trudge to school took in a short cut via the unsavoury part of Jalan Besar. There were many back alleys in the area where hookers plied their trade. My daily journey also passed a makeshift coffee stall, and even at the ungodly hour of seven in the morning, some of the women would be having coffee and breakfast, probably after finishing their night's business.

They were wicked and would call out to me in their gin-cracked voices, making suggestive remarks and gestures. I was so nervous that I persuaded a neighbour's son, who was in the same school, to walk with me along this route. Years later, this street called Desker Road would become synonymous with the sex trade, and every mention would send us pubescent boys into sniggering fits of laughter.

My Personal Barber

Some people brag about their personal trainer and the *chi chi* set have their personal shopper. For most of my childhood I had a personal barber. Until the age of seven I never went to a barber because my barber came to me, so there! He was called Muthu, a tall, Indian gentleman with a debonair manner. He always wore a spotless white *dhoti* and tunic, and a pair of leather sandals. In one hand he'd carry a leather case containing his barber's tools, and in the other a rolled up black umbrella.

He had the knack of knowing exactly when my father, brothers and I needed to have our hair cut. For one thing, we never found out where he lived and we had no telephone, let alone hand phones. Like clockwork he would turn up on our doorstep every so often and cut the family's crops. When he'd finished, he would spend a few minutes giving us a hefty back massage, then whip off the protective cotton wrap-around and powder our necks. All for fifty cents each.

Sometime in the early 1950s he left for India for good, but not before visiting our house to say goodbye and coyly suggest we give him a going-away present. Actually, he specified watches, and not one but several to give to his sons and daughters. It was only then that we found out he had left his family back home in Tamil Nadu so he could earn a living in Singapore. Such dedication and discipline are rare today, and I can still see his face in my mind's eye. I cannot help but smile when I read about superstars paying their personal hairdressers thousands of dollars just for one haircut. Where are you, Muthu?

Our Personal Milkman

No, we did not have a milk cart pass by our door each week. We had a personal milkman, even if he was just a Punjabi who'd lead his cow to our doorstep every week. We got our milk rations straight from the udder. Mother loved milk, and as we waited he would flip out his three-legged stool, perch on it and proceed to milk his placid bovine. The milk was expressed into a small tin pail then transferred to a glass jug. Mother would then gently boil it for hygiene reasons. The cowherd's hands were none too clean to look at, but at least we got fresh milk, such that you do not get today.

Sometimes we would persuade him to let us try the milking and he would comply, albeit unwillingly. I would give him an extra ten cents (each jug of milk cost thirty cents but it was enough for three or four glasses). My attempts at milking were clumsy and often only resulted in viscous dribbles. It required a certain knack and you had to massage the udder a little before tugging at the teats. It was fun, but messy.

Some years later the cowherd sold his cow and began to turn up with a goat! Mother did not like switching her drink, and the rather mangy goat had a peculiar gleam in its eyes every time they stopped by. The milkman stopped coming when tinned milk—Bear Brand, I remember—could be bought from the local shop. At other times we had to depend on condensed milk for our coffee. We never drank tea with milk, but condensed milk became rather a vile spread on sandwiches, something I still loath to this day.

Soaps and Scents

During my childhood, bath products ran the gamut from bars of carbolic soap to latter ones called Sunlight and Ayam. Mother would cut a square from each bar and this was all the cleanser we had. It was really rough on the skin and smelled like medicine. There was little else available, and we even used the same soap for laundry. It was only years later that we had scented soaps like Palmolive and Lux, two brands that became iconic.

As for toothpaste, it came in little round tins and was coloured pink. I cannot remember the brand name, but it was slightly minty and you had to scrape it with your toothbrush before using it. Mother had her own formula that I never understood. We used wood as fuel to cook with, and after the wood had turned to fine, grey ash, Mother would collect the top layer to use as her toothpaste! She didn't even bother with a toothbrush, but instead found a twig the thickness of a finger, bashed in one end to form a rough brush and from then on cleaned her teeth with it. It must have taken off a layer of her gums but she did it for years.

Years later we were able to buy branded products like Darkie and Kolynos. The former was taken off shelves worldwide in the 1970s for being politically incorrect, but someone cleverly put out a similar brand under the name of Darlie. The objection was to the picture of a black man in a top hat, like something out of *The Black and White Minstrel Show*.

Perfumes, only imported ones, were expensive and hard to come by but Mother and my aunts were adept at making their own infusions. It was my job to go round the neighbourhood and hunt for highly scented blossoms like jasmine and other tropical flowers. Mother and my aunts would steep them in a mixture of rose-water then boil the liquid for a few minutes. This would then be put outdoors—to catch the dew, Mother said—overnight, then strained through thin muslin.

The Nonya ladies would anoint themselves with this lightly scented perfume whenever they went out.

Some years later I found a little bottle that I mistook for some sort of perfume. I dabbed it on my neck and nearly fainted from the uric odour. It was smelling salts, meant to revive someone who has fainted. I had done the reverse, to my gagging discomfort! I later found out it was called *beh jio,* which literally translates as 'horse urine'. In actual fact it was a highly concentrated ammonia. I never raided Mother's dressing table again.

She also had a veritable collection of strange creams and lotions, but the one she'd had the longest was something given to her by a Malay neighbour. It was an ointment called Tonic Chap Gajah (Elephant Brand Tonic) but I never knew whether it was supposed to be drunk or rubbed onto the skin. Mother had accepted it out of politeness but had never used it.

For her muscular aches and pains she relied on something called Pak Fa Yeow (White Flower Ointment) that was very popular. It was a pungent oil that you rubbed onto any part of your body that ached. Once, I had a stuffy nose and used it, to my chagrin. My skin started to feel like it was burning and I had to wash the oil off using gallons of water.

The universal panacea in our home were Zambuk and Tiger Balm, both of which still exist today. Sometimes Mother would buy a bottle of what looked like wine but it had a snake in it! Apparently she would use it for her aching joints and it lay behind her bed for years. It looked horrid and smelled awful. I never knew what the snake was for, but she insisted it did her a power of good. Even today men in China drink snake bile in the hope of acquiring endless virility, so there must have been a reason for this serpentine wine.

Mother used to have frequent massages from a Malay neighbour called Wak Wak, who was a grandmother trying to earn pocket money. Whether the weekly rubs she gave Mother worked or not,

I never knew, but she was practically a permanent feature in our house. At other times she would come bearing this or that home-made ointment and persuade Mother to let her use them on us. As a result, Mother's bedroom always smelled like a dispensary. Wak Wak had weird home cures you wouldn't believe.

When one of us suffered from skin ailments like ringworm, which was often in my case, she would suggest home cures that amounted to torture. Ringworm was the bane of my childhood on account of the fact that I often played barefoot outdoors. The symptoms were extremely itchy soles peppered with tiny dents.

Once, Wak Wak suggested that I take the thorny branch of a rose tree and scrape the soles of my feet with it. Mother believed her and subjected my feet to the most excruciating pain. All I got were bloody feet but the ringworm soon subsided, making Mother more respectful of Wak Wak's cures.

When I contracted ringworm on my groin, probably from being unwashed most of the time, she rubbed an oily, gritty substance on it that made me wince. First of all it was in a very sensitive and private area, and secondly the substance was apparently a mixture of ash, ginger and powdered sulphur. I found out years later that sulphur is the best treatment for ringworm. The ash and ground ginger did absolutely nothing except make me pong like a wet market. Where this woman learned her herbal skills from, I never knew. Probably some village witch doctor or *dukun*. It is probably the reason why *lor kun* means 'doctor' in Hokkien, its derivation most telling!

Betel Nuts and Other Stains

Mother herself often looked like she had been in a bloody battle as her lips were always stained a flaming red from the endless chewing of *sirih*. This was a favourite Nonya addiction, much like smoking, and Mother would wrap these little leaves with a mixture of ground betel nut, gambier and a smidgeon of white lime. She chewed them day and night, staining not only her lips but her teeth and gums as well. This was supposed to be a mark of Nonya beauty but I doubt that Father considered it alluring, given the fact that he was attracted to other red lips that were the result of lipstick, but more of that later.

All of Mother's cronies and my aunts enjoyed this habit, and each would never be far from a little enamel spittoon, used solely for the purpose of spitting gobs of red juice caused by chewing. It was a custom practised by early Polynesians thousands of years ago, which then filtered down to India and became common among Hindus in Thailand, Indonesia, Vietnam and Myanmar. The Malay word for betel nut is *pinang*, after which the Malaysian island of Penang is named.

Considered an auspicious ingredient by Hindus, the betel nut is used along with the betel leaf in religious ceremonies and also as a social offering to guests. Betel nuts are chewed mainly as a euphoric stimulant, attributed to the presence of psychoactive alkaloids. Chewing betel nuts is believed to increase the capacity to work but more importantly it is a cultural activity much like drinking coffee.

Mother would cut her betel nuts with a sharp pair of secateurs called *sarota,* made specially for the purpose. She would then wrap the shavings in a betel leaf along with lime and sometimes cloves and cardamoms for extra flavouring. This was more a Hindu practice. It was common after chewing to swipe the mouth with a ball of loose tobacco, and I saw that most of my Nonya relatives would have one of these balls sticking out from their mouths. I never understood the purpose but it was de rigueur among them, whether they were simply chatting or playing mahjong.

Each Nonya had a special container for all the paraphernalia and it was usually made of lacquered wood or brass. I still have in my possession Mother's brass thingy that is a treasured keepsake.

Nonyas were also seen with a square of batik cloth, like a large handkerchief pinned to their sleeves purely for wiping their mouths. These would be stained red over the years but they were an important item in Nonya fashion. As for the spittoons, they are very much a collector's item today and you can still find them in antique shops in Katong, Malacca and Penang. They are no more than the size of a large coffee mug and many are beautifully enameled with motifs of birds and flowers in brilliant green, red and yellow.

Strangely, though, my grandmother did not indulge in the same habit but was fond of her hand-rolled cigarettes. When she became blind with glaucoma in later years, she would ask one of her grandchildren to roll them for her. I blame it squarely on her for starting me smoking when she came to live with us in the late 1950s. Of course I rolled her cigarettes but could not resist smoking the odd one. Actually, the main reason why Mother asked her to come and live with us was because she nearly set fire to Grandfather's house several times.

She would sleep on a large platform and, being nearly blind by then, would often simply stub out her still-smouldering cigarette butts on her mattress. Once, the mattress caught fire and if it had happened at night when everyone was asleep, she would have gone up in smoke. Whenever she smoked at our home, Mother would make sure she had one of her little spittoons on standby just in case Grandmother did her usual sightless and mindless stubbing.

Perky Memories

My memoirs are not really to chronicle the horrors of war or its aftermath; we know enough about this today given that every day, somewhere in the world, atrocities are being perpetrated in the name of one cause or another. I prefer to perpetuate happier memories instead. When you are six or seven, life does not rest on gloom and doom but rather on the brighter moments, on the perks and highlights, however small they may be. One such perk came in the form of an unexplained aunt to whom we would run for comfort and sustenance.

We had any number of such relatives, for many had fled their homes in Malaya and elsewhere in Singapore, and had come to live with us. It was meant to be temporary but a few stayed on for years afterwards as their own homes no longer existed. In more than one comforting sense, our family was really extended as there could be as many as twelve people living under the same roof. This unexplained aunt had a son of her own, born around the same time as me.

She was motherly, buxom of stature and a prolific milk producer. Mother was too distraught to breast-feed (what with constantly having to evacuate during bombings) and was only too glad someone else could take on the duty to lactate. 'Aunty Milk Bar', as we were to call her in later years when she reminded us of her milky largesse, would chide us often: 'Humph, if it had not been for my milk you would have become a skinny devil.' See what I mean about nicknames?

She was also something of an expert in home remedies and we were subjected to many holistic treatments that were sometimes successful but more often foul and reeked. If any child suffered colic or stomach ailments, she would grind shallots and ginger and heat the mess in a muslin bag. This would then be unceremoniously slapped on the patient's belly, and he or she had to endure the ignominy of walking around smelling of burnt onions. It happened to me more times than I care to remember.

This aunty had a cure for everything, even dog bites! In our neighbourhood there were many mangy strays that we would often torment, only to earn a bite or two on our ankles and derrières. Once when it happened to me—honestly, today I am an avid dog lover but I was an ignorant eleven-year-old then—I ran home shrieking and clutching my behind, that now had a small chunk missing. Aunty

Milk Bar leapt into action and hurriedly heated up some rice that she promptly slapped onto my wound. The rice quickly became a blood-soaked lump. She exhorted me to feed the guilty dog with it. 'Why, for heaven's sake?' I asked between sobs.

'You silly idiot, don't you know that if the dog eats the rice that contains blood caused by its bite, you will heal instantly!' It was a medical diagnosis of the most mystical nature, but I was not about to go after a mangy cur that had just had part of my rump for its lunch, much less hope that it would eat the bloody lump of rice.

Once, I nearly severed my thumb while sawing a piece of wood trying to make a toy gun. The pain was excruciating and I ran into the kitchen to try to stem the blood that was spurting from the wound like a red fountain. Aunty Milk Bar was just preparing some *sambal* and, quick as a medicine woman, she heated a wad of raw *belacan* and rubbed it onto my thumb. She wrapped it in a length of not-too-clean kitchen towel and instructed that I not remove the dressing for four weeks. Too traumatised to question yet another home cure, I silently obeyed. And the miraculous thing was that I did not have blood poisoning or any other side effect. The thumb healed—probably from being cauterised and the salt in the *belacan*— and I had a new-found respect for this ingredient. Don't try it at home, though.

Rule Britannia and First Mother

As I have already mentioned, First Mother was Father's principal wife, a little lady no more than about four feet eight inches tall. She had a son, who unfortunately died at the age of one, and two daughters, one adopted and the other biological. It must have appeared odd to friends whose domestic arrangements did not follow this custom, as some of my classmates often asked: 'How come you have two mothers?'

It was too complicated to explain so I simply replied, 'Two for the price of one!' and left it at that.

First Mother was feisty and full of fun while my own mother was more sombre and a disciplinarian. They had respect for each other, with Mother belonging to the old school of thought that didn't question the status quo as long as we were well provided for. However, if it had not been for First Mother, we wouldn't have had any fun at all. When I longed to own a pair of roller skates—all the rage then—my mother vetoed the idea. It was First Mother who went out secretly to buy me my first pair. She would also take us on trips to the cinema because Mother would not allow us to go. Their relationship was firmly one of first and secondary wife and my mother kept to her place, such was the hierarchy.

The first movie First Mother ever took me to was showing at the Sun Talkie cinema that, even then, Mother still barred us from. I still remember the film: *Shane* starring Alan Ladd.

First Mother had plenty of stories to tell, some funny and others completely baffling. She frequently mentioned a certain Prince Alwi who had visited Singapore some years earlier.

'Who is Prince Alwi?' I asked, as I had never heard of such a dignitary. I thought he was from some Middle Eastern sultanate but no, First Mother said he was from *chor keh* (the Mother country). This meant England because during this time many Singaporeans had been conditioned to refer to England as Mother Country. However, I was still baffled as the European history I'd learnt in school had never mentioned an English Prince Alwi.

Years later I discovered that she had completely mangled the title Prince of Wales to Prince Alwi as a dialectal pronunciation as she spoke no English. He was Queen Elizabeth's grandfather and one of the several titled Prince of Wales over the centuries. There are quite a few in the British Monarchy, Prince Charles being the current Welsh honcho. First Mother was at least single-minded in her loyalty to the

British Crown. She also kept many of the commemorative silver coins minted with the Prince's image, and treasured them so much she had them made into buttons for her blouses. At least she was able to hold her beloved Prince Alwi to her bosom!

My Boxer Rebellion

And so the 1940s rolled on and the big news of the time was India's independence from Great Britain. I remember it was 15th August 1947 and the small Indian community in our kampong were all celebrating dressed in full war paint. Since I was only five, the political significance was lost on me. For some curious reason, Father joined in the celebrations, and even put a white dot of wet powder on his forehead. He was a man of the people and whatever mood of the day, he always joined in effervescently.

Sometimes he would even wear a white *dhoti* as if to make a statement that he was one of the people. Actually, Father was looked up to as some kind of community leader during the post-war years, which also gave him licence to play a paternal role with all the neighbourhood kids. Wearing a *dhoti* did have its awkward moments, though. One blustery day it somehow loosened and fell in a limpid pool around his ankles. At least he was wearing clean underwear.

I think Father was the original hippy. In fact his enthusiasm for all things knew few bounds. After the liberation of Singapore in 1945, he acquired a few nylon parachutes that had been left behind by the departing Japanese army. These were a pale cream colour and almost entirely non-porous. They had to be in order for the chutes to work. What did he do with them? He made Mother sew them into shirts for us to wear. Silky they were, but silks they were not. As for comfort, can you imagine wearing a shirt made from non-porous nylon that trapped in the humidity and heat? We felt like we were walking saunas. It was mortifying at school when, during PE, my shirt would billow out, making me look like a mini galleon in full sail. The parachute chords did double duty as belts. Such was our sartorial heritage, courtesy of the Imperial Japanese Army and though I can forgive other atrocities, this I still cannot. Even today, going into the sauna at my gym brings back these stultifying memories.

There were other sartorial elements foisted on me and my brothers that, in retrospect, were not too bad. Mother was a deft needlewoman and made good use of unwanted flour sacks from the local grocery shop. Ever ingenious, she fashioned these into underwear for us. It was good, stout cotton after all. Come to think of it, we were wearing the first designer underwear, even if the label read 'Heng Tai Flour Mill' across one side. Eat your heart out, Calvin Klein. There was one problem though; the fabric used often caused a rash in the most embarrassing places and I rebelled against wearing the underwear. You might say it was my boxer rebellion—not the Qing Dynasty one in China, though the trauma was not dissimilar.

Slurping Rewards

Father was really generous when he was pleased. I usually did well in primary school, and if my report cards came back without any red marks (red marks meaning you'd failed), he'd ask what I wanted as a reward. He would give me money which was usually what I wanted. One year when I came first in my class, he gave me the ultimate choice: Would I like a Mickey Mouse watch or a month's supply of *kway teow* soup? There was this hawker stall in our neighbourhood that served a superlative version and one that I occasionally patronised when I had the requisite twenty cents for a bowl.

The prospect (even till this day) of enjoying my favourite dish for a whole month was too delicious to turn down. Who needed a watch anyway? And so it came to pass that my name was written on the hawker's stall for a whole month. My siblings still rib me about being a greedy devil. It seems I cannot escape my past that easily.

At other times, if Mother was lucky in her daily game of Chap Ji Ki (see 'Gamblers Anonymous', p205), something that she indulged in for as long as I can remember and until her dying day, my brothers and I would be treated to some hawker delight or other. My favourite was satay but I cannot say if the satay man returned this sentiment. When times were hard, and we had just enough money to buy perhaps a few sticks at ten cents a stick, we would incur the satay man's displeasure. This was because we would pay him for the satay but then proceed to demolish the sliced cucumber, *ketupat* (compressed rice dumpling) and gravy accompaniments that had been laid out for liberal helpings. Mother was a little more ethical and would order at least ten sticks for the three of us, but we still ate more of the accompaniments than decency allowed.

If the late-night *kai choke* (chicken porridge) man passed by our house—usually at 11 pm—we would be treated to a steaming bowl of his delicious congee. The custom was to not actually leave the house to buy our supper. Instead, we would holler at the hawker then lower a basket from our upstairs window. In this would be the requisite number of empty bowls and money. When full, we would then hoist the basket back up without opening the front door. Since it was always a very late hour, this seemed a very sensible thing to do.

Rickshaws

Singapore's first mode of public transport was known as *khan chiu chia,* which literally translates as 'hand-pulled vehicle'. It was no more than a special bicycle with a side car that could seat two comfortably, more if you squeezed children on board.

The common belief is that they originated in China. Not true, for they were derived from rickshas, which were first used in Japan around 1868 at the beginning of the Meiji Restoration. The word ricksha comes from the Japanese word *jinrikisha—jin* meaning 'human', *riki* meaning 'strength' and *sha* meaning 'vehicle'. Despite being wholly dependent on manpower, the Japanese found that these were nonetheless faster than the earlier form of palanquins or sedan chairs that needed two men to carry and move them.

Another hypothesis is that the rickshaw is the handiwork of an American blacksmith named Albert Tolman, who invented the vehicle in Massachusetts, USA, in 1848 for missionaries in Japan. Yet another interesting theory suggests that the rickshaw is the invention of a Mr Richard Shaw, an unemployed taxi driver from Birmingham, England. This is unlikely, given that rickshaws were in existence long before taxis.

Another hypotheses has it that it was the Japanese who invented the term when the social upper classes in the mid-nineteenth century used the mode of travel when the aforementioned palanquin became passe. Credit for the invention was given to three Japanese men: Izumi Yosuke, Suzuki Tokujiro and Takayama Kosuke. There is evidence that the Japanese government had granted them the license to make rickshaws. The seal of one of these three inventors was also required to be on each license to operate a rickshaw.

By 1872 there were some 40,000 rickshaws operating in Tokyo alone and the trend soon spread overseas*. By 1880 rickshaws could be found in Simla, India, then twenty years later in Calcutta. They were initially used by Chinese traders to transport goods but in 1914 the Chinese applied for permission to use rickshaws to transport passengers. Pulling them was often the first job for migrating peasants. The vehicle was also adopted in China in the late nineteenth century but had disappeared by 1949.

Rickshaws were brought to Singapore in the 1930s, when

*Source: Powerhouse Museum, 2005; The Jinrikisha story, 1996

most immigrants lived in enclaves and were segregated under the leadership of a *kapitan* (captain) who took charge of the internal affairs of each community. At that time Singapore was divided into separate areas according to the different dialect groups. As time passed, some immigrants became successful merchants and traders in Chinatown, Commercial Square, Chulia Kampong, Kampong Glam and European Town.

Coolie agents were middlemen who helped these traders and merchants find workers from India and China. These Indian and Chinese workers became the first rickshaw pullers in Singapore, most being wiry and hardy. I just about remember riding in a rickshaw as a small child. The pullers either ran barefoot or, at best, wore rope-soled sandals. It must have required tremendous strength and stamina to hotfoot it across the searing tarmac roads. Each rickshaw had a collapsible roof that could be lowered but when it rained, passengers would be drenched as the sides were open to the elements. The pullers wore conical hats that came to be associated with the coolie brigade. By the early 1950s there were no rickshaws left in Singapore as another form of vehicular transport came on the scene: the trishaw.

Ronggeng, Joget and Pythons

Father's proclivities for female company and dancing also extended to another realm: that of Malay culture. At New World Amusement Park there was a nightly performance given by a troupe called the Joget Moden, or Modern Dance Troupe (*joget* is the Malay word for 'dance'). As a true-blue Baba, Father spoke fluent Malay and Indonesian and supporting this troupe was a frequent pleasure for him. There was one fundamental rule: the Malay female dancers were not allowed to have bodily contact with any male. They would simply dance on the stage and invite like-minded men to join them in their rhythmic movements to the sound of gongs and violins. But there was absolutely no bodily contact.

I remember each dance cost fifty cents and Father must have spent a few dollars in a few hours. The absence of hanky panky did not bother him much as he truly enjoyed the simple pleasure of music and movement. In fact he was an amateur musician himself and a member of a local band called the Merrylads. He could play the violin, after a fashion, the keyboard and a strange instrument that he blew through his nostrils. It looked like metal *ha gau* (pouch-shaped dumpling) and gave off the strangest tinny sounds.

It was Father who made us all study music as there was an old beat-up piano in our home. My elder brother went on to finish his keyboard studies and became a music specialist during the 1960s and 1970s. My second brother studied the violin but was forced to give it up one day when a fierce flood in the area washed away his instrument. Me, I was made to join a local dance school, more of which I will relate later.

New World wasn't just a cultural platform, for during the late 1940s and well into the 1950s it was home to a rather risqué attraction, the likes of which you do not see today. A winsome and well-endowed lady called Rose Chan gave nightly performances dressed in no more than a bikini and a most unusual accessory: a six-foot python with which she would do things that would send temperatures soaring among the mostly male audience. Today, she would be a star in Las Vegas, or at least Bangkok's Patpong. Among the Malay-speaking Babas, Rose Chan was known as the Ulah Ulah Queen (*ular* meaning 'snake'). There are a lot of similarities between her hip-swivelling and that of Hula dancers in Hawaii.

The show was not advertised as a striptease act as Rose did not divest herself of her skimpy clothing. Her forte was to tease and writhe with her snake to the music of Xavier Cougat and his Latin band. Her pièce de résistance was to arch and twist herself around her python to the strains of 'Cherry Pink and Apple Blossom White'. This chic-a-chic-a-boom rhythm became forever associated with this form of burlesque. Men in the audience were known to throw flowers and occasionally gold bangles onto the stage. She would pick these up (the bangles, not the flowers!) without missing a beat and go on to perform to uproarious applause.

In later years she also trained two of her nubile daughters for a threesome act that brought the house down, for there were now three scantily clad women with three pythons. Rose went on to make a fortune and could often be seen driving her posh American car, a Pontiac. Oldsters today still talk about Rose Chan, for she was an icon in her day.

And so Father whiled away his spare time with his bevy of favourite dance hostesses. This polite moniker was often used by a man when he introduced his latest squeeze to his business associates. Theirs was a rarefied world of pulsating music and tinkling laughter, a unique inner sanctum that few wives were privy to, unless they had devised a scheme to trail their husbands. Some did, and were rewarded with their husbands storming off to acquire even more mistresses. Mother knew which side her bread was buttered and left Father to his own devices.

Except one day when I was about seven. Father had gone out for the evening and returned home very late. He had forgotten his key and rapped on our front door in the wee hours of the morning. Door bells were non-existent then. Our house was built in such a way that our overhanging balcony had a kind of vent to allow us to peek down in case there were unwelcome visitors. Mother and First Mother, who was also a little miffed by his behaviour, filled a pail with water and poured it through the vent, drenching Father to the skin. He fell to the floor in a drunken, wet stupor and was left there until the next morning. The next day both my mothers packed their bags and left for Grandma's house.

Gold, Glorious Gold!

Oh yes, Father's fondness for gold was not confined to teeth, or to offering gifts to his paramours and assorted dance hall women. He also attributed it to names. All the boys in our family have the middle name of Kim, which means 'gold' in both Teochew and Hokkien dialects. At least Father had the foresight to tag on more meaningful names to these. My elder brother is called Kim Swee (Golden Water), my middle brother is Kim Hay (Golden Fire) and me—well, I had the ignominy of being named Golden Mud, or Kim Tho. Actually, as explained to me much later, it means Golden Earth. Some cold comfort.

It seemed we were named after the three elements of Water, Fire and Earth. It should have been noble except that I had to bear the brunt of being taunted endlessly by schoolmates who said I would never amount to anything with a name like Mud. Of course they, the philistines, failed to see the symbolic significance. In my later years I chose to refer to myself as Earthy. But no, one evil friend disclaimed this and said I was simply Muddy.

What Father actually did for a living, the family never really understood. It had vaguely to do with draughtsmanship, rubber, tin and rambutans. Oh, he also dabbled in orthodontics, or was it dentistry? We only discovered this 'hobby' one day while playing in his office. In a drawer among his various draughtsman's tools we discovered a large tin in which were complete sets of gold, silver and enamel dentures, tins of denture powders and tombstone-like loose teeth. Thank goodness he never practised on us but one time, First Mother, in a fit of pique, put glue on a set of dentures she knew belonged to him. For several days afterwards Father's face was set in a grim, tight-lipped snarl.

Given that Father also had only one good eye—the other was glass, on account of a war injury—he really resembled an ugly

43

gargoyle when crossed. He also had the disconcerting habit of falling asleep without first taking out the false eye that could not be shut. So whether he was really asleep or not, we were never quite sure.

We only cared about this state of affairs because Mother had the habit of wanting us to raid his overall pockets for any spare cash when he was asleep. She wouldn't do it herself and usually egged on me or one of my brothers to do so. I would tiptoe into his room but was never able to get up enough nerve to rifle through his pockets as his glass eye was always glaringly open. Or was it his good eye? I never waited to find out.

And so life rolled on, and when Father was awake he could be quite fun and generous.

Re-laxatives

Whether it was protective instinct or male bonding, I never gave any explicit information to Mother about Father's extra-curricular activities, other than whether he had won or lost at mahjong. Perhaps it was because I was always too winded from gagging after the doses of castor oil that Father forced on me and my siblings on a weekly basis. Perhaps he knew the oil would fog my mind enough for me not to spill the beans, even if I spilled everything I'd eaten several hours earlier.

Memories of this castor oil ritual still live in the deepest recesses of my mind, or rather my stomach. He would line us up, mouths open, and pour the vile stuff down our throats, throats that did everything they could to reject this laxative that tasted like sump oil. We would suck on limes to kill the foul taste but no matter what we did, the castor oil would repeat itself throughout the day. Needless to say, we did not have many close friends.

Apparently Father had something to do with a rubber estate somewhere in Johore Bahru. His connection was enough to warrant frequent visits, often with me and my brothers in tow, during school holidays. While other children were taken to the zoo or overseas for holidays, we were given the rare treat of seeing how rubber was tapped. During those stays, we would usually be stirred from a deep sleep at the bone-chilling hour of four in the morning.

So geography lessons were a cinch for us as we learnt, first hand, how to cut the thin bark of a rubber tree into a chevron shape, see the white rubber sap trickle down into rough-hewn cups and later collect them to be deposited into large pails, and in turn into vats. We learnt, too, how it was smoked then shaped into pliable sheets. The husky, peculiarly pungent smell still evokes memories whenever I change my car tyres today.

Father must have been convinced that the regular doses of castor oil did wonders for growing limbs and decided that I would benefit even more if I took up tap dancing. One of his business associates, Mr Yap Pheng Gek, lived in a house on Keng Lee Road and his daughter, Maudreen Yap, ran a dancing school in their capacious hall. It was to here that Father firmly steered me when I was barely seven years old. He bought me a pair of tap shoes and ordered me to stay and learn or face the prospect of more castor oil.

So I did, for a couple of years, making like Gene Kelly only with much less aplomb. Maudreen was a fierce dance teacher who was never out of her powder-blue dance togs: a short skirt and ballet slippers. She smoked like a chimney and put us little tots through paces that threatened to turn us into pretzels. Anyone who has been through a tap or ballet school will know the rigours of practising for hours in an attempt to become more flexible. The ultimate aim was to turn stiff-jointed, awkward children into double-jointed angels who could do the splits without putting a hair out of place.

As the months went by I did learn how to tap dance and even took part in a concert at the Victoria Memorial Hall, where I took my turn as one of the dancers in a chorus line. I remember the music to this day; it was 'The Skater's Waltz' by Strauss and I managed to strut my stuff without missing a beat. The smell of the crowd and the roar of the greasepaint did not quite transform me into Nureyev but I did enjoy the annual Christmas parties Maudreen and her father threw. At least *I* did, but I don't about one of the other students, as I will explain.

By the time I had spent a few years toe-tapping, Father had passed on and Maudreen kept me on in the class out of charity as Mother simply could not afford the fees. Ballet and music lessons were really the realm of the middle classes, and I for one was getting tired of putting up with snide remarks from snotty kids. They were all ferried to the classes in shining limousines and I came by in the family trishaw! Father did not know it but he could have driven me to therapy, had it not been for my feisty spirit.

Anyway, for every Christmas party each kid had to bring a gift-wrapped present, which were all placed in a pile in the centre of the dance hall. At the end of the party, each child would take away one of the presents, any present as long as it wasn't the one he'd brought. Given that by now our family circumstances were a few dollars short of impecunious, my bring-along Christmas present was—wait for it, wait for it—two tins of Ayam Brand sardines! And the parents of these posh kids were of the ilk that loved to show off their wealth. I do not know what the other presents were but I do know what I took home with me: a beautiful and probably very expensive battery-powered toy speedboat.

I could not wait to run it along my favourite longkangs but my thoughts were with the poor kid who got my sardines. I was still at the school the following year and practically rebelling against more bone-crushing practice sessions when I chanced upon a conversation between two mothers.

'You know, last year some stingy miser gave his child two tins of sardines for the Christmas draw and my poor Adeline was in tears.

She had brought a beautiful walking, talking doll that cost me S$50 and got back stinking fish that must have cost fifty cents!'

The other mother replied: 'I know, I gave my Norman a chess set but luckily he took home a very nice picture book of *Grimm's Fairy Tales*. I don't know what kind of people send their children here, must be either stingy or too poor!'

I know what kind, dear lady, I was tempted to say. The kind that have no time for such uppity pretensions.

There were other mishaps too that probably made Maudreen wish she had not extended her charity to me. One time we were rehearsing at a hectic pace for another concert and one of the routines required us to tumble and somersault across the dance floor. I was waiting on the sidelines dying for a pee, but the routine was taking forever as some fifteen children had to be put through their paces, and only those who performed properly would be selected for the final line-up. When it came to my turn, my bladder was in meltdown mode and I tumbled across the parquet floor trailing a watery wake.

All the kids guffawed and Maudreen nearly choked on her cigarette. It was the most humiliating moment of my young life. My dancing career ended on a rather soggy note, but I cannot eat sardines today without a gleeful chuckle. Years later I happened to work with a radio colleague who had been in the same class, and we mulled over these funny moments. She saw the funny side of it and no, she had not had the misfortune of receiving sardines as a Christmas present.

Cuisine Canine

When Father returned from one of his weekend sojourns—one that my brothers and I had not been dragged along to—we discovered another one of his quirks. He returned in his beat-up, old, made-in-England Ford car with his personal assistant-cum-chauffeur Ah Seng, who was a Hakka. The Hakka, who settled around the harbour and port areas of Hong Kong, had the reputation of liking dog meat, I swear. Well, as it turned out Father had run over a stray animal and had seen fit to bring it back home. It fell on us to remove the carcass from the car boot. This chore did have its compensations as, more often than not, the boot would also contain the odd bag of rambutans, some fragrant tree-ripened durians, sometimes mangosteens and, less frequently, a dead jungle animal Father had shot. Over the years we had the revolting chore of dragging from the boot dead iguanas, mousedeer, a brace or two of wild ducks, snakes and on this particular hot, sweltering day, a dog.

As my brothers and I pulled at the tail of what we thought was a wild animal, we soon realised that it was very much a stray mongrel that evidently had no home as it did not have a dog collar. Apparently Father had run over the stupid mutt along the Causeway and instead of driving on, had somehow been persuaded by Ah Seng to bring it home for dinner!

Our Hakka friend did not want to pass up the prospect of enjoying his favourite stew, claiming that since it did not have an owner, why waste good meat? The unfortunate task of cooking it fell upon my mother's quivering shoulders—quivering as much from humping the heavy beast as the nausea of preparing it with ginseng and ginger. Dinner that night was a grim passage but Father would not hear of any of us turning down the gooey, gelatinous portions slapped onto our plates. Ah Seng slurped up every morsel remarking: 'Eat more, good for asthma.'

Father may have been weird but he was not cruel—at least not physically. Aside from subjecting us to regular doses of castor oil and the occasional carnivore meal of unspeakable degustation, he would devise ever more inventive ways to punish our misdemeanours. One punishment still reeks in my memory after five decades. There were any number of spittoons around the family home, most of which were used by Mother as receptacles for the remnants of her betel nut and jungle leaf concoctions. Among the Nonya ladies of her genre, chewing a mixture of betel nut, gambier and lime all wrapped up in a paisley green leaf called *sirih* was a social habit.

There were also other large spittoons which we used as night receptacles for urine as the only toilet we had was at the back of the house through yards of sinister gloom that we, as children, would rather not traverse. These spittoons were invariably sloshing with reeking liquid. As punishment, Father would make us balance one of these on our heads while standing on a chair, until we had learnt not to misbehave in any way that displeased him.

Even if our neighbour's children displeased him they would be put through the ignominy of this pungent torture. Of course, we didn't dare move for fear of being drenched in urine—Father would make sure each spittoon was a filled one! I've been told I have good carriage but little do my friends realise how I came about this. Think about the African women who spend most of their lives carrying pots and other receptacles on their heads. I guess I owe my elegant stance to piss pots!

Hazy School Daze

In Singapore the education system was very much based on the English template. Every child had to go through Primary One and Two in a lower primary school, then on to Standard One to Five (later changed to Primary Six) in an upper primary school, before earning a place, after an Entrance Examination, at a secondary school, where we then went through Standard Six to Nine (this was later changed to Form Two to Five). Thence we moved on to Lower and Upper Sixths before attending university.

My teachers were almost exclusively from England, Scotland or Ireland and the headmistress in my lower primary school on McNair Road was a formidable Scot called Mrs McPherson. Behind her back we called her Mrs Fierce One as she pulled no punches when it came to punishments. Politically incorrect or not, she thought nothing of whipping our backsides with a ruler if we stepped out of line. And if you played truant, God help you, for you were kept behind after being whacked. This was called 'stay in' and was a real stigma. Mothers would cringe with shame if one of their sons—there were no co-education schools yet—was taunted with 'Ah Seng stay in, Ah Seng stay in!' I took great pains never to smudge my reputation as this would only have brought me more whacks from Mother.

First Mother was very good at getting on the good side of Mrs McPherson, probably in the hope that she would look on me with more benevolence. She was very good at 'tatting', a kind of knitting skill that transformed wool into a little doll's dress. She would then stick a plastic doll's head on the dress. The whole thing would be placed over a coffee pot or teapot as a cosy. First Mother was constantly producing them and gave several to the headmistress, who appeared pleased with them; as a Scot she must have been a tea drinker. Call it graft, bribery even, but I was never punished by her, despite the odd misdemeanor. When I finished my primary education at that school, Mrs McPherson presented me with a brand new suitcase, the kind with two hinged locks, for me to use for my next years of schooling.

As for my upper primary-school days, these flashed by in a blur of confusion. This was largely because of the ogre of a headmaster we affectionately called Bulldog on account of the fact that he had a mien like the squashed face of a bulldog and the body to match. Short on stature, he was long on philosophical gems that went right over our heads every morning at assembly.

Picture the scene: Several hundred tots from six to eleven years old, dressed in starched white shirts—the starching I will deal with later—brown shorts and Meltonian-chalked shoes, gather in the hot sun wishing they were somewhere else. Bulldog comes down the wooden stairs of the central block with several other grim-faced teachers who look like they could eat us up with hate.

Bulldog holds up his hands as if in supplication to some unknown deity and proceeds to intone such profound words that we never ever fathomed in all the years we were there, trapped like squirming ferrets.

'Good morning, boys,' he thunders down a megaphone. If the gathered throng does not reply immediately he thunders again: 'I said, "Good morning, boys." Are you deaf, or what? And why were some of you late? You know that punctuality is the essence of humanity. How will you ever achieve anything if you cannot be one step ahead of Old Father Time?'

By now the furious sun is melting the starch in my collar and it begins to stream down my chest and onto my groin, making me want to scratch. But we are not allowed to twitch even one iota. Only when assembly is over and we march into our classrooms can I spend the next five minutes enjoying an orgy of scratching, to the extreme irritation of my form teacher Miss Osman.

I remember that, like Bulldog's disciple, she would thunder at me with fire issuing from her thin, brown lips. 'Have you got ants in your pants, or what, boy? You will burn in hell if you play with yourself, you know!'

To which the whole class would snigger and chant: 'Itchy balls, itchy balls,' and Miss Osman would thunder even louder that we would *all* burn in hell for such profanity. And so it went on for the next few hours until tiffin time, when I would escape to the comfort of the tuck shop and my favourite macaroni and chicken soup.

A Coffin For My Pencils

Father must have saved a bundle not buying us toys. My first ball was a walnut-sized lump of excess raw rubber sap scraped from the rim of a cup attached to a rubber tree. It was brown and hard and bounced like no manufactured ball did. It also did double duty as an eraser at school. In fact, I'm not sure whether Father was plain mean or just enterprising, as I rarely had store-bought things during my childhood. However, one item in particular was the object of much discourse among my Primary Two classmates: my pencil box that Father had crafted himself.

It was a foot-long, miniature Chinese coffin with a sliding lid. It also became a formidable weapon, for whenever I was bullied I would brandish it threateningly, and the superstitious among my classmates would flee for fear of being hexed. It was my teacher who saw this in a different light.

'At least, my boy, given that your Arithmetic and English marks are so bad, you could always become an undertaker.'

I failed to see this allusion, for to me it was just a pencil box.

Nuns and Sins

My cousins all went to mission schools and some of the nuns who taught in the convent in Katong lived in a large, rambling bungalow near Grandfather's house in Siglap. In the front yard of this property was a large, prolific jambu tree which grew close to the fence. On frequent occasions the neighbourhood kids, my five cousins and yours truly would break the commandment 'Thou Shalt Not Steal'. Without the slightest sense of guilt we would climb up the fence and purloin whatever fruits we could reach.

We usually did this when there were no nuns about, but one day along came one of them in her black habit, looking like a fearsome penguin as she bore down on the perpetrators. My oldest cousin was already up the fence, standing on the shoulders of a neighbourhood boy, when the nun shouted—yes, shouted—at him. Jesus, I thought that these good women never raised their voices, except in prayer. Anyway, she wagged her finger at my cousin who promptly dropped down on his knees exclaiming in breathless nervousness, 'Please, Jesus, may I *curi* (steal) the jambu!'

I thought it distinctly odd that, despite years of Christian conditioning, catechism lessons and God shops, none of my cousins had embraced the faith. Even my other female friends, who'd spent all their formative years in various convents, were apt to feel the same. One, who later became my editor, said that, if anything, she was more hell-bent on committing sins because of the stringent rules set by the nuns. She was quite funny when recalling some memories: 'Just imagine, all the commandments but not one that preached "Thou shalt not have sex willy-nilly." If there is a willy that is willing, why not?'

Music and Movement

Of all my early school lessons, I enjoyed music lessons the most. We did not learn music as such, but the period was devoted to sitting around a radio in one of the teaching halls with the music teacher in attendance. Mandatory classes called Music and Movement had been programmed into all primary-school syllabuses by the Ministry of Education. The then radio station had a schools broadcast division that produced programmes for teaching the appreciation of music. This division was headed by a lady called Mrs Aisha Akbar, who many Singaporeans of indeterminate age today will remember.

At that time I was in my upper primary class. I was transported to a magical realm via music like Tchaikovsky's 'Peter and the Wolf' with narration. Other stories were told through music, and once every so often Mrs Akbar would do the school rounds. A redoubtable lady, she would sit at the piano, wearing glasses that Elton John would pay a fortune for today, and make us go through the movements in time to her music.

'Stand up!' she would trill as she played a rippling cadence of notes. 'Sit down, wave your arms and stand up again!' It was fun, needed no brain power and we could fidget as much as we wanted. Years later, when I joined the local radio station and was posted to the school division for a few months, it was a tremendous surprise and joy to find out my boss was Mrs Akbar! She had been a child piano prodigy and when she started doing the school rounds, she was only in her early twenties.

As fate would have it, over forty years on and Aisha has become a friend and, like me, is now also living in London. She is in her seventies and we meet up once in a while to chunter about the past. When I last visited her in Twickenham and she asked me to sit down, it sent goosebumps down my arms.

School songs were a delight for they were, to me, real music and not like the heavy metal stuff you get today. We sang songs like 'The Ash Grove', 'Juanita', 'The Happy Wanderer' and 'Mr Ling'. This last one still rings in my memory, the words and music very much still alive in my mind.

> 'Oh, Mr Ling, we'll sing-aling-aling
> With all our hearts to you.
> We'll sing-aling-aling and tring-aling-aling
> And tring-aling-aling for you!'

Such innocence and a childhood not beset with coarse language and meaningless drivel. I'm sure my peer group remember this.

Excursions were another primary-school highlight for they meant we could get out of the stuffy and humid classroom. When parental consent had been obtained, we would assemble, usually on a Saturday, in the school yard, all eager beavers packed with sustenance like sardine sandwiches, apples and a favourite orange drink called Green Spot. The excursion might have only been to a local establishment called Thye Hong Biscuit factory, but to children of a young and impressionable age, it was most absorbing and educational. We saw how flour was made into batter with sugar and other additives, fed into machines, and emerged as biscuits. I wonder if children today know, or care, how biscuits are made.

It fuelled childish curiosity, taught us about the manufacturing process and how things were made. It was this insatiable curiosity that prompted me to pursue a career in journalism. I am still intrigued by what is involved in the production of a box of chocolates, what makes a clock tick and the million and one things we all take very much for granted. With good teachers and a core curriculum, education can make a man. These formative years can make all the difference between a well-turned-out boy and one who ends up on the street hustling DVDs.

My Aboriginal Links

My family had always suspected that Father's genealogy had something to do with Aborigines. Apparently he was Indonesian Chinese by birth, dark-skinned and spoke not only Indonesian but several Aboriginal dialects, notably Sakai and Negrito. How do I know this? As an optional extra during our rubber estate sojourns, he would take us, his three sons aged seven, nine and ten— my three sisters had by then married and were much too old for such jaunts—to stay at a Sakai settlement somewhere in the depths of the Johore jungle.

Adventure holidays today have nothing on this, I assure you. There we were, my brothers and I, terrified out of our wits, being escorted by Father and his Indonesian friend who was cradling a Sten gun, heading into the depths of a gloomy clearing after travelling for what seemed like days in a jeep. When we alighted in a small clearing on the edge of a jungle where there were attap lean-tos and tin shacks, we were met by a gnarled old lady who looked a hundred years old. Her hair was chalk-white, and on her left hip she was cradling a small child. On her right hip, nestled in a twist of grubby fabric, was a fearsome parang.

We relaxed a little when Father greeted her like a long-lost friend and soon other faces began appearing from within the gloom of shacks and dappled treetops. Father had brought with him some cheap batik cloths, mirrors and plastic trinkets, and the Sakai families were soon swarming around the gifts that now lay gleaming and glinting on a woven mat. Our Indonesian escort never loosened his grip on his Sten gun, and we were soon hauled up into the tree houses where, as Father explained, the Sakai slept at night for fear of snakes and other poisonous creatures of the tropical jungle. I spent one sleepless night in such a tree house. It should have been fun, but the thought of being eaten alive by a python or poisoned by a scorpion's bite never left me for one second.

Lau Pok Car

While Father was alive we were fairly well off and our family car, beat-up though it was, was a source of neighbourhood envy. Owning a car in the early 1950s was a rarity indeed, even one as cranky as Father's old Ford. Among the affluent Chinese, the aspiration was to own either a Fiat or a Ford. These were the only two imported makes of vehicles. Where I lived they were called Piak and Pok. To this day any jalopy is called a Lau Pok Car—an old Ford, if you prefer.

Ours was unprepossessing to say the least. It was black, with left and right turn signals in the shape of orange plastic 'wings' that were supposed to pop out when a button was pushed. Except that they often did not and we had to reach out with our hands to manually prise one or the other out as required. On rainy days this was a really sloshing task. Still, it was a moving car and provided many hours of play, even while stationary.

Sadly, Father died not long afterwards, on a day and under circumstances that Mother described as 'being dragged by the devil to the eighteen tortures of hell!' No, she wasn't being insensitive. Anyone who ever visited the old Haw Par Villa before it became a bastardised theme park know what I am referring to.

It was the fifteenth day of the seventh lunar month, the time when hungry ghosts spend their time on earth going every which way. Actually, they had the licence to be among mortals for the whole month but it was this day specifically that we had to mind where we went—if we went out at all—or we ran the risk of incurring their displeasure. Anyone who subscribed to the belief that the dearly departed walked the earth—and many of us did—were fearful enough not to do or say anything to displease these 'ghosts'. And on the mid-month day, the ghosts were particularly bad tempered, it seemed.

So Father, stubborn and unbelieving as he was, refused to listen to Mother's pleas not to go to work that day. He had been involved in some construction job in Penang Lane and wanted to see if his workers had done the job properly. Being Taoists, none of his workers went to work that day for fear of some unknown fate. Not too long after his departure, there came a knock at our door.

It was a policeman. He didn't mince his words.

'Is this Mr Tan Ah Kau's house?' he asked Mother. She nodded, speechless and fearing the worse. 'Are you Mrs Tan?'

'Yes,' she replied whereupon, without ceremony, the policeman simply said: '*Tuan sudah mati*!' ('Your husband is dead!')

Mother let out a shriek and screamed: 'Stupid old turtle, I told him not to go out. Now he has been taken by the hungry ghosts. *Alamak, Tuhan tolong* (Dear God, help).' She was inconsolable and rained curses, not on the hungry ghosts, but on Father for his stubbornness and disbelief. For weeks afterwards we were not allowed to leave the house except to go to school. Once, I sneaked out to Mount Emily for a swim and came back to face a flogging for taking such stupid risks.

Did I not know that there were ghosts everywhere, ready to take stupid children into hell? Her wrath was more than enough to curb my need for sporting activity. Still, we found devious ways to escape the confined existence she would rather us have. Brought up a cloistered girl with no education, she knew only of the world that existed within the boundaries of the home. She hardly ever ventured out, apart from the daily trips to the wet market, and saw little reason for her children to seek the pleasures of the outside world.

Grandfather, the Opium Smoker

To call someone an opium smoker—rarely heard today—was not a derisory remark, such as *apian sai* (opium turd) which was used to refer to people who were nerdy and skinny. Grandfather really was an opium smoker, and had been since he was a young man, according to Grandmother. He made his fortune in the 1920s from property, and built a large rambling house in Nallur Road, Siglap, yards from the seashore. Adjacent to this was a kind of annex, normally for housing cars even though there were few cars in Singapore then.

Instead Grandfather used it for storing odds and ends, mostly unwanted furniture and, most oddly, a small coffin! We knew that early on in his career he'd been in the business of selling coffins. When he struck it rich by buying up large chunks of property in Siglap and Changi, he gave up the coffin business, according to Grandmother. Grandfather never spoke much to us and spent most of his waking hours in a state of opium-induced torpor.

Sometimes he would ask his grandchildren to light his opium pipe for him. The pipe was like a Middle Eastern hookah that he would fill with little rolled balls of cooked opium called *candu*. These were much cheaper than raw opium. He would then deeply inhale the opiate fumes and an expression would form on his face that was as near to complete peace as we could gather. In today's terms we would probably say he was 'zonked out' or 'high'. This was the 1940s remember, and opium was not classified as an illegal drug. Indeed it was freely available if you had the contacts. Grandfather died sometime in 1947.

Many years later, sometime in the 1960s, I visited his house with a few classmates. We were intending to spend a few days cycling in the area, and it seemed logical to stay in the small wooden bungalow that Grandfather had built for my father just by the beach. We had biked all the way from town and I told my mates to put their bicycles in the annex while we stayed in the bungalow. What I did not anticipate was that the small coffin, unused and left over from Grandfather's shop, was still there, having become the nesting place for Grandmother's chickens.

When one of my classmates pushed his bicycle into the annex, it must have startled the chickens. Squawking, they leapt up in a flurry of feathers. Taking one look at the coffin, my classmate hurled his bicycle in the air and ran out screaming as if he had just seen a ghost! We still talk about it today as he has been living in London for the past thirty-five years and we meet up now and then.

Opium Dens

Opium (*Papaver somniferum*), was a significant part of general trade during Singapore's pioneering years. Encouraged by the British colonial government, the country reaped heavy profits from opium licences. Many Chinese coolies—a term derived from the Chinese *koo li*, meaning 'bitter labour'—succumbed to this vice as they tried to escape from the harsh reality of their mundane lives. Despite this addictive drug being banned in 1943, the opium trade continued clandestinely, so the death penalty was introduced in 1989 for opium dealers and peddlers in order to put a complete stop to it.

For many years, opium was used in herbal medicine in China and early Malaya to treat a range of illnesses: asthma, cancer, catarrh, coughs, diarrhoea, hypertension, insomnia, rheumatism and even snakebites. First cultivated in China, India and other parts of Asia, particularly the Golden Triangle, it was mainly consumed locally or peddled illicitly in other countries.

In nineteenth century China, opium smoking was an accepted social grace by both the elite and the poor alike. The practice of offering an opium pipe to a visitor was a simple one, akin to that of serving tea. When the Chinese migrated to the Straits Settlements around the mid-nineteenth century, they brought the habit with them. According to historical records, there were some 20,000 Chinese who made up the majority of the local population, and of these some 15,000 were addicted to the drug.

The Chinese who migrated were mostly coolies with little family support, scarce entertainment and a life of ceaseless grind. For many of them the habit was a form of escape from their harsh reality, rather than a form of social grace. However, it proved an expensive and addictive habit. An increase in the price of opium led to an escalating crime rate. Many resorted to theft and abduction to support their habit. Although opium dens could only operate with licences issued by the government, there were many other illegal operators with close ties to secret societies.

Many opium dens were located in town houses, with some in rural areas that were no more than attap huts. The town dens were concentrated in Chinatown, along Pagoda Street and Trengganu Street. Dens in Tanjong Pagar, the Rochor areas around Sungei Road, Duxton Street, Amoy Street and Beach Road were still in use right up until the 1970s, despite the earlier ban. Prior to this they had the licence to operate until 9 pm. However, most smokers would retire to makeshift quarters inside these dens to continue their vice till midnight. The rooms inside were lined with wooden benches. Men in pairs shared a dim lamp between them and smoked leisurely whilst lying on the benches.

The trade fetched profitable returns and was supported by the colonial government of the time. It was such a roaring business that from 1898 to 1906, the average annual revenue from opium was forty-nine percent of the total income of the Straits Settlements. Singapore saw the rise of opium syndicates during the mid-nineteenth century as opium and spirit farms, where tincture of opium was produced illegally, grew increasingly common. The same was true in Johore, Malacca and the Riau Islands. Violence between various triads often erupted from everyone's desire to control the opium trade.

Ancestor Worship

Every birth certificate has a section marked 'Religion', and in Singapore in my day if you were not a Christian, the information that would automatically be entered would be Buddhist. I do not know if this has changed today, but in my time it was assumed that Buddhism was the only other alternative to Christianity. In truth, most Singapore Chinese subscribed to Taoism rather than Buddhism, which is a totally different discipline.

I shan't go into a lengthy discourse, but it is suffice to know that ancestor worship is common in Taoism, and pays homage to the pantheon of deities, goddesses and fairies of ancient Chinese mythology. True Taoists do not regard these figures as part of mythology and regularly pay abject homage to their favourite deity. The God of Heaven is the supreme commander and it is to him that most offerings and prayers are made, especially during Chinese New Year.

When I was growing up, especially during the 1950s, there were other sideshows related to Taoism, including ceremonial rituals I witnessed among Chinese mediums. During the month of the Hungry Ghosts, our neighbourhood would resonate with the clash of cymbals, gongs and flutes as troupes of these mediums performed some rather gory acts. Most people watching were fascinated by the assortment of mutilation and flagellation that took place among some mediums, not unlike the Hindu Kavadi carriers.

During this month it was common to see walking along the roads two mediums carrying an ornate sedan chair on which was seated the effigy of a minor deity. If what we saw was to be believed, the violent rocking of the sedan chair was due to the deity making it so. The carriers were in a trance.

Elsewhere, in specially erected tents, even more gory tasks were being performed. We often peeped through the tent seams to see what was going on. One ritual in particular that we saw was that of a medium piercing both his cheeks with a six foot brass pole. Not a drop of blood was spilled, I kid you not. After this, the medium would sway and prance along the streets while believers would follow in awed silence. Sometimes mediums would slash their backs with sharp swords, again with bloodless impunity.

The climax of these Taoist activities was when a medium would scale a tall ladder as high as twenty feet. Perfectly normal activity you think, but the rungs of each ladder were not made of wood but razor sharp knives facing upwards. Again, whether by mystic design or otherworldly dictates, not a drop of blood was drawn. If you have ever seen Hindu devotees fire walking, you'll not be sceptical about these displays of mind over matter. By the early 1950s most of these rituals were banned because some children imitated these mediums with fatal consequences.

Ancestor worship is still practised today but with much less fervour. Instead Christianity became the preferred choice among the educated classes. As an intrinsic part of Chinese beliefs, these rituals are mostly memories today.

Sam Sui Women

These hardy women were among the Chinese immigrants who came to Singapore as early as the mid-nineteenth century to seek their livelihoods. Hailing mainly from the county of Sanshui province in Guangdong province—hence their name—they were women of Hakka and Cantonese stock who had taken vows of spinsterhood. Apparently they did not like the yoke of motherhood and opted for their single status so they could travel and seek their livelihoods elsewhere. Nanyang, as Singapore and Southeast Asia were then called, was an attractive destination where they could realise their potential. While my life's path did not cross theirs too often, my father ran a small building contracting business, and had occasion to employ these doughty and hard-working women via his sub-contractors. They were most distinguishable with their trademark red hats fashioned like a square nun's whimple. They also wore nothing but stiffly starched black *samfoo*s and trousers with a coarse apron tied around, like a large bib. On their feet they wore rough-hewn sandals fashioned from pieces of hard rubber cut from used tyres and fastened with a strap. This must have been the original recycling effort!

It was largely by the sweat of their brows and on their strong backs that early Singapore was built. Some 200,000 Sam Sui arrived on these shores between 1934 and 1938 and more continued to arrive until 1949 when emigration was declared illegal in China. They took on heavy jobs like brick carrying and other manual jobs that would have floored hardy men. Their lives were extremely plain, almost ascetic, but they were not known to moan, even though the money they earned was meagre.

No job was too tough or too far away from their homes and many ventured as far as Malaya to work in tin mines, on rubber estates and construction sites. Some even took on jobs as domestic maids and child minders. These Sam Sui women would eventually discard their red hats, heralding a new brigade of migrant workers known for their unstinting devotion to their employers.

By the late 1940s and well into the 1950s their bobbing red hats were a common sight on the Singapore construction scene as they carried out their onerous tasks. Nothing fazed them: piles of bricks to be carried, high scaffolding to be climbed or holes to be dug belying their small physical stature. Their homes were mostly shared quarters in cramped shophouses along Upper Chin Chew Street, Upper Nanking Street and Eu Tong Sen Street. Their routine was unchanging; up at the crack of dawn, their breakfast was a very basic meal of rice and tofu—curiously many Sam Sui women, despite their rigorous lifestyles, were vegetarians—before going to work.

Their lunch was even more sparse, again consisting of rice, tofu and fresh vegetables as these were readily available in Chinatown. If they had one vice, it was smoking but they only smoked self-rolled cigarettes with crude tobacco. They toiled from sunrise to sunset and went back to their rooms—often several to one tiny hovel—and to their kitchens to cook their evening meals. Most of these rooming houses had one small, cramped kitchen used by many. As the years went by, they were to form associations, sisterhoods that were like support groups and they became a close-knit and rather insular lot.

They rarely mixed with other migrants, especially those who did not speak either Hakka or Cantonese and were wary of strangers in their midst. They were also known to be rather aggressive when crossed and had no other purpose than to work hard and save money so they could return home to China when they got old. There was never any intention of making Singapore their home but by the late 1950s many were too old and feeble to travel and died here.

As late as 1996 there was a Sam Sui Kun Association that looked into the welfare of these migrants who were, by then, well into their eighties and nineties. The association provided free travel for seven

Sam Sui women in the same year to see their hometown and relatives and also to pay respects to their ancestral graves in China for one last time.

My father had a personal assistant-cum-chauffeur who spoke Hakka, a dialect not dissimilar to that of the Sam Sui women. He would often follow Father to one of his construction sites on Penang Road, sadly the same place where Father fell from a building he was inspecting in 1953 and died. Years later Ah Seng, as he was called, related the conversations he'd had with one Sam Sui woman there. I'd only been eight at the time and too young to converse with them, but by the time I reached secondary school they fascinated me.

Ah Seng's Story

One Sam Sui woman that Ah Seng knew was in her late sixties, a rather delicate and frail old lady. She escaped an arranged marriage when she was fifteen.

'Life back home in Sanshui was very hard. I worked in a sugar cane field from morning to night for very little money. My friends were better off and they did not have to face the prospect of marrying a man they did not know. For all I knew he was ugly and would beat me.'

She said all this without the least rancour and even managed a chuckle or two when she expressed her relief at not being the wife of an ogre. Her parents were relentless in wanting to marry her off. At that time married women in China had to toil even when they were pregnant, some working right up to the weeks before giving birth. Some even died because of this.

'In Singapore I can earn my own money, so who needs a husband?' she snorted while rolling one of her many cigarettes. 'Nobody can control me now.'

In addition, and perhaps most significantly, Sam Sui women were not subjected to the crippling practice of having their feet bound, like one of my relatives who spent her whole adult life hobbling about. This was so that Sam Sui women could work efficiently and, in any case, only women of a higher caste had their feet bound as it was meant to make them walk in a ladylike fashion.

When asked by Ah Seng what she thought of this practice, she snorted again.

'Humph! It was so that they could not run away from their husbands who only wanted to sleep with them and give them many children!'

Life in Singapore was, in many ways, better than in China. Sam Sui women were independent, proud and believed they were as good as, if not better than, men. That their lives were full of hardship seemed not to deter them as that was what they had chosen, not what had been chosen for them.

The Longkangs of My Life

Longkangs, or monsoon drains, were truly conduits of pleasure. It would cost nothing to zigzag across the sloping sides of the drains when they were swollen with brackish water. Sometimes, when we felt reckless, even the presence of foul sewage did not stop us from enjoying the pleasure of such sport. Besides, many monsoon drains at that time were bountiful with tropical fish. One particular type was extremely prolific and spawned like manic rabbits. We called them 'giving birth fish' as I do not know their real name.

After tiring ourselves out pounding the sides of the drain, it was enormous fun to dip old jam jars into the murky water and try to catch these little fish. Occasionally we would catch brilliantly coloured Rasbora, probably strays from the many tropical fish shops around the neighbourhood. When our pockets jingled, we would buy Siamese Fighting Fish, so called because of their pugnacious nature.

They would even peck at their own reflections on the jars and rip their lips to shreds. When two were placed in the same jar, it was a battle to the death. If one fish emerged the victor, we would fawn over the owner of that fish as it meant we could use his champion to fight another day, usually for a little money on the side. If we could not afford to buy these fish, we would just stand in the shop and watch them, enthralled for a few hours.

Of other toys we had precious few, mostly just rubber bands. I had a small fortune of these. I would plait them in thick strands and keep them in an old biscuit tin. For a game, we would draw a large square on a pavement and, standing about six feet away, attempt to throw a handful of these bands within the square. Those that fell outside the square would be claimed by the next thrower and those inside would be retained.

And that was how we spent the idle hours after school, if we were not losing our marbles. I had marbles by the score, smooth grey-veined white stones plus a coveted champion that could knock all others for a loop. Like the rubber-band game, we would use chalk to draw a square on beaten earth. Then we would place a pile of marbles in the square and attempt to 'shoot' them to send them flying. No money was involved, only the pride of owning a champion marble.

1950s

Our Trishaw Man, Khan Chia Peh

In local Hokkien parlance, *khan chia peh* means 'trishaw puller', a rather endearing term really as he was held to the bosom of many Singaporeans. We used to refer to the three-wheeled vehicle as *sar leng chia,* an essential means of transport for most Singaporeans up until the late 1950s and early 1960s. By the late 1940s, its predecessor, the rickshaw, had been phased out and replaced by these bicycles with side cars. At the beginning, these new vehicles were called cycle rickshaws on account of the fact that they evolved from the original rickshaw. Buses then did not operate a comprehensive route and were a far cry from those we see today, so the trishaw served as the ideal mode of transport.

Car ownership was the exclusive domain of the rich but there was some one-upmanship involved. In our family we had a personal trishaw man who ferried my sisters to and from school. Generally seating two, a trishaw could accommodate several more; you could carry a baby or two on your lap, and a small child could crouch at the front of the trishaw. This didn't happen often as trishaw men were not too keen about risking a heart attack by peddling a 300 lb load—the total weight of a family of four or five.

Trishaws were the favourite mode of transport for Nonya ladies not given to walking long distances for the simple reason that they wore heeled slippers and fairly tight sarongs that made it difficult to negotiate uneven roads. The truth was my mother and aunts were rather languid people for whom exercise was an alien activity and best left to men like trishaw pullers.

Every neighbourhood had its own brigade of trishaw pullers who, during their breaks, would simply perch on their bicycle seats, put their feet on the handlebars, cover their faces with a battered straw hat and snooze for an hour or two. It was remarkable that they didn't fall over. Once, during Chinese New Year, my wicked neighbour, an evil child, lit a fire cracker with a long fuse and attached it to the toes of a sleeping trishaw man. When it exploded, did he wake up? No, he simply shook his foot and continued sleeping. He must have been really exhausted.

Trishaw men usually cycled for hours without much respite. Local temple authorities did have a charitable heart and would arrange, at different distances along some streets, a tea stop under a makeshift shelter. Each stop had a large earthenware urn filled with cold tea so trishaw men could slake their thirst, and then some. Sometimes a particularly knackered trishaw man would not only drink the tea, but ladle cups of it to wash his face and hair! These 'tea kiosks' were still around in the 1960s, and as kids we also got up to some mischief. We would used the tea to wash our marbles and tops after play!

Even prostitutes had their personal trishaw man, a downscale version of the taxis employed by the high-class courtesans of the cabarets. Near our home were two local 'guesthouses'. This was really a euphemism for brothels. At the courtyard of each there were usually two or three trishaws at rest, and when we passed by on our way to school we could sometimes see well-dressed and heavily made-up women entering the buildings. Mother warned us to never go into one of these guesthouses, knowing who dwelt there.

It only fuelled our curiosity and we would sometimes sneak along the sides of the hotels to try and peep through the windows. We never saw anything or anybody as the windows gave only a view of the hallways. What we sometimes did was chat with the trishaw pullers, and the stories they told were fascinating. One chap, Khan Chia Peh, regaled us about his life in China twenty years earlier. He had come from Fouzhou—as many of the trishaw pullers did—and spoke a dialect akin to Hokkien.

He had been a farm worker, toiling from dawn to dusk for a pittance and living in a shack with his parents, six brothers and three sisters. Often they had little food other than watery rice porridge, a few pickled vegetables and some fish. Life was gruelling and when he turned eighteen, he took advantage of the open door policy initiated by the British and moved to Singapore. He had tried many jobs, from manual labour to fishmonger's assistant, but when I spoke to him he'd found his niche as a trishaw man.

'Now so good as I do not have to peddle for many hours. My client only uses me a few times at night and the rest of the time I can sleep. Sometimes when I introduce her to a businessman, she pays me more money and tips!' These trishaw men were rather like mobile pimps. I saw fit to ask him what kind of business his client was in to have customers. His reply was rather cryptic, but kind. 'You, small boy, don't worry about such things.' It was part of my early education about the murky side of humanity.

Khan Chia Peh was also fastidious about his personal hygiene. Near the guesthouses in Farrer Park, the government had built a public swimming pool. It cost twenty cents per entry and it was here that I spent many happy, splashy hours. At certain times of the day, when Khan Chia Peh had been cycling and carrying other passengers, he would make for the swimming pool and jump in wearing only his under shorts of striped cotton. He did not and could not swim as such, but rather soaked in the shallow end then proceeded to clean himself with a cloth. The pool staff did not impose rules about regulation swimwear until they noticed that it was often filled with trishaw men and other sundry manual labourers using it as a bathhouse! After that a sign went up stating: EVERY SWIMMER MUST WEAR PROPER SWIMMING TRUNKS OR HE WILL BE ASKED TO LEAVE THE POOL! It was written in four languages: English, Mandarin, Malay and Tamil. The message must have hit home, as in later years I never again saw trishaw pullers bathing there.

I used to walk to my upper primary school, which was only one street away, but during my early primary years, my school was a few miles further on and we had to use a trishaw. Though Father had a car by then it was used exclusively by him for business. The thought of ferrying us to school never crossed his mind and we didn't have the nerve to ask. Five mornings a week, my first mother would accompany me to my primary school in McNair Road—my two older brothers were already attending classes at an upper primary school in Rangoon Road and didn't need a trishaw—and return home in the same trishaw. She would arrange for the trishaw man to pick me up after school, sometimes unaccompanied and sometimes bringing her along. She did this when she wanted to catch up with the mothers of the other kids. If she decided to wait for me to finish school, she would gather with a few mothers on the front patio of a neighbouring house. She always carried a pack of Chinese playing cards called See Sek, which means 'four colours' in Hokkien as they came in red, green, yellow and white. She and the other mothers would spend the hours that I was in class gambling. Even Khan Chia Peh joined in when he didn't feel inclined to do any peddling.

You could say that I had my personal trishaw man for a few years. Most rides cost twenty cents for a short ten-minute ride but this would increase, depending on the distance. Our arrangement was on a weekly basis, but I never knew how much my personal transport cost as Mother dealt with it.

Many years later I heard that Khan Chia Peh had died, and by the early 1970s this mode of transport had all but died out. Today it is purely a quaint tourist attraction costing about S$20 per ride. Trishaws have become an indelible part of Singapore's history, but the most curious thing is that now in London and New York, trishaws have become a form of 'green transport'. Long may they last.

Taxi Dancers

Curious title, no? Taxi dancers did not refer to cab drivers who did break-dancing during their breaks, but rather to professional women who charged for dancing with randy old men like Father. Young men didn't patronise these women for it wasn't about the joys of tripping the light fantastic, as such. These were young women who had been groomed to be light on their feet and ensconced in what were known as cabarets in one of the three World amusement parks I grew up with: New, Happy and Great. The taxi reference was probably due to the fact that each woman had her own private cab that would take her to wherever she was destined after she'd got her prey, so to speak. Trishaws were beneath taxi dancers as the latter were too well dressed, being in a class that demanded elegance to snare their prey.

These amusement parks were sprawling acreages designed to host exhibitions and other sundry fairs but were best known as dens of iniquity. In 1966 Happy World had a name change and became known as Gay World, which Western tourists found most bemusing. They thought Singapore had become so liberal as to accord a special place for the gay community!

Great World and New World were known for their restaurants and cabarets. Our home was near to New World in Serangoon Road and Father usually frequented the cabaret shows there. The women were a mixed coterie of exotic blends. Many were believed to be orphans, adopted by spinsters who were very single-minded in grooming their young charges to become dancing girls as a means to continue their financial solvency.

All the girls were slim and pretty in a way that made them stand out as potential mistresses for rich, dirty, old men. Indeed the very raison d'etre of their existence was to snare a wealthy sugar daddy so everyone was happy—except the sugar daddies' wives if they ever found out. Father was a prime target for this match made in a dance hall.

The cabaret girls did not, heaven forbid, regard themselves as hookers—even if they had been groomed all their lives to hook some well-heeled patron—but were happy enough to be called courtesans. A rose by any other name must at least be fragrant. And indeed they were, reeking of heady perfumes, with scarlet lips and painted talons. They were at least a notch above their lesser-pedigreed sisters, the hookers of less salubrious stomping grounds who did not have their own taxis but trishaws! Times were hard and the meagre earnings they picked up from occasional passengers did not quite add up to what their hooker patrons paid them.

Such was the social divide of a world resonant with different rhythms. Dancing women were experts at the waltz, tango, foxtrot and quickstep, usually to the music of one Victor Silvester and his Ballroom Orchestra. Exotic and exuberant Latin dances like the rumba, samba and cha-cha were still a decade away. Father and his business cronies were not necessarily a great big heap of testosterone. They were of the ancient school of male chauvinists who exercised their inalienable right to have their cake and eat it; in short, a wife or two or four and as many mistresses as their bank accounts would allow. It could have stemmed from Imperial China when emperors had a many as a hundred concubines.

On the Buses

Our bus system may have seemed adequate in the 1950s, but compared to today it really made life very difficult. Before Merdeka Bridge linked the city with the east coast, travelling to and from these two districts was tantamount to spending half a day on the road. Whenever I had to visit my grandparents, or simply wanted to eat out in Katong or Changi, it entailed a convoluted journey that taxed both patience and bodily comfort.

I had to take a Singapore Traction Company (STC) bus. STC was an ironic name for a bus company, considering the fact that strap-hanging when the bus was full was practically a kind of traction—like the medieval torture of stretching the body!

How well I remember this convoluted route. First I had to take an STC number eighteen bus which would stop just outside the Convent of the Holy Infant Jesus. Fast forward four decades to the time when I visited Singapore again after being away for ten years. Imagine my confusion when I saw in the convent's place an edifice to gourmet pretensions called Chijmes.

'Whoa!' I said to my colleague in the publishing firm I was working for. 'Someone has misspelled "chimes", adding a "j" for some stupid reason.'

'No, you idiot,' my colleague replied full of mirth. 'The initials stand for Convent of the Holy Infant Jesus. Now who's stupid?'

What sacrilege, I thought, but change is what modern Singapore is all about.

Anyway, I clearly remember there was a bus stop next to a breadfruit tree within the grounds of the convent. After alighting from the number eighteen bus, I would take the STC number ten all the way to Katong and alight outside the Roxy cinema. From there I then had to take a red Tay Koh Yat bus number two and then take a third red bus number three to Siglap. The whole journey took all of an hour and a half. It cost twenty cents for the first leg, fifteen cents for the second and ten cents for the last. In 1956 Merdeka Bridge was still a vague notion in the minds of urban planners.

If my final destination was Changi, it meant a fourth change, which was like waiting for a milk train! If I got there in an hour and a half it was good, but usually it took about two hours. The whole journey cost a handsome thirty-five cents in all but what a saga!

It didn't help that the bus from Siglap to Changi, and from Changi to Siglap, was popular with market traders, so it was like a travelling menagerie with chickens, ducks and the odd piglet carried in baskets by the traders. You would pay your money to the ticket collector who would then give you a little piece of paper torn from a large roll he had in a metal box. My mother, who suffered from travel sickness, found it exceptionally gruelling but she had little choice. A trishaw puller would have had a heart attack if he'd attempted this prolonged journey, not that Mother did not try persuading her regular trishaw man to do so.

One of my aunts found travelling on the buses easier, and the tales she had to tell after some journeys! Apparently some men deliberately strap-hung near women and each time the bus jerked and swerved—which was often given the state of some rural roads—they would swing with the rhythm and somehow brush their lower bodies against an unsuspecting woman's anatomy. When it happened to my aunt one time, she did what any decent woman would do: she took a large gold pin from her hair bun and jabbed it at whatever part of the man's body that happened to be where it shouldn't have been. She chortled with glee when it rammed home.

'I tell you, it must have poked his privates for he yelped and got out very quickly at the next stop. I think it was on purpose!'

There were other hazards to bus riding that one would not care to be involved in today. Bus drivers did not seem to have any particular regard for passenger safety, and quite often would drive off before passengers had alighted properly. On many occasions a passenger would trip, fall on the road and get separated from his basket of live chickens as they escaped and caused almighty mayhem. What a hullabaloo it was trying to corral squawking, frantic chickens in a bus.

There was one occasion when I was returning from Granny's farm in Changi. On the same bus there was a lady carrying a basket of durians. Suddenly the bus jerked violently and came to a screeching halt as the driver tried to avoid a jay walker. The passenger's basket tipped over and the durians fell out, rolling to the front of the bus, whereupon a male passenger had the misfortune to fall off his seat and land squarely on one of the thorny fruits. It was a painful sight, but much more so for the poor man.

There was relief all round when the first *pau wang chia* (pirate taxis) came on the scene and the comfort level of long journeys went up by many notches. Most of these taxis were illegal, hence the pirate tag, but they were most welcomed by popular mandate. The German manufacturers of Mercedes would not have been too pleased if they had known their beloved cars had been thus relegated. In later years I was eternally grateful for them during weekly jaunts between my army camp in SAFTI and the nearest bus station in Changi.

The Ang Mo Syndrome

When the British and other expatriates were in Singapore in the 1950s, Saturday nights became something of a political situation. If you went to a late-night show, especially if it happened to be raining, trying to flag down a taxi was an exercise of teeth-clenching futility. Often desperate late-night revellers would stop a taxi only to be confronted with the taxi driver's pointed comment of, 'I only take ang mo!' This was a very irksome situation for locals as foreigners never bargained—meters had not been introduced yet—and were also good tippers. Locals, on the other hand, never failed to haggle.

It became a sensitive issue, compounded by the fact that some anti-colonials were already seeing red about other elements of fraternisation. Domestic maids, especially the black and white *amahs*, would only work for Europeans as they paid top dollar. A syndrome developed called Ang Mo Kang (European Work), and lasted until the 1960s when most expats decamped. It became a kind of misplaced pride among foreigners that really got up the noses of locals. It sure fanned the flames of political discontent. But it was no good fuming at the taxi drivers for they had to earn a living.

Shopkeepers had a similar attitude, especially those in tourist areas and places where expats had clustered in residential enclaves. These shopkeepers would not give locals the time of day. Once I went into a steak house somewhere in Changi that was heavily patronised by British army personnel. My friends had heard about their steak and chips and we asked to see the menu for the day's special. The waitress's opening remark had me nearly jumping out of my chair to bop her one on her smug face.

'You want our special today, very expensive you know!'

Ouch.

Devils of the Deep

The 1950s were fraught with different fears as the memory of the occupation faded. It was a time for rebuilding broken homes and families. There was no television, and radio was still in its infancy. Entertainment venues were scarce, and the few cinemas were mainly Capitol, Cathay and Alhambra Theatres. Haw Par Villa (Tiger Balm Gardens) had been endowed on the Singapore public by two wealthy Chinese brothers, Aw Boon Haw and Aw Boon Par, whose names meant Tiger and Leopard respectively. There were the Botanical Gardens, the three aforementioned amusement parks and government bungalows. The more sophisticated of society had their watering holes, such as Paradise Nightclub in Pasir Panjang and other urban clubs which only the affluent could afford to patronise.

I remember Haw Par Villa the most vividly as it was the first and only theme park, albeit of a resoundingly Taoist nature. One of the displays there was a gruesome tableau which graphically portrayed the twelve tortures of Hades (Hell). We were absolutely fascinated by the hapless fate of those who'd committed crimes, even in mythology. The cement and alabaster figures on show portrayed hideous methods of torture that left nothing to the imagination. Thieves had their hands not just cut off but ground in granite mills. Liars had their tongues pulled out and chopped up, and murderers and other assorted hard-core criminals were portrayed being torn limb from limb. Most Singaporeans were enthralled with all these horrid representations. Perhaps we had a ghoulish sense of humour but it was entertainment of sorts. Video nasties these days really are no different.

As for my fear of the Chinese Hades, I recall one incident that had to do with a particular marine tableau. There was a deep pool in which resided effigies of many mythological creatures; weird mermaids and other undersea creatures that would have brought a smile to Steven Spielberg today. Just imagine Indiana Jones and the Twelve Tortures of Hades!

I remember I had gone on an outing with my cousins and proudly taken along my Brownie camera, as taking pictures on outings was de rigueur. I got a bit bored simply taking pictures and decided to do something to liven up our outing. So I climbed down into the pool—it had no water but the bottom had been painted a symbolic blue—and as my cousin primed my camera, I planted a kiss on what appeared to be the statue of a human-cum-crustacean sitting within a clam shell with snakes coiled in her hair. To cut a long story short, when I showed the picture to Mother, thinking she would be amused, she shrieked and began to chastise me, the likes of which you've never heard.

'Ayoh! Why you so stupid and reckless? Now this *hum* (clam) monster will take you for her husband. Do you not know that you never take pictures with these creatures? Now I have to go and pray in the temple and beg her not to take you to her watery hell.' By that she meant I would meet an untimely death i.e. as the monster's husband. The subsequent rituals she performed to remove this most evil hex also required me to surrender the shirt I had been wearing that fateful morning. This she incinerated with joss papers—it was my best S$5.95 CYC too!—and I had to drink a foul tea brewed with the charred remains of my shirt and the papers.

Oh Lord, as a spotty sixteen-year-old I should have been so lucky to snare a wife, what with my Brylcreemed (or was it Tancho?) hair. But my cousins cackled with laughter, quipping that at least I would have all the clam chowder I could eat for free! Naturally I did not meet my watery death, but I learnt never again to show Mother pictures of what I'd done.

I went back to Haw Par Villa sometime in 1991 to see if the scene of my early irreverence was still there. The place had been transformed into a theme park and where there had been a fearsome dragon guarding the main gate, there now stood a huge effigy of Mickey Mouse. Frankly I preferred the Twelve Tortures of Hades as at least it reflected a culture I was familiar with.

My Lampu Days

Going to the cinema was a weekend must for most as it was true escapism, whatever the movie. We booked our tickets and dressed to the nines: S$1 for front stalls, S$2 for back stalls and S$3 for the upper circle. I remember the Rex Cinema in Serangoon Road where the after-cinema treats were satay, *kambing* soup and *rojak*. It was a favourite stomping ground for many years afterwards.

If you went on a date on a Saturday night, it would invariably be to a cinema showing, thence to a place for supper. When my sister—the youngest among the girls and twelve years my senior— went on a date with her fiancé, I would invariably be the *lampu,* or streetlamp. This meant I was the chaperone and would shine a light on her fiancé if he had any salacious designs on her comely *samfoo-*

clad form. It was simply a precaution among traditional families: their unmarried daughters should never be alone with a man, even if they were betrothed.

So I would be sent on this weekly mission ostensibly to report back to Mother if my future brother-in-law did anything remotely lecherous. Whether he did or not I cannot recall with too much lucidity as he kept me well fed—and distracted—with copious amounts of *keropok*, *rojak* and whatever else I fancied, which was usually a lot. With resulting dyspepsia and a belly full of my favourite hawker dishes, I wasn't about to betray my provider.

Mother would grill me endlessly: 'Did he touch her? Did her hold her hand when they were walking?' and so on. All I could do was reply in the negative and looked forward to more burping weekends. Mother was paranoid, if nothing else. She went as far as reinforcing the snap buttons on sister's *samfoo* to make it difficult for her fiancé to try anything untoward. He was, however, a perfect gentleman and to the best of my knowledge never so much as played footsie with her under the cinema seats, let alone mess with her buttons. They are still married after fifty-four years.

Paradise of Sing-Song Girls

By the late 1950s, Singapore was a popular destination and meal ticket for many sing-song girls from Taiwan and Hong Kong. These girls were of a totally different genre from those of Father's era. They really set the entertainment scene that was to last well into the 1960s and 1970s. These pioneers were mostly at Paradise Nightclub in Pasir Panjang, to which the swains of the day would head every Saturday night. I do not know why there was always such a large concentration of beautiful women from Taiwan, but they all seemed to prefer Singapore. As one friend quipped, they were 'over here, over-paid and over-sexed'. Singapore swains had their tongues hanging down to the floor.

And they were all singers, at least during the night hours. Rumour had it that they were high-class call girls during the day, but since I did not move in the inner circle of wealthy businessmen I never found out the real truth. Given their stunning beauty and hourglass figures, they had no trouble snaring any man. Most were comely, but Shirley Bassey they weren't. For some inexplicable reason they had names like Lulu, Fifi, Mimi and Fanny.

Many a Singapore businessman considered having a Taiwanese singer as arm candy, a proud achievement. Many of these girls did extremely well for themselves and this must have encouraged others to follow over the next two decades. So to Paradise we swooning males and the plain gauche like yours truly would go, pockets jingling, hearts thumping and other appendages throbbing, to be more succinct.

Much as I didn't understand a word of Mandarin, the singers' only language, I enjoyed their melodious crooning—until they began to sing English songs for which they had neither had elocution lessons or indeed understood the fine nuances of phrasing and meaning. To say that they butchered English is an understatement. They would persist in singing songs not native to their tongues and fractured them something awful. 'Blue Moon' became 'Brue Moo' and 'Let's Make Love' was mutated to 'Rats May Ruv'. 'Jingle Bells' became transmuted to 'Chingko Bear' and other torturous linguistic crimes were committed. Still it was fun to request for songs like 'Supercalifra gilisticexpialidocious', at which Fifi's attempts to enunciate the words sent us into hysterics.

These girls actually created a name for themselves, and if a local girl became something of a flirt she would be described as a 'Taiwan singer'. I actually got to know one of them who was a friend of a friend. She turned out to be a decent sort and had come to earn a living so as to support her brothers and sisters back in Taipei. She said that in one month she could earn enough to pay for her siblings' school fees for a year. I thought it very noble and she earned my respect for her mission.

Obiang Cha-Cha

As the years progressed, these songstresses moved to other urban spots such as Orchard Road and nightclubs patronised by the chic crowd and Taiwanese businessmen, naturally. As for obiang, I believe it is a bastardisation of the popular Off-Beat cha-cha that was all the rage. Off-Beat, or OB, was a dance which required one to dip and jiggle one's behind in a most provocative manner. It became the signature rhythm of guys who couldn't dance, and singers who couldn't sing. And BO was when one jiggled and passed wind at the same time! I leave you to deduce why this was so. Nonetheless, with the advent of Sunday Tea Dances at which I was a frequent patron, it became the thing to do.

Dancing schools were also all the rage, and one such school became well documented. It was run by a Mr Lau Poh San who was a dance demi-god among the OB crowd. People packed into his classes to learn the latest rumba, cha-cha, mambo and other exotic Latin American moves. It was a pulsating time for all, and home dance parties became a common social highlight. His two children, Sunny and Betty, went on to win scores of medals for ballroom dancing.

There were few live bands as such, and most dancing was done to the sounds of gramophone records or vinyls. Some years ago I gave away a whole stack of them to charity, little realising that they were collectors' items and worth a pretty penny. Among my stash were Stanley Black's *Latin Rhythms*, albums by Xavier Cougat and his mambo group, Trio Los Paraguayos and Tito Puente.

It was an exciting era for those enamoured by swaying, bopping, languid dances and women dressed to match with flounces, hoop earrings, huge plastic flowers in their hair and other Latin paraphernalia. I remember well such vocal luminaries as Grace Chang and Chang Chung Wen, both stunningly beautiful singers and actresses, the latter from Taiwan. In fact, Chang Chung Wen earned the cachet of 'The most beautiful animal in Formosa' (Formosa was the former Portuguese name for Taiwan). I also remember Grace Chang, who was known as the Mambo Queen and graced many a cinema screen with her sexy moves. Her fabulous side-swept big hairdo became iconic, and was copied by women for decades.

Ten Cents a Movie

When Father was still alive he had an 8 mm projector that he would use to show black-and-white films. The movies were always silent as he did not have a sound system, even if talking films had been available. Our family home had a capacious hall and when he set up his projector, we would be inundated by dozens of kids and their parents who could not afford to go to proper cinemas. They would all sit on the floor and be enthralled by cartoons, but it was the aftermath that caused my mother to seethe.

Some of the children would leave the place where they'd been sitting awash with their bodily fluids and other unspeakable deposits that Mother would have to mop up, cursing Father for his generosity as she did so.

'You'd think what this is a public cinema. No manners, these children and their parents,' she'd grumble. The children had probably been too mesmerised by the movie to bother asking for the toilet.

Near our home was a house belonging to a well-to-do family who exercised the same generous spirit. They too had a projector but instead of letting neighbours into their home, they set up a screen, using a stretched bed sheet, on their forecourt. We could then perch on the railings of their fence and watch the movies. The only snag was that the film was back to front so every action was reversed from left to right and vice versa. Still, it was free but clinging to a fence for several hours wasn't exactly comfortable. However there was a sweet bonus. Just beyond the fence was a rambutan tree and during the fruiting season we would help ourselves to the fruits while watching the films. Who needed popcorn?

After Father passed away, Mother was even more fiercely protective and we had to have a very good reason if we wanted to take in a cinema show. Not that we had to venture further than the local playing field which, once a week, became the site for a travelling cinema. As the forerunner of cinemas, these travelling cinemas were more than adequate. In any case, the cinemas downtown entailed a bus ride that, even though it only cost twenty cents for one journey, was beyond even our slim pockets. It cost much less to patronise these rustic travelling ones.

The screen was a makeshift affair, no more than a large sheet of white cloth stretched between two bamboo poles. The 'walls' of this first walk-in cinema were simply a temporary picket fence of canvas, but oh the joy of sitting on the grass through endless episodes of *Zorro's Black Whip* and *Jungle Jim* for only ten cents!

All we needed was ten cents and a thick wad of old *Tiger Standard* newspapers that we could put on the damp grass and sit on, and we would be enthralled for several hours. If the operators decided to run two episodes of some heroic epic on the same night, we would be charged a discount price of fifteen cents.

One time the organisers got really ambitious and decided to use CinemaScope to crank out the film *Quo Vadis,* which was screened on a sheet stretched across four bamboo poles. The epic starred Robert Taylor and just as he was about to kiss his screen lover, a gust of wind whipped by and blew down two poles, enshrouding the front two rows of viewers. The organisers learnt their lesson as we all demanded our money back. Never again did they show a film on a wide screen.

When it rained, there was the usual pandemonium but did the organisers stop the screening? Of course not. Viewers, armed with umbrellas, simply sprouted a sea of brollies and it was the most irritating thing to try and see the screen over their tops. Still, it was the only form of cinema we had until a few years later.

As I have mentioned, somewhere along Serangoon Road, where the amusement park called New World was located, the Sun Talkie cinema had been built. Although talking films were already the vogue, many films were still silent, especially those starring Charlie Chaplin. For the luxury of sitting on proper seats—actually they were rough-hewn wooden benches—we had to pay fifty cents, which was a lot of money then when our school pocket money was usually no more than twenty or thirty cents a week. In fact I had to save for a few weeks in order to accumulate this amount.

But at least the Sun Talkie cinema had a roof, unlike the makeshift one we were used to, so we did not have to bring umbrellas. There was, however, no attendant toilet and to relieve ourselves we simply left the large hall and found a handy bush or shrub outside. Well, the males did. I do not know how the girls managed but anyway, few young girls were allowed out to the cinema and if they were, they probably went to the toilet before taking their seats. At least I assume they did, for relieving themselves in shrubbery was not at all acceptable behaviour.

The 1950s was also a time when triads were ominously present. One had to be very careful not to so much as stare for too long at any guy who appeared to be one of them. In fact, many a fight would break out as a result of these staring matches. There were several sects and each had their own secret signals and codes. When I was still in secondary school, a few of the less studious students were enlisted by triad gangs and we lived in fear of being recruited or subjected to protection money.

Whenever I brought home a classmate, Mother would give him the third degree.

'Are you a *samseng* (gangster)?' she would ask outright.

I used to caution her and say that even if my classmate was, she shouldn't be so bold as to confront him so directly. I did hear of some gory incidents where triad members would gather in one place and battle it out with knives and bicycle chains studded with nails. It was a nightmare era for the police.

Once, when I accompanied Mother to the market on her usual shopping trip, we witnessed a horrifying incident. We stopped by a noodle stall and ordered our usual breakfast. Just as were eating, a man came hurtling past us and collapsed in a bloody heap at our feet. He had a knife sticking out of his back. Mother jumped up, gripped my arm in terror and told me to run. I protested that I had not finished my *tar mee pok* and she screamed, 'What? This man has just been murdered and you want to continue eating? You mad, or what?'

Well, my noodles had cost me thirty cents and I had barely finished half the bowl.

Snow White and the
Poisoned Char Siew Paus

Movie theatres were a godsend throughout most of the 1950s as there was precious little entertainment around. Capitol Theatre was the stomping ground of just about everybody as nearby was an ice cream parlour. It was also a stone's throw from the Esplanade where post-cinema activities were concentrated. The seafront was the perfect setting for courting couples and the original Satay Club offered sustenance for those less romantically inclined.

In Singapore at that time there was no local film industry to speak of, apart from a small studio that churned out Malay films. Imported American movies were still a decade away and we had to depend on a slew of feature films made in Hong Kong and Indian movies that ran the gamut from the sublime to the ridiculous. The former were based on set plots that rarely changed but for the main leads.

Female idols were the beauteous Lin Dai, Li Li Hua, Pai Lu Ming, Betty Loh Ti and Margaret Tu Chuan, to name but a few. The male matinee idols were Peter Chen Ho, Yuen Chuen and Chiao Hung. Peter was married to Lin Dai and Yuen Chuen was married to Li Li Hua and you get the picture about the scene. The plots were right out of soap operas: girl meets boy, girl marries boy and mother-in-law throws the monkey wrench into the works. The whole story was usually drawn out over hours of heart-wrenching singing.

Favourite costume dramas were classics like Diao Chan of *Romance of the Three Kingdoms*, *Love Eternal* and *Madame White Snake*. These epics were invariably of the ancient Chinese historical genre but they were lapped up by audiences. Some were set to music that simply added to the overall length of the films. If there was a death scene, the heroine would perform at least two songs during her death throes; and this with a knife in her heart and blood spewing out of her mouth. Still she sang and flopped down theatrically only after the last strains of the orchestra had died. We quipped that it took three songs for Lin Dai to die!

And these were just the films in Mandarin. Those in Cantonese that I recall brought more mirth than any others before them, and they weren't supposed to be comedies. They were only hysterically funny because of their story lines. Imagine a Cantonese version of *Snow White and the Seven Dwarfs* starring the delectable Lee Heong Kum as Snow White and Chay Yin as the prince. These two Cantonese thespians were the 1950s version of Jet Li and Gong Li, if you like.

Anyway, as the story goes Snow White's evil stepmother decides to do away with her because her enchanted mirror tells her that

Snow White and not her is the fairest in the land. Spitting nails, she transforms herself into a harridan and goes to the forest where Snow White loves to play with the animals. In the original fairy tale, Snow White is enticed to eat a poisonous apple. In this Shaw Brothers production, she is offered four *char siew pau*s tainted with poison.

I remember I found it hilarious that Snow White manages to eat not one, but all four, of the *pau*s and proceeds to sing several songs before gasping and dying. The prince comes along but does not kiss her because at the time the film was made, this was disallowed in Chinese movies. Instead he sings to her, not just one aching song but several, before she disgorges the poison *pau*s from her throat. It seemed that the audience didn't particularly care that she had eaten all four poisoned *pau*s but still managed to come back to life. And the background music? Beethoven's 'Fifth Symphony'.

Indian movies sat firmly on the ridiculous side, being all of four hours long and with plots that have not changed for the past fifty years: boy meets girl, boy sings to girl and both sing in unison to the accompaniment of a whole chorus that suddenly appears. They always live happily ever after but not before more singing and dancing into the Mumbai sunset.

Technical accuracy was certainly not a strong suit of this cinematic genre. One movie had a boy and girl courting and singing while riding bicycles. It mattered little that the scudding clouds behind them were moving at a speed much faster than the speed of the bicycle, and they weren't even holding onto their handlebars. Still they managed to get through half a dozen songs interspersed with dancing. Where had the bicycles gone? Nowhere apparently, but mysteriously came back into the picture after a while. These films were not comedies, but one had to laugh at the guileless nature of Indian romantic movies.

Malay films firmly followed the domestic mould, with story lines built around home life, endless tea drinking and sobbing maidens. A friend who worked in the industry said that if you could cry, you could become a Malay film star. Famous names of the time were Neng Yatimah, her daughter Rose, P. Ramlee, his wife Saloma, Maria Menado, comedian Wahid Satay and that was it. They were invariably in every movie, just with different plots and costumes. Essentially they played themselves.

Neng was the quintessential matriarch, with Rose as the ingénue. Ramlee was the 1950s answer to Frank Sinatra as he could hold a tune, Saloma was the Marilyn Monroe of Malaya, Maria was the sexpot and Wahid Satay the fall guy. Oh yes, there was also an Indonesian import in the form of Siput Sarawak, the mother of the famous Anita Sarawak who people today might know as one of the best entertainers of the 1960s and 1970s.

And there you have it. Film sets were invariably *kampung* houses, love was wrenched out through songs and after much sobbing and tea, the young hapless couple would be seen sitting on a rock somewhere in Siglap looking into each other's eyes. As they swooned and crooned and appeared to touch, the camera would pan over their heads and you would see a couple of butterflies flitting and flirting. What lovely symbolism, and the censors would never lose any sleep over salacious content.

Actually I had my fifteen minutes of fame thanks to the very friend who told me about crying in Malay movies. He managed to get me and my cousins jobs as extras in one of the half a dozen *Pontianak* movies Cathay Kris studios churned out, starring Maria Menado. A *pontianak* is a Malay ghoul, much like Dracula but of the female gender. Like Dracula, she is believed to like to suck the blood of handsome young men who fall for her charms when she is in human female form. When she turns evil, she becomes just a hideous head with no body, only entrails. The only weapon against her evil is a long nail that one has to drive into her head, if you are so lucky.

Anyway, when it came the scene in the film where Pontianak was chased by the villagers and her hut set on fire, we, the extras would shout and egg everybody on. We were paid S$10 for an afternoon's work but I never saw myself in the movie as the scene must have ended up on the cutting-room floor. Ah, the joy of fleeting fame. By the way, when Pontianak was in the form of a beautiful female, she loved to eat *rojak,* invariably sold by Wahid Satay. He met his untimely death when Pontianak sucked his blood dry, but not before she had eaten all the *rojak* he'd offered her. Years later, at a friend's home, I met up with Maria who had retired and still looked stunning at sixty something years old. She was eating *rojak,* as per her film persona, and we had a good laugh.

Monkey Business

I have the sharpest memories of a patch of green in Tanglin which acted as the backdrop to many an exciting outing. Well, these outings were exciting to us—we would torment the hundreds of monkeys there, some positively feral, and endlessly pose for photographs dressed in our spanking 1950s threads. At that time for men it was fashionable to wear skin-tight trousers, Buddy Holly spectacles and put lots of Brylcreem in the hair. The girls were into circular skirts and cancan petticoats that got caught on just about everything, from bus doors to cinema seats.

For the girls it was considered chic to pose with the circular skirt arranged in a perfect circle on the grass and one finger coquettishly positioned under the chin. The boys would stand peering through spectacles, looking like nerds—today's Ah Beng has nothing on this— and sometimes have to sit on the edge of the girl's skirt so as not to muss it up. Snap taken, we would then set up a picnic corner and begin to entice the monkeys, not that they needed any encouragement. Some were so bold as to come and snatch our sandwiches. We would slosh them with orange crush and they would snarl and bare their teeth. It was fun, if not rather cruel, but it was the 1950s after all, and political correctness was not an issue.

Bungalows and BBQs

When holidays beckoned and listening to fractured English pop songs paled into insignificance, the race was on to rent one of the former colonial houses located by the sea at Pasir Ris and Tanah Merah. The rules were that you had to ballot for it, and only civil servants were eligible. The waiting list was long and categorised into divisions one, two and three, which was undemocratic to say the least. Well, it followed the British system that we'd inherited, and hierarchy extended beyond your place of work. If you weren't part of division one, you would make sure you had friends who were, but actually division two bungalows weren't too bad either. Whenever one of our crowd managed to secure one, we would all invariably pile into it. BBQs were the order of the day, and we would make sure we had a record player or two, a mahjong table and all the paraphernalia needed to spend a salubrious week by the sea.

However, these bungalows did have some irksome downsides. Their electric hotplates took forever to heat up and the mosquito squadrons were hell bent on sucking our blood. So mosquito nets and scented coils were also important gear. It was an innocent time; our crowd were not into 'snogging', to use a modern term, courtships were sedate and no hanky-panky was condoned as usually the parents of the person who'd secured the bungalow would also join us.

It was as much youthful fun as family togetherness, a time when the focus was on good food, water sports and endless mahjong sessions. These events were the one activity that Mother fully endorsed, despite the fact that among us young adults, hormones were never far from the surface. There was little libidinous behaviour and romance was of the old-fashioned variety. Walks on the beach and listening to songs by Connie Francis and Doris Day were all the help we needed to fan the flames of gentle passion. Besides, smooching on the beach came with the risk of being eaten alive by mosquitoes.

What was nice about the bungalows in Tanah Merah was their proximity to my granny's fruit farm in Siglap. This was the era of my youth that most shaped my penchant for food and tropical fruits. Living in London these past twenty-five years has only intensified my longing for durians and mangosteens, fruits that cost an arm and a leg in Britain. I still cannot eat a mangosteen without feeling nostalgic about those in Granny's farm.

Halcyon Days

After Father died, First Mother and our biological mother took to spending more time with Mother's mother in her sprawling beachside home just yards from the sea along Nallur Road in Siglap. What used to be a sun-bleached strip of pristine sand lapped by the gentle ebb and flow of coastal tides is now an unrecognisable private housing estate; the zealous government land reclamation project has all but obliterated my memories of those carefree days and balmy nights.

For me that time was the beginning of my peripatetic life, full of fun and frolic—and a few accidents. Halcyon were the days when we could jump into the sea at any time, and during this period, I first learnt to swim. I was about ten. One of my male cousins had borrowed a rickety sampan from one of the fishermen living with his family in one of the many attap huts nudging the seashore. My cousin coaxed me to go fishing with him one morning and, unaware of his real intentions, I agreed. As soon as we were out in deeper water he shoved me overboard chortling, 'This is the only way to learn how to swim.' I must have swallowed a gallon of salt water but, hey presto, I learnt how to tread water in just a few minutes.

Other joys I recall were when we, Mother included, used to

scrape the soft sand on the beach looking for little clams called *remis*. When we had bucketfuls of them, they would be born to the kitchen where they would be pickled with soy sauce, garlic and vinegar. I have not eaten these for several decades. They were delicious.

Granny's Durians

The most fun we used to have was at Granny's fruit plantation. I still remember the glorious joy of climbing up mangosteen trees that were no more than the height of a one-storey bungalow. Mama, as we sometimes called Granny, was chatelaine of one small section of a fruit plantation owned by our maternal grandfather. It was about a hundred metres inland from the sea and close to Grandfather's family home. Apparently he gave this little plantation and all that was on it to Granny to stop her nagging him to curtail his opium-smoking habit, a lifelong indulgence that we found most fascinating.

In reality, the plot of land Granny had wasn't a plantation as such, but rather a smallholding that my maternal grandfather had planted with a few durian, mangosteen and jambu trees. There were also many rambutan, mango, soursop and starfruit trees.

These were the most precious years of my teenage life as the plantation was also close to my grandfather's large rambling home, built in the typical Peranakan style. At that time the area was still unpolluted by the detritus of the petroleum industry.

Granny was a true-blue Peranakan who only wore the elder Nonya's costume of a long tunic and sarong. She taught us much about determining the quality of each type of durian, how to spot a wormy mangosteen, trap a grass snake, catch a swift-swimming catfish in the stream that ran across her smallholding and many other rustic secrets. She also had a vocabulary that would have made a sailor blush, and on many occasions would used her pungent Peranakan curses on people she didn't like. When she was crossed, she would raise herself to her full height of four feet six inches, with an indomitable spirit to match, and let fly with enough ripe expletives to turn the air blue.

She spent most of her days tending to the dozen or so fruit trees that dotted the smallholding. We never ran short of home-grown durians, rambutans, mangosteens, *langsats*, *chiku*s, guavas and mangoes. The durian trees were beyond our reach as well as the soaring rambutan trees. A wizened old lady who spoke little Chinese, Granny manned the place all on her own. She would collect any durians that dropped upon ripening and sell them to the local market fruiterers. Of course she would pick the choicest mangosteens and rambutans and it was from these transactions that she earned pocket money. But it was her durians that gave us the most pleasure. She even had names for each tree, as the fruits each bore were distinctly different to one another.

One was called Lau Chairn (Old Green), and it bore large durians, rather like the Thai Mon Thong we know of today. The flesh was not as soft as it should have been, harder and not butter-like. Granny's favourite tree was called Eu Chi (Fine Thorns) and it bore smaller, exquisitely flavoured fruit with the slightly bitter edge that true durian lovers adore.

At that time there was no particular way to harvest durians other than to wait for the fruits to fall from the tree of their own accord. We would watch and wait for the familiar thud, signalling that one or more durians had dropped from their great height. Like hares, we would race to the spot and swoop upon them. We were never allowed to eat the good durians and Granny kept a close watch on the natural harvest. The ones that cracked upon falling would be our treat.

Occasionally Granny had help from a neighbour, a skinny middle-aged man who would help gather the durians when we were not around during the school holidays. When we were around, this devious man took great pleasure in crying wolf. He would go to a particular spot, away from Granny's humble attap hut, and throw a large stone or brick in the air. When it hit the ground it made much the same thud that a durian would. We would race to the spot only to see him grinning from ear to ear, holding up his stony 'find'!

Granny never needed to shop for fresh herbs as the farm also had clumps of lemon grass, pandan leaves, chilli bushes, lime leaves, turmeric leaves and chives. It was a culinary school of the most bountiful and aromatic kind, and also the place where I learned to blend spices under her tutelage. The heritage she passed on to my mother and me is what has enabled me to chronicle all that I can remember.

The little hut she lived in during the fruiting season was no larger than a garage today. It had a large raised platform that she used as a bed and community area. Here she would peel onions, prepare vegetables and also sleep on a linoleum cover. The platform was at least chest high and underneath it, running the whole perimeter, was a storage space where she kept unripe fruits. What an aromatic ambience in which to live—the fragrances of a dozen tropical fruits intermingled with the scents of lime leaves, lemon grass and frying spice pastes.

Flying Fox Curries

One pesky problem that plagued Granny was the constant presence of fruit bats, or flying foxes. These toothy fruit-loving flying creatures could devastate an entire rambutan tree in one night, which was the only time they would emerge from their daylight slumber to scavenge for food. They would lay waste almost any ripening fruit and the only way to bring them to the ground was with catapults that we were very adept at using. They were fashioned from the supple branches of a tree called the Tembusu. Our rough-hewn weapons were whittled down so we could grip them in our palms. We would then cut two lengths of stout rubber from the inner tubes of car tyres, and attach them to a small square of canvas that cradled the lethal pebbles. My cousins and I would fill our catapults with small stones, aim them at the flying foxes and shoot. The ensuing velocity and impact would literally puncture the wings. Some we missed but when the aim was true, the bats fell to the ground, snarling and spitting like mini vampires from hell. A brace or more would be borne triumphantly to Granny's kitchen where she would proceed to cook the most delicious curry, sousing them with spices and coconut milk in her clay pots.

Nothing that we caught was ever wasted. Everything, from small pythons to frogs, would be turned into a gustatory delight. You have not lived until you have eaten flying fox curry with rice, durian and *sambal belacan*. To this day I drool at the memory of this gourmet treat.

Bringing down flying foxes was a particularly vicious joy. As they wreaked havoc on Granny's fruit trees, we felt little sympathy for them. We usually aimed to catch them during the day when they slept, hanging upside down from branches. As they were usually engorged with fruit at this time, they would fall like plummeting stones when hit, still alive and snarling like miniature hounds from hell. One hefty club with a stick would stun them, then Granny would bear them gleefully to her kitchen where she would skin and gut them like chickens. Some were indeed as large as chickens and tasted of gamey beef.

Granny would then sauté a spice paste of coriander, chilli, turmeric, aniseed, onions and garlic, and simmer this, along with the joints of the bats, in coconut milk for several hours until they became tender. Today, flying fox curry and durians with rice are only a delicious, if dim, memory.

On days when peace reigned, flying foxes simmered in pots and there were delicious durians to be had, Granny's place was a culinary, fruitful paradise. She would cook her curries in earthenware pots called *belanga*. Sometimes she would catch the occasional catfish from the stream and this too would end up as scrumptious *asam pedas*, enriched and soured by the sour starfruits from one of her trees.

Our diet was esoteric to say the least. Granny's little plantation was a veritable cornucopia of exotic viands, supplemented by many herbs and vegetables that grew in her backyard that was also home to chickens, ducks and geese all being fattened for festive feasts.

How I miss her belimbing tree which bore sour fruits related to the carambola or starfruit. She would have us pluck these green fruits, that also went by the curious name of 'pig's teats' as they vaguely resembled porcine mammary glands. Granny would slice and salt the fruits, squeeze out the tart juices and cook a delicious prawn curry that I still cook today with a substitute ingredient such as aubergines. Alas, there is nothing like belimbing.

Although Granny's real home was a large seafront house, she preferred to spend most of her time in her little attap hut among her beloved fruit trees. Sometimes, if she caught a suspicious-looking person snooping about, she would wield a parang at them, the same parang she often used to dismember the odd snake that happened to slither by!

On one occasion she heard some rustling noises amid a copse of fruit trees some distance from where she was. Armed with nothing more than her trusty parang and a hissing carbide lamp fashioned from an old Ovaltine can filled with lumps of grey carbide fuel, she ventured out to find the intruders. I shudder to think what might have happened if Granny had caught them. As it turned out, they must have fled when they caught sight of this wizened figure, face contorted with fury amid the carbide glow and wielding a fearsome weapon.

The stream that crossed the smallholding was teeming with catfish that loved to feed at estuaries. Although they were smaller than the ones in the sea, if you tried to catch one you still ran the risk of receiving a very painful jab from the spike protruding from its head. The spike contained a mild poison that could cause excruciating pain, but the prospect of Granny's catfish curry with tamarind more than compensated for the risk factor. There was nothing quite like Granny's coconut rice and catfish in tamarind and turmeric gravy, all downed with her equally delicious homemade *tapeh* (fermented rice).

Indeed, there was always a large vat of this potent brew fuming under Granny's bed. She would take glutinous rice, steam it and sprinkle yeast over the grains with a little sugar. Within a week the pungent smell of the fermented rice would assail our nostrils, even as we approached the plantation from the main road fifty yards away. In her backyard Granny also grew tapioca from which she would make tapioca *tapeh* that was positively alcoholic.

Most of the time we had the glorious privilege of sitting on the fork of a mangosteen tree and eating the fruit straight off its branches. Or we'd race to claim the durians that had become ripe and fallen from the trees of their own accord. This was a delicious game, for whoever got to the fruit first got to eat the choicest bits. However, I do remember a few mishaps that, luckily, did not befall me, despite my alacrity whenever I heard the characteristic thump of a falling fruit.

A cousin, not very agile on his feet and apparently with a death wish, had the misfortune of standing under one particular durian tree when a fruit chose to drop from its horizontal branch. The durian delivered him a glancing blow to the head and he had to have a few stitches to the wound. The moral of the story? Don't stand under a durian tree known to have ripening fruit. To assist us, Granny taught us some valuable lessons about how to identify which tree was ready to release its fruit. I forget her advice with the passing of time but during those halcyon days, I never once experienced this painful thorny mishap.

Fruity Battles

We revelled in the many episodes when something got up Granny's sarong and she turned into a harridan of shrieking mien that frightened off even the flying foxes. Adjoining her fruit farm was another smallholding that belonged to a buxom country farmer's wife who I remember as Ah Heng. She seemed to be constantly lactating, her ample bosoms bouncing under her loose *samfoo* whenever she climbed her own fruit trees to harvest their ripened bounty.

We took great joy in leering at her—at least my older cousins did—and she would swear at us with language that does not bear repeating. She was also less than ethical about which fruits were hers. A little stream marked the boundaries of the two farms, and some of the boughs from Granny's trees would hang over her side. I remember one stout tree in particular that Granny was fond of as it bore large, fleshy fruits called *buah binjai*. These were much like mangoes but I haven't seen any for over forty years.

If the *binjai* dropped on Ah Heng's side, and if she thought no one was looking, she would steal them and hide them under her *samfoo*. Since she was already of ample proportions, she often got away with this misdeed—we could never ascertain if her undulating movements were from her breasts or the stolen fruit! One day Granny caught her red-handed and the ensuing battle was a raucous bout the likes of which I haven't seen since. Granny rose to her full height of four foot six or something and ranted in Malay and some Teochew at the lady thief.

What a palaver! They screamed so loudly at each other and gesticulated so wildly that soon a crowd formed. To back up Granny we joined in the verbal fray, but Ah Heng's sons were rather more menacing. At one point Granny, her voice hoarse from the tirade, lifted up her sarong and cursed with all the might she could muster:

'Nah you can see my privates (this is my translation as her words were too ripe for publication) and may you never strike lottery for seven years!'

Where she learnt this from I never found out, and I know Granny had never seen an Italian film where curses like those were accompanied by lurid Neapolitan gestures. Anyway, it worked as Ah Heng was of a superstitious nature. She promptly hurled the fruits across to our side and ran off with her brood. My admiration for Granny's feistiness immediately went up several notches.

We were to see more of this feistiness in other clashes. One in particular involved another peasant farmer's wife, who lived on a neighbouring smallholding and was also wont to stealing our fruits. Once, Granny caught her trying to get away while girding her blouse around what looked like an extremely large durian. Granny gave chase with a gait that belied her small stature, caught the offender and pushed her to the ground with the durian on top of her quivering stomach.

'You want to steal my durians, huh? Well, take it then,' she shrieked at the woman, pressing the durian down on her exposed stomach. Together they made enough noise to wake the whole neighbourhood. The woman in question limped away with a bleeding navel, much to granny's delight, and we all had extra durians that day. The upshot of it all was that there were no more thefts.

Every time we had a durian feast, there was a ritual that we had to observe. Granny would take an empty durian casing, fill it with tepid salted water and insist we drink it all. This was supposed to counter the heatiness of durian. It must have worked for we never suffered from a surfeit of the fruit, that was known to cause spots and acne.

Grandpa had also built a small wooden bungalow right by the seafront, its front yard kissing the lapping waves. He would spend his time there whenever he needed to collect rent from the many tenants that lived in the attap huts dotting the coastal reaches. The whole area was like a sprawling estate with no particular parameters. Grandpa's house cast a noble shadow across the rustic neighbourhood. It was affectionately termed 'The Big House' by all his tenants, who were mostly Hainanese fisher folk who looked upon Grandpa as a venerable *lau chek* (old uncle).

By the 1960s the house was gone but the memory of its spacious, airy interior is still fresh in my mind. When I visited China in 1992, a feeling of déjà vu took me back three decades when I saw some houses in Beijing that looked very similar. Each house had a very wide frontage with an overhanging porch, on either side of which were raised ledges supported by fat, curvy, glazed, green portals. It was on these ledges that we whiled away boring afternoons when it rained. The porch was covered with terracotta tiles throughout and many times we played our favourite game of 'balloon' or hopscotch.

First we would use a piece of chalk to draw three large squares and a half-moon-shape cap, the whole looking like a large mushroom. On either side of this were two squares that formed a 'T' with the column of three squares. Each player had a flat stone. He would hop on one leg on each square, hurl the stone into the next square, pick it up still on one leg and traverse the whole grid without ever putting both feet on the ground. It was an endless game and great fun.

Beyond this porch was the main hall that I remember to be rather gloomy, with light coming in from only one window set high up in one wall. On either side of this capacious hall was a large doorway and heavy beamed doors that led into yet another room, the secondary hall. This kind of 'Big Hall' and 'Second Hall' were characteristic features of houses owned by the merchant classes. Through another large doorway was the cavernous kitchen, a square that embraced a large atrium open to the sky. Overlooking the perimeter were the overhanging balconies of the upstairs living quarters. This perimeter was so wide that it was able to remain dry during a thunderstorm, even though rain would fall right in the middle of the atrium and be washed away by drains that ran the entire length of the square.

Set into one side of the covered area was the kitchen proper. This was no more than a raised brick area in which stood several charcoal-burning red sandstone ovens called *hang lu* (*hung lo* in Hokkien). On each *hang lu* stood a wok or pot. On the floor were Granny's favourite implements, including a large *batu giling* (slab of granite) with its own granite roller that was used to grind spices to pulp. She would use this if she had to make a large amount of food for a festive meal or special occasion. For daily use she preferred a *batu lesong* (pestle and mortar). Whenever we visited the house, Mother would spend most of her time in the kitchen, cooking up a storm with a few of my other aunts.

Early most mornings, it was a most delicious treat to go down to the beach where, come drizzle or fierce sun, Mother would spend hours scraping the damp sand for *remis* (bean clam). She would gather buckets of these small clams to pickle in soy sauce, garlic and chilli. They were scrumptious when eaten with watery rice porridge.

At the crack of dawn I would be up with the first rays of the sun. Dressed in a pair of ragged shorts and a singlet, I would go to watch the fishermen bringing in their catch. Most of them owned *kelong*s (fishing platforms) about a few hundred metres out to sea. Here they manned their nets overnight. And what a sight when they rowed their *sampan*s ashore—*sampan*s which could seat two, five or even eight people. They would come crunching onto the shore where many *kampung* folk would be waiting with their bamboo shopping baskets.

The bulk of the fishermen's catch would be sold to market traders but there would always be enough left over for the pots in the village: silvery *ikan parang* (wolf herring), *ikan sembilang* (catfish), *ikan bilis* (whitebait), crabs, prawns, bivalves, squid, horse mackerel and dozens of other briny delights. I also remember *geragau*, microscopic shrimp that Granny would ferment in bottles to make our favourite Nonya dish of *cincalok*. There is nothing quite like fried *ikan parang* with *cincalok* and a good squeeze of *kesturi* lime juice.

Mother would transform catfish into ambrosial *kuah lada* (literally chilli gravy) with *brinjal* or lady's fingers. If we had a few cents in our pockets, we would buy a scoop of tiny squid, rush to the *kampung chai tau kway* man and persuade him to toss them in with the fried radish cakes so loved by all. He would grumble that the squid ink made his pan all black but usually relented when we paid him ten cents more for his trouble. My cousin would point out that his pan was black anyway and he would pretend to want to hit him with his ladle. He was nonetheless a kind hawker and we did give him regular business.

Brooklax and Running Fishermen

My cousins would concoct many ways for us to amuse ourselves. One of these was rather evil in hindsight, but at that time it was a source of great mirth. My eldest cousin would buy boxes of the laxative Brooklax and offer them to the fishermen as 'chocolates'. The fishermen were simple folk for whom chocolates were a rare treat, luxuries from town. They would greedily gobble them up, often a whole box per person.

Come the next morning, we would visit their attap homes to learn from their wives that there would be no fishing that morning. Barely being able to contain our laughter, we would politely enquire why this was so, only to be told that the men had gone down with mysterious trots. The wives blamed it on evil spirits that their husbands must have crossed. And so we fled, racked with helpless laughter. It was an unkind jape that was not tinged with evil—only the thoughtless need for fun. Till today I cannot look at a Brooklax tin without smiling at the memory.

'At least they were not constipated!' was my cousin's cheeky defence. I wondered a lot about what he was learning from the Christian brothers who taught him. He must have spent hours devising wicked schemes to make life miserable for quite a few people.

When the tide went out we had a rather unenviable chore. Out on the second bank and just before the *kelongs* that were secured to the seabed, there were scads of seaweed floating about. We would collect them by the ton, drag them across the shallows and dry them in the sun. After a few days we would sluice them down with fresh water, then dry the seaweed in the sun again, this time for weeks until it looked like pale golden straw. The seaweed was then used to make beloved *agar agar* for Chinese New Year. Mother would boil, clarify and sweeten them before dividing them into jelly moulds. These were again baked in the sun until they turned a tawny golden colour.

This was the pace of life during our school holidays—a balmy episode of endless culinary surprises, salt water brews to dispel the gaseous result of too much durian, redolent pots of flying fox and catfish curries, all amid the dusk chorus of what seemed like a thousand chirruping cicadas. It is this 'creek creek' melody that still comes to life when I shut my eyes and recall those carefree years of my childhood.

Rites of Passage

If Father was an unbeliever, there were others in our family who set total store by geomancy, feng shui et al. My maternal uncle, Mother's elder brother, had four daughters, all of whom were educated at the local convent school. As much as each family liked to see its daughters married off, there were obstacles of impossible dimensions.

Tua Koo (Big Uncle), as we addressed him, was of the old Taoist school and he would not allow any daughter of his to leave the house after school, much less go on a date. When each daughter reached about seventeen, he would seek a matchmaker to find her a prospective husband, but it was an irksome time for my cousins who must have been chafing at the bit. Each potential spouse was given the third degree and questioned about almost all of the yin and yang tenets of Taoist providence: Was he well educated? Was he a good provider? Did he have a squint? Was he bow-legged?

The litany of negative elements was endless and reached beyond the boundaries of common sense. Big Uncle truly believed that a girl born in the year of the tiger could not marry a man born in the year of the pig as she would eat him up (meaning he would die a premature death and leave her a widow). The man had to speak the same dialect, Teochew, he could not be a Christian, have floppy ears or buck teeth (this symbolised his previous incarnation of being a beast) and so on and so forth. As a result of his demands, all four daughters ended up as spinsters. They were still living together the last I heard about ten years ago. They would be in their late sixties today, if alive. Alas, we lost contact but I do feel for the poor dears.

According to folklore and ancient Chinese custom, we were not supposed to celebrate birthdays other than those that exceeded the fiftieth milestone. This was in accordance with the ancient custom that no mortal was deserving of a birthday celebration until he or she was half a century old. It was deemed that one could not achieve any wisdom before this age. The birthdays we were allowed to celebrate were at fifty-one years old, sixy-one years old, and so on, each marking the passing of yet another decade.

I can only remember celebrating our parents' fifty-first and sixty-first birthdays as they both died before their seventh decade. The requisite birthday meal was a bowl of noodles cooked in sweet syrup with two red-dyed hard-boiled eggs. After Father passed on, we became more modern and insisted on celebrating every one of Mother's birthdays. Of course she objected, claiming it was not necessary. Actually it was for economic reasons more than anything, as she did not believe in spending money at a restaurant. She also never understood the significance of birthday cake and when we once foisted this on her, she protested vehemently that only dead people had candles burned in their memory.

We never did it again.

Nonya Weddings

A Nonya wedding was a full-blooded traditional Peranakan affair with all the rituals and trimmings. I have learnt much from participating in these rich ceremonies and have, in fact, made full use of my knowledge of the Nonya heritage as a food writer and chef.

When it came to the important wedding banquet, one simply did not go to a restaurant or hotel function room. The Nonya Long Table feast was reserved for this and the preparation of food would take the family weeks.

Months before my sister's wedding in 1953, Mother would dry sliced cucumbers, cauliflower, cabbage and shallots in preparation for her splendid *acar,* the epitome of Nonya pickles and one that I make frequently. *Acar* is a supreme example of Nonya cuisine and one that was very much a labour of love for Mother. She would select shallots and garlic of similar sizes and dry them for days in the sun. The fattest green chillies would be chosen, slit open and stuffed with a spiced blend of grated green papaya. It would all then be blanched in vinegar and then tossed in another spiced blend. This *acar* could keep for months and tasted better with each passing day.

Sister's banquet required the help of many hands and these we did not lack. There were any number of aunts, relatives and even neighbours who pitched in to help. I really bemoan the passing of this tradition as community spirit does not exist today in the same measure.

The different rituals involved in a Nonya wedding are too numerous to chronicle here—they are deserving of a separate book altogether. It is suffice to know that the wedding went on for many days, even weeks. There were enough highlights to bring a smile to most, especially when it came to bargaining over the dowry. Although the question of the dowry was largely symbolic, the matchmaker employed to do the bargaining took it very seriously. She conveyed the message to my sister's intended husband's family, who were not of the same heritage and beliefs but politely conceded to her demands.

The dowry didn't consist of just cash, per se. It usually had to also include jewellery, a roast pig, lengths of sugar cane and all sorts of ritualistic items. Fundamentally, the idea was based on the tenet that no family would give away a daughter without adequate recompense. In a few cases these demands would result in minor warfare and even threats to break off the engagement! Other customs were less taxing on the Nonya soul, like Mother exhorting Sister to not smile or eat anything throughout the day's celebrations.

Poor sister had to pretend she was sad to leave the family and any happy countenance and ingestion of food would reflect her joy. Apparently getting married was not a joyful occasion for any Nonya woman. As was the custom, Mother made Sister eat a bowl of *bee tai mak* (droplet noodles) first thing on the morning of the wedding. This was supposed to sustain her for the next twelve hours of festivities. If Sister had growled, it would have come not from her throat but her stomach.

Throughout the wedding I was doing financially very well as, being the *koo kia* (little uncle), red packets were pressed into my palms from every quarter. I began to think that all those months of being my sister's chaperone during their courtship had paid off. Not so, for as soon as the wedding was all over, Mother demanded I give all the red packets to her. Money was tight and she was determined to replenish whatever she had spent.

On my brother-in-law's side the wedding celebrations were full-scale as his family were well off. They had three separate dinners: one for family, one for business associates and a third for anyone who had missed the other two! My aunts and other elderly family members stuck to their age-old habits of never attending dinners outside the home. Even if we had invited elder relatives to an outside banquet, they wouldn't have turned up. Heaven knows why but this was their custom.

One could not just send an invitation card either. My two mothers had to personally visit every relative to invite them. This was regarded as mark of respect. Not doing this would have resulted in a no-show.

A Wake! A Wake!

Father's funeral was not so much a wake as a neighbourhood party. Call me old-fashioned or even a fuddy-duddy but I feel it is important to remember the elements of Taoist culture in our hearts and minds, even if are not believers. Many people in early Singapore lived their lives steeped in superstition. Even today, there are many cars with the registration number 888. These numbers are supposed to bring good luck and prosperity—the phonetic pronunciation of eight sounds like *fatt*, Cantonese for prosperity.

But I digress. I learnt much about the rites of passage when Father died and the wake was held at our home. I remember there being a heated argument about which way the coffin should face. According to Hokkien lore it should face the door but according to Teochew custom, the coffin should be at right angles to the door and some such superstitious flim flam. If the coffin was not correctly aligned, the departing soul could not leave the house.

Since Mother was of Teochew stock, she insisted we follow her instruction but First Mother, who was Hokkien, protested that

Father was also Hokkien so we had to follow his order. Mother spat back and said that we should ask Father what he wanted. At which First Mother retorted that how could they, he was dead! And so it went on until the Taoist priests we had employed to take care of the rituals said we could compromise and lay the coffin at an angle so everyone would be happy!

I wasn't especially pleased when I and my siblings had to feed Father symbolically. It was nerve-racking lifting a spoonful of food to his grim mouth and practically forcing the grains of rice through his pursed lips. It was all ritualistic but it had to be done while we chanted the words: 'You brought us up, we are now sending you to heaven with good food!'

We also had to cry on command, especially when another visitor came along. This was to show our filial piety and sorrow, never mind that my thoughts were more with my fighting fish and spiders. I was too young to feel the loss and could not cry on demand. So one aunt was instructed to pinch us extremely hard whenever the tears had to be turned on. I hated her for months afterwards as she had sharp fingernails that really dug into my bottom. I cried from pain not sorrow, but it mattered little as long as we were seen and heard to be howling. In other wakes in Chinatown, professional mourners were employed to howl out loud—for a price.

Mourning clothes were also irksome to say the least. Being the eldest son, Elder Brother had to wear a sackcloth tunic and untreated raw muslin trousers. We were spared the sackcloth but even the muslin was extremely uncomfortable as it caused the skin to itch. We were also not allowed to wear normal shoes but a pair of rustic rope sandals I had only ever seen Sam Sui women wear. Was it a penance? I never really understood all this masochism. Elder Brother also had to carry a long bamboo pole with a paper lantern hanging from one end. He would lead the way when all Father's children circled the coffin several times while priests chanted prayers.

I remember similar scenes taking place at my grandfather's wake some years earlier. My first uncle, Grandfather's eldest son, had to wear similar sackcloth garments and carry the same bamboo pole. During periods of rest, my cousins would wield the pole and play-fight, pretending to be Robin Hood and Little John. My aunt gave them hard thwacks from the same pole for being so irreverent. Much as I was sorely tempted to play-act at Father's funeral, I did not have the nerve for fear of being pinched even harder.

After the burial we had to burn stacks of paper money so that Father would not want for anything in the other world. Each son and daughter had to burn a paper chest filled to the brim with folded paper money fashioned from gold- and silver-tinted sheets. These we would fold into little boat shapes, each boat representing S$1. If we curled up the ends, it was S$10. This we did with alacrity as we did not want Father to be skint. Mother, however, had other ideas.

'Silly old turtle, why give him so much money when he didn't give us much? Do not fold them into S$10,' she would berate us. It was funny and sad at the same time, as later we would sneak downstairs and curl up the edges of each paper boat without her knowledge.

Then there was the paper house that must have cost a pretty penny even then. It all went up in smoke and we hoped that Father would smile down on us for giving him such a handsome abode. The practice of paper objects at funerals still goes on among believers, and the paper houses of today are replete with limousines, chauffeurs, swimming pools, hand phones and computers. Hades never knew better urban planning.

Cremations and Burnt Offerings

Cremations were not preferred by staunch Taoists who believed a body should go to the next world whole and not barbecued. However, by the 1970s cremation was common practice as cemeteries took up precious land that had to be converted into real estate or used for HDB flats. I am fast forwarding here but I experienced this type of burial first-hand when my eldest sister died. She was cremated at Kong Min San temple in the Thompson area. It was a moment of extreme sadness punctuated by nervous laughter.

Her husband, who had earlier been injured in a motorcycle accident, suffered mental lapses and was wont to acting confused. After my sister's cremation, that took several days as the kiln was wood and not gas fired, we had to gather at the temple to collect her gruesome remains. The temple priests gave us chopsticks to pick up what bones had not been incinerated and put them in a jar. This jar would then be placed in the temple and marked by a tablet inscribed with her name. Anyway, my brother-in-law was seen picking at the ashes and chortled that he could pick up the largest pieces and we couldn't.

'See, this must have been her hip bone and that must have been her ankle bone!' he announced with innocent glee. His children drew him aside but did not chastise him as he was not himself.

I recall in later years one of my schoolmates worked at the Mount Vernon Crematorium as a superintendent. One day, well meaning no doubt, he asked me to convey a message to my family and friends to the effect that he would give a fifteen per cent discount to anyone who wished to be cremated! It was a message that I had no desire to pass on, pardon the pun.

For a while my second brother also worked at this crematorium and when I wondered why he'd chosen this career path, I did not have to look very far into our past. When we were still at secondary school, we used to walk past an Indian cemetery somewhere along Race Course Road. As was the practice then, Hindu cremations were performed in the open air, with the corpse laid out on a funeral pyre stacked about eight feet high.

One time we were walking past when a cremation began. Not

wishing to witness this rather stomach-churning ritual I snuck away, but Second Brother's curiosity was really fuelled.

I was keen to avoid the scene and hung around far enough away. When Second Brother returned a few minutes later he was ashen-faced, so I asked him what was wrong. Spluttering he said that he had seen the corpse rise up from the pyre as if it was still alive, amid furious crackling, hissing and spluttering. Much later an Indian friend told me that this was normal because muscles contract when burnt causing a reflex action. Second Brother was traumatised by the sight and perhaps, as a gesture towards catharsis, decided to work in a crematorium. So much for idle curiosity.

Chinese Wayang, and Food, Glorious Food

We may have a slew of food courts and hawker centres today, but I truly miss the hawkers of the 1950s who were of a genre now confined to history. This delicious heritage had its beginnings in the street operas of Singapore, known as Chinese *wayang*. During the festive months such as the Hungry Ghost Festival, Lunar New Year and Cheng Beng (Festival of Brilliant Light or All Souls Day), several troupes would set up stages in different areas for two or three days.

Food stalls were scattered in the vicinity of the stage and what a joy it all was! The oyster omelette, *char kway teow*, duck porridge, *rojak*, ice cream *potong* and *ngoh hiang* of today owe their existence to this rich celebration. When there weren't any performances, it was natural for the food sellers to hawk their dishes around the island, mostly in the areas where they lived.

I recall one of my favourite stalls seemed to prefer operating underneath the opera stage. This hawker sold soy sauce braised duck but the main attraction was his little gaming table. We would take it in turns to rotate a wooden rod mounted on a circular board etched with numbers. Tied to one end of the rod was a piece of string and a metal weight. If the rod stopped at say number nine, you might win a duck's neck or claws. If it stopped at number twelve, the golden number, you would win a drumstick, and so on. This was called *tikam*. Unfortunately a whole duck was never put up as a prize. The game cost about thirty cents each time. For some reason the weight would invariably stop on a number which only offered the scraps as a prize. We suspected the hawker tampered with the weight but never had any proof.

The other disconcerting thing was the toilet habits of the opera cast. Each stage floor was constructed of wooden planks with crevices in between. As there were no portable toilets then, an area on the stage was screened off for this function, and no guesses as to where the rank streams ended up: through the crevices, straight down to the ground, and not too far from the duck stall. But nobody turned a hair.

The troupes and their cast had fans that followed them all over the island, Mother included, no matter how far or how inconvenient. Her favourite troupe was called Lau Sai Toh Guan (see 'The Wayang Years', p118). This was the number-one troupe of the time and its stars were worshipped by many fans. This was especially true of the principal actress who always played male roles. I remember her name still: Gek Choo. Her counterpart, who only played female roles, was called Poh Choo and together they went on to win thousands of fans throughout the 1950s.

I still remember the scene.

Dusk has fallen and in a small clearing somewhere in Siglap a crowd begins to gather, taking their seats on small stools in front of a brightly lit stage. As the first sounds of the opera orchestra begin to rise and the ornate curtain opens, a hush falls over the crowd. By now a few hundred people have gathered, all tightly packed together, some sitting at the front but most just standing in rows. The music swells and soon the stage is alive with colour, pageantry, movement and singing. Thus begins the enactment of a historical classic that will go on for some four hours.

Costume dramas of this era were gloriously colourful and drawn from many classics like *The Monkey Goes West*, the chief characters unchangingly reflecting mythical warlords, courtiers and concubines. There was a great deal of singing—all of four hours—but the operas that drew the largest audience were those depicting tumultuous battles between good and evil. There was a wicked minister who always wore black make-up, a princess whose dress always had a pair of silk 'water' sleeves which she could toss about when she was singing and gesticulating, and a grand hero who had four imperial flags attached to the back of his costume.

Opera Roles

Chinese opera has a large variety of dramatic roles, which generally fall into four categories: the male, the female, the clown and the painted face. The male's role is either civil and scholarly, or military. He can be young or old. The female's character can be one of many: the virtuous young woman (often a tragic heroine), the flirtatious lady, the female warrior or the elderly, dignified woman. Training was rigorous, even tortuous, and could last a lifetime.

Costume designs dated back to the Tang, Song, Yuan, Ming and Qing Dynasties and were ornate. Often authenticity was sacrificed for dramatic impact. Headdresses for female roles were extremely fancy, studded with sequins, pearls and other glittering embellishments which audiences loved.

Make-up was also elaborate and one of my greatest joys was to be allowed backstage to watch it being applied. I had an uncle who knew one of the opera owners and arranged for this special treat. But it was the performance itself that was mesmerising, never mind that I did not understand a word of classical Teochew which was quite different from the Teochew I spoke at home. It was fascinating to watch the actors' every moment synchronised to music, to hear melodic phrases accompany tragic events or see the entrance of a beautiful princess. Every action on stage was governed by the rhythm of the strings, woodwind and percussion.

Story lines were drawn from the cultural wealth of Chinese literary classics and history. I loved the stage movements. A certain gait implied that the actor had travelled a great distance. Or an actor would come on stage in a 'carriage', which was no more than a number of flags. It was exaggerated mime but it transfixed us nonetheless. Props were minimal; one soldier represented an entire regiment and actors relied on the audience to understand the symbolic power of a few objects. A short stick with ribbons symbolised a horse, black silk represented gales and the toss of a water sleeve indicated anger or joy.

The Wayang Years

Though Chinese *wayang* (street opera) dates back to the late nineteenth century, I feel it important to chronicle some of its history here.

As early as 1880 in Singapore, there were permanent theatres situated in Tuo Poh (Big Town), the present Chinatown area. One road was even named Wayang Street. There were two main troupes, one performing in Cantonese and the other in Hokkien. By the time of the Japanese Occupation, both theatres had seen their heyday. The buildings were converted into shops that in turn gave way to People's Park Centre in the late 1960s.

The 1920s saw the arrival of three more troupes: Lau Tiong Chia Soong, Lau Sai Toh Guan and Sin Sai Poh Hong. All were of the Teochew dialect. Throughout the next three decades Chinese operas in theatrical halls, temple compounds and village clearings were an integral part of cultural life for the Chinese. However, by the late 1950s social and political unrest in the region threatened the survival of many Singapore-based troupes whose livelihood depended on touring neighbouring countries. A large proportion of their revenue came from performances in Thailand, Malaysia, Vietnam and Indonesia where there were large Chinese communities.

At home, increased urbanisation contributed to the decline in the number of professional troupes. In the 1950s most of Singapore's population were living in rural areas. An opera performance during the festive months was an event eagerly anticipated. Our family could hardly talk about anything else if a troupe was scheduled to perform in our street or at Granny's *kampung*.

In most rural areas, an open market was part and parcel of the opera experience and the cacophony of sounds, both from the opera performance and the vendors, created a marvellous ambience akin to that of a village fair. In fact, a village fair is a good way to describe it. Sadly though, as Singapore became more densely populated and urbanised, many villages were first turned into SITs (Singapore Improvement Trusts) and then HDB (Housing Development Board) estates. This inevitably reduced the number of shows the troupes could stage in any one year. Some troupes disbanded and street opera became virtually extinct. While it lasted, Chinese *wayang* was the legacy of a rich cultural tradition that had taken root more than 160 years earlier. There has been a small revival since, but the performances have nowhere near as much ambience as they used to.

The British Era

Throughout my school days, between 1949 and 1959, we were still a British colony. Therefore we had little choice but to sing 'God Save the King', and then 'God Save the Queen', and wave the Union Flag on the occasions that demanded it. We didn't know enough about Britain to be pro- or anti-monarchy, but Queen Elizabeth II's coronation in June 1953 came with terse orders from the British High Commission. I was eleven years old and just about to sit for my Entrance Exams that would take me into secondary school. My pocket money was still only twenty cents a day.

The day of the parade downtown was fraught with excitement, especially among the Eurasian and expatriate communities. Many had already booked seats at venues such as Whiteaways Building in Shenton Way and other colonial buildings that had views of the parade. We did not have the same privilege but were ordered—yes, ordered—to buy at least one Coronation commemorative thingy. On offer were miniature versions of the Royal Sceptre, the Orb and even the Coronation Crown. We were also ordered not to say anything, apart from 'God Save the Queen', during a special school assembly on that day. What did they think we were going to shout? '*Balik kampung* (Go back to your village)'?

The commemorative sceptre was a kind of brooch about four inches long and cost me two weeks' pocket money. I opted for this as it was the cheapest item amongst the array of Coronation tat. Sorry, but when you have only twenty cents a day for sweets, being made to spend S$2.50 on a mock-jewelled accessory that an eleven-year-old boy has little use for was distinctly undemocratic. I have never understood why people get excited about commemorative items such as mugs, coins and other useless objet d'art that only end up in the back of a drawer.

What I did understand was the need for discretion when expressing views about my country's British rulers. For sure I appreciated learning Shakespeare, reading Wordsworth and waxing lyrical about daffodils and meadow larks. This was tropical Singapore and I had never seen a blessed daffodil before, much less felt passion for it.

However, I was taught well by English, Scottish and Welsh tutors. One of the many songs we had to sing during assembly in my secondary school was a traditional Welsh folksong called 'Sospan Fach'. It was only years later that I found out that *sospan fach* means 'little saucepan' in Welsh. The song catalogues the troubles of a harassed housewife. Why it was chosen as a school song I'll never know. For a long time I thought it was a double entendre meaning 'sex in the kitchen'!

What I never understood was the lack of education we received about our own Asian history and geography. Even our roads have English names; I was born in Oxford Road, bought groceries in Cambridge Road and played games in Dorset Road. However, I have to admit that being steeped in British mores at such a young age helped no end when I decided to settle in England in 1983. By then I was more familiar with Jane Austen and Enid Blyton than the Empress Dowager.

I do remember some lessons about the Malay heroes Hang Tuah and Hang Jebat, but I can recall only one Malayan history book. It had been written by an English schoolmistress named Margery Morris. I learnt a lot about spring, summer, autumn and winter but nothing about typhoons and monsoons. My brothers and I played Monopoly endlessly, and were buying and selling properties in Mayfair and Park Lane decades before I set foot on English soil. Today I take great pride in boning up on Singlish, having missed out on its evolution in the 1980s and 1990s. I believe one can only benefit from learning about other cultures and not being insular.

Relations and their Honorific Titles

The 1950s was a rich and comforting era, full of extended families. Growing up in one that was a mesh of traditional Chinese and Peranakan mores was perplexing, sometimes frustrating, but always fascinating. Within the hierarchy, the honorific titles we used were set, though most of them have now eroded. I feel it important to at least remember how we used to address our elders and each other by using proper titles, and not just shouting, 'Hey, you'. No one ever bothered to write down these titles, so below is my attempt, however inadequate. I grew up with Hokkien and Teochew as the main dialects and my list reflects both. I find the Western use of titles totally lacking as everyone is either an uncle, aunt, niece or nephew. But this doesn't give you any information about what the precise relationship of that person is to you. You may not find these honorific titles useful, but their use does go back centuries, making them deserving of a place in our history.

Father's sister—Ah Kor
Mother's sister—Ah Ee
Brother's wife—Ah So
Sister's husband—Che Hoo
Mother's sister's husband—Ah Tiong
Mother's brother—Ah Koo
Mother's brother's wife—Ah Kim
Grandfather's brother—Chek Kong
Children by your son—Lao Soon (inner grandchildren)
Children by your daughter—Gua Soon (outer grandchildren)
Male cousin (younger)—Pio Tee (Pio Hiah, younger)
Female cousin (younger)—Pio Muay (Pio Cheh, elder)
Son-in-law—Kia Sai
Daughter-in-law—Sim Pu

Woman's father-in-law—Tio Lang
Man's mother-in-law—Tio Erm
Man's father-in-law—Ching Keh
Woman's mother-in-law—Cheh Erm
Grandfather—Ah Kong
Grandmother—Ah Ma
Great grandfather—Chor Kong
Great grandmother—Chor Ma

I do not know what gave rise to the rather derogatory phrase 'Your grand *chor kong*' as an expression of incredulity. Nor can I shed any light on the oft-used curse, 'Your grandmother's *kondek* (chignon).' Regardless of where they came from, these phrases are very rich. Even when mourning the death of a relative, family members used to wear armbands of different colours, each colour indicating the precise relationship of that person to the deceased. In other words, sons wore black, daughters wore blue and daughters-in-law wore blue with a red dot. The list is exhaustive and not too important today as few still follow it.

The Nonya Heritage

The 1950s were also golden years for the Straits Chinese. Although their heritage is timeless, this period saw the greatest evidence of their culture and traditions. It is the heritage of my life, and spanned most of my early years until the culture was diffused somewhat.

The First Nonyas

Nonyas are variously known as the Straits Chinese or Peranakan, the latter meaning 'born of the soil' in Malay. The men are called Babas and collectively they are termed Nonyas and Babas, which is often contracted simply to Nonya(s) for easier assimilation.

The term Straits Chinese relates to geography rather than history. For many years there were Chinese fishing villages in the Malay Archipelago. The South China Sea cradled many ancient civilisations, with the lure of spices attracting Roman mercantile fleets and Egyptian traders alike. Galleons and junks all had to pass through the Straits of Malacca, the strategic waterway between the Peninsular Malaysia and the island of Sumatra. In the early sixteenth century the Portuguese began casting their beady eyes on this spice-rich region. A pitched battle for supremacy ensued between the ruling sultanate and the European interlopers; Malacca fell and was to remain in Portuguese hands for the next one hundred and thirty years. Meanwhile the Dutch, who were entrenched in the Indonesian port of Batavia (Jakarta), joined the fray and wrested Malacca from the Portuguese in 1641. They stayed until the British East India Company appeared on the scene in the early nineteenth century.

Among the assorted European empire builders, buccaneers and upper-crust merchants came two audacious men who leapfrogged over each other's acquisitions with their incursions into Southeast Asia. They were Francis Light and Stamford Raffles. Francis Light planted the British flag in Penang in northwest Malaya in 1786 and Stamford Raffles founded Singapore in 1819. Soon afterwards, the Chinese, mainly Hokkien-speaking peoples from the Amoy province of South China, began arriving to these areas in large numbers.

When the first Chinese arrived, they did not bring their women folk with them. They had no desire to make Malaya their permanent home, but had come to get rich quick and then go back to China. Perhaps to satisfy biological needs, the nouveau riche married or cohabited with local women of Malay communities. In time, larger numbers of Chinese arrived and gradually their emotional bonds with China weakened as fortunes were made and permanent homesteads established. In the centuries that followed, the bloodlines of Chinese, Malay and other races fused together even more.

A Baba or Nonya was the descendant of a Chinese–Malay union, and spoke little or no Chinese but rather the Peranakan patois. He practiced a religion that was a mix of ancestor worship and Buddhism, his female counterpart wore Malay costume and they enjoyed a cuisine that was almost all Malay with overtones of Indonesian and Indian.

In theory three communities of Babas evolved more or less simultaneously in Indonesia, Penang and Malacca. The Singapore group were really an offshoot of the Malacca community. As such their cuisines became a rich mélange of Chinese, Malay and European elements.

My maternal grandfather was born of the soil but his father was not. His wife, my maternal grandmother, was a true-blue Nonya, had skin the colour of pale chocolate and spoke mostly Malay with a smattering of Teochew. My mother and her siblings grew up in the rambling family home in Siglap that Grandfather had built in a style that was part Chinese and part Peranakan. You can still find many of these kinds of homes in Malacca and Penang but sadly mostly are gone in Singapore.

In the 1940s this was a grand and sprawling house that we romped around in with much joy. Weddings and other festivities were celebrated there in true Peranakan style, the cavernous kitchen always the scene of bustling activity. Everyone would pitch in to help grind, pound, cook and bake a dozen and one cakes and savoury dishes.

My father was born in Indonesian Borneo and was also very dark-skinned, spoke fluent Indonesian and also Malay but had kept his Teochew intact. My first mother was not a Nonya, born in Penang, but became a Nonya by osmosis and learnt to speak fluent Malay as well as her musical Penang Hokkien.

Many of my aunts could not speak a word of Chinese and only learnt because they were frequently immersed among relatives who did. Some Nonyas had strange habits. One aunt always slept on a lacquered brick pillow so as not to muss up her elaborate hairstyle. This was a chignon piled high on the top of her head and studded with gold ornaments.

Being elder, she wore a long tunic and *sarong* known together as a *baju panjang*. Mother wore a *sarong kebaya*, the blouse being a shaped, shorter garment. On special days or when she was going out, she would wear one that had fancy embroidery called *sulam*.

Men folk or Babas only wore Chinese trousers or jackets with frog buttons, but by the 1940s most had adopted Western style clothing. Mother never wore trousers in her life as these were deemed unladylike. By the 1960s most traditional Peranakan outfits had given way to Western modes as women went out to work and found their Peranakan garments too constricting. I must applaud Singapore Airlines for sticking with this mode of dress for their stewardesses as it has kept the tradition very much alive, despite the curious fact that the SIA version was designed by a Frenchman, Pierre Balmain! At least the patterns follow the basic shape.

The Patois

When I was growing up, Malay was the lingua franca in our home, although both Hokkien (my father's dialect) and Teochew (my mother's) were spoken. When my aunts visited, everyone spoke almost entirely in Malay. The patois was a rich blend of mostly Malay words but Chinese words were liberally incorporated and pronounced with a typical Malay twang.

Nonya weddings, while reflecting Chinese culture in rituals and traditions, had traditions with Malay and some Chinese words. For example, the ritual of threading the bride's face—this was the removal of facial hair with a thread wielded by an expert Nonya and could be very painful—was called *chionh tau*. The bride's entrance into her chamber at her new home was called *chin pang*, literally meaning 'enter the room'.

Even though I got married in 1968 and had a fairly modern wedding, there were a couple of busybody aunts who demanded to know what my bride had brought with her by way of jewellery. They still subscribed to the notion that every bride had to come to her husband with all her worldly goods—namely gold and jewels. I decided to do a mean thing and asked them to come into our room to see what my bride Dorothy had brought. There, hanging on the wall, was her A Level certificate.

My aunts were miffed and complained to Mother that I was being rude and how could the girl come with only a piece of paper? Fortunately Mother knew better and soothed their irritation, saying education was far more valuable than gold bangles. They went away not really satisfied with her explanation and grumbling under their breath, '*Mana boleh, tak ada berlian, emas dan cincin, kertas ini buat apa?*' ('How can, no diamonds, gold and rings, what good is this piece of paper?')

The patois also contains many catch-all words and pithy phrases that defy translation. I paraphrase and explain them below as best as I can.

Celaka—a common and mild swear word you use on children, its origins unclear.

Cekik—a word used to scold a child for not eating fast enough. A coarse version of the word 'eat'.

Cekik darah—literally 'suck blood' and uttered to convey exasperation or extreme irritation.

Cekik leheh—in the same genre as above but literally meaning 'strangle my neck', as in choking frustration.

Oh puchot!—an exclamation used when one is startled, accidentally drops something or bumps into someone. There is no translation.

Latah or *melatah*—this really is bizarre for it refers to a condition when a lady is startled or poked without warning, and she lets off a stream of curses and obscenities. Often her swearing will go on for minutes without stopping. This condition seems to afflict only Nonya ladies of advanced years or a nervous disposition. I loved doing this to one of my aunts who would dance and leap about like she'd been tickled mercilessly.

Ho mia—actually a direct translation from Hokkien and Teochew. It literally means 'good life' but is used only as a counter retort. It is similar in to the phrase 'I should be so lucky!'

Macam tok po—literally meaning 'looking like a dishcloth' in Teochew and alluding to someone wearing something quite ugly or unfashionable.

Jangan cakap banyak—literally meaning 'don't talk so much' in Malay and really telling someone to shut up.

Mulut bocor—literally meaning 'leaking mouth' in Malay, alluding to a gossipmonger.

Mai ex si borak—literally meaning 'do not brag or boast' in a hybrid of Hokkien and Malay. *Mai* means 'do not' in Hokkien and *borak* means 'talk big' in Malay. I do not know where the words *ex* and *si* come from, possibly from the English 'to exaggerate'.

Lenggang kangkung—the origin of this phrase is unclear. *Lenggang*

ABOVE *The wedding picture of father and first mother, the exact date being unknown. A diminutive Penang-born lady, she died some ten years ago at the age of 92. She had borne father only two children, a boy who died at birth and my half-sister who is still robust at 82 today (she's the one dressed like a boy in a following plate).* (Photo courtesy of Terry Tan)

ABOVE *Father posing beside a biplane that we never actually saw him pilot. He was the original poseur and liked to impress his cronies with stories of his derring-do. He was wealthy before my brothers and I were born so he could have learnt to fly before the war. We knew he did fight the Japanese, losing an eye in the bargain. His war effort also saw the recycling of stifling parachute fabric for our shirts!* (Photo courtesy of Terry Tan)

BELOW *Father in his horse and carriage during an era before cars were available. His favourite outfit was a white Chinese-style tunic and trousers. He had many Indonesian friends who owned their own carriages but whether father actually owned one we never did find out. By the time we came along in the 40s, this mode of transport had gone the way of history.* (Photo courtesy of Terry Tan)

RIGHT *An original Ford, one like father owned and that gave rise to the Hokkien reference of* lau pok *car (old ford car). As in the desire among businessmen to own a* Piak *or a* Pok *(a Fiat or a Ford) the first foreign cars in Singapore.* (© Collection of Wong Kwan / National Archives of Singapore)

RIGHT *My half-sister with hair shorn to look like a boy to escape any Japanese soldier's lecherous designs. Her outfit is an echo of father's favourite white tunic suit. Taking family photographs like these was very popular then, all posing stiffly. Studios had the invariable chair for subjects to sit on and this kind of pose was classic.* (Photo courtesy of Terry Tan)

LEFT *My first claim to stage fame as a little soldier boy during a concert put on by the dancing school father had sent me to when I was barely seven years old. I didn't enjoy the celebrity status at all, given that my dancing school mates were all snobby middle-class children and I had gone over to the wrong side of tracks after father died.* (Photo courtesy of Terry Tan)

Above *Travelling medicine men were the mobile dispensaries of the 1950s. Many were veritable circus acts with herbalist performing acts of remarkable fortitude, swallowing iron balls and the like. Diagnosis of ills and dispensing of medicines were offered at this 'clinic' where you had to squat on the roadside as the medicine man did.* (© Collection of KF Wong / National Archives of Singapore)

Below *Samsui women, the red-hatted manual brigade from South China on whose hardy backs Singapore was largely built. They did not care for men, swore to spinsterhood, lived ascetic lives and did back-breaking work that even men would not do. In their heyday, there were thousands of them in every sphere of construction, climbing up rickety scaffolding, hoisting heavy loads of bricks or working deep in the ground during piling work. The three samsui women below find themselves out of place in 80s Singapore.* (© Collection of Kuo Sheng Wei / National Archives of Singapore)

ABOVE AND BELOW *Typical 1940s and 50s hawkers selling food, household wares and other sundries that hung from both ends of a long, supple wooden pole. These hawkers trudged the streets of Singapore until the mid-1950s when trishaws and bicycles made their life less grueling. Many were bent double with years of such heavy yokes.* (Both images © National Archives of Singapore)

RIGHT *Haw Par Villa, the original Chinese/Taoist theme park that gave us much pleasure in the 1950s and 60s. The most fascinating attraction was a tableau depicting the eighteen tortures of hell. It was a gruesome depiction but people flocked here most weekends to have their pictures taken with strange creatures from ancient Chinese mythology. I did to my chagrin as it incurred the fear and wrath in my mother that I would be taken into the underworld for doing so.* (© National Archives of Singapore)

ABOVE *Built in 1903 to house Singapore's rickshaws, the Jinrikisha building still stands in Tanjong Pager; a historic testament to the beginnings of the island's public transportation system. For more than forty years, it was a bustling central depot for rickshaws that at their height numbered more than nine thousand. The word Jinrikisha comes from the Japanese language;* jin *meaning "human",* riki *meaning "strength" and* sha *meaning "vehicle" It certainly needed human strength to pull it. Today, the building is a busy commercial mall with restaurants, karaoke lounge and shops.* (© Collection of Arshak C Galstaun / National Archives of Singapore)

ABOVE *Great World Park that was the scene of many exhibitions and also cabarets where nubile dance hostesses charged for the pleasure of taking the floor with them. In reality, they had their eyes peeled and talons sharpened to hook sugar daddies. Today, it is a modern shopping mall that reflects very little of this colourful past.* (© National Archives of Singapore)

BELOW *New World Park in Serangoon Road that pulsated to the rhythms of nightly Malay* joget *music and the gyration of one Rose Chan, Singapore's first and best-known burlesque dancer with her famous python act. We lived very near here and most nights father would be here soaking up the atmosphere and likely as not, ogling Rose Chan when not doing his favourite* ronggeng. (© National Archives of Singapore)

ABOVE *A solid state radio, the predecessor of the transistor and many homes had one. Television was decades away and this was the only means of knowing about current affairs. Most were the size of a toaster but some were as large as ovens and just as heavy! We had one, a Philips that mother would ration for only a few hours a day. It was useless explaining to her that it cost very little to have it on.*

BELOW LEFT *Brylcreem, the brilliantine of my callow youth that caused rivulets of grease to stream down our neck on hot days. One had to plaster hair down with the stuff to look anywhere like the Teddy Boys of the day. It did do a marvelous job flicking up locks and giving gauche young men some semblance of hirsute sexiness.*

BELOW RIGHT *Green Spot, an iconic drink that was the drink at parties and during Chinese New Year. Our favourite treat was to dunk love letters* (kueh belandah) *into this drink and suck the delicious orange squash up. It was the only non-gaseous bottled drink then.*

describes a walking gait and *kangkung* is the vegetable water convolvulus. *Lenggang kangkung* refers to the slow, ambling gait of a Nonya lady who never walks fast if she can help it.

Sampai mati—literally meaning 'until death' in Malay and refers to something that is futile ie. '*Sampai mati,* cannot strike lottery!'

Other patois phrases, while mostly in Hokkien or Teochew, were exclusive to the community and trotted out every so often for emphatic meaning.

Yeow siu—another phrase whose origin is unclear. It is a most pithy curse, meaning 'greedy devil' and used only when you are extremely angry with someone.

Tua pek kong tolong—*tua pek kong* is the God of Heaven within the Taoist pantheon of deities, and *tolong* is a plea in Malay. Together they are used to convey a prayer of salvation in difficult circumstances, especially during gambling sessions when one wants good cards.

Chianh tok—literally 'to invite to a dinner' in Hokkien and refers specifically to wedding banquets ie. 'Where you *chianh tok* for your daughter's wedding?'

Your grand *chor kong*—a really multi-lingual hybrid that is used as a curse. It has no particular rationale as *chor kong* means 'great grandfather' and the phrase is often used to express disgust or incredulity.

Gua sim kua—literally meaning 'my heart' in Hokkien as a term of endearment to a beloved.

Family Retainers and Washerwomen

When my elder sister was born in 1926, my father was rich enough to be able to employ a family retainer. Ours was a lady from China who had left her homeland to seek her fortune elsewhere. She'd left her husband and several children at home to fend for themselves. She never elaborated on this as I suspect it must have been very difficult for her. When she came to us she was already in her forties and still robust. We called her Hokkien Sim (Hokkien Aunt). For some inexplicable reason, ladies of her time did not reveal their names. Hokkien Sim became my sister's minder and when my sister grew up, Hokkien Sim took care of my elder brother.

By then she was in her sixties, wizened and extremely dotty. Her eldest son ran a timber business in Fujian province. He married and had many children of his own, but Hokkien Sim was too attached to our family and would only visit him occasionally. She had many funny stories to tell and by then she was more candid about her departure from China.

Her story went that she fled from her husband because he only regarded her as a lowly woman good for two things: bearing his children and tending to him. She regaled us with stories, such as how he tried to seduce her as she was cutting sugar cane in a farm where they both worked.

'The silly old fool insisted that I give in to him right there and then in the cane field. When I protested, he forced me down. I took a length of cane and pushed it as hard as I could into his crotch and ran away. I never saw him again.'

Her stories had us splitting with laughter, though she seemed to embellish many of the details. She doted on my eldest brother who was already the recipient of much mollycoddling, being the Number One Son. She would crack crab claws for him when we had crab for dinner, debone his fish and chicken and generally spoil him rotten, much to my annoyance.

Before our father died, she would lecture us interminably about who should help carry his coffin when he did die. It was a topic I didn't care to pursue, but she had plenty of others up her blue cotton sleeves. She wore nothing else but rough, blue, cotton tunic-like blouses and black silk trousers. Her hair was always in a small chignon at the back of her head, held together with an enormous gold pin that she had saved a whole lifetime to buy. It was her only hedge against poverty, apparently.

In the 1950s, just about every family's laundry was taken care of by a passing brigade of washerwomen. These daughters of migrant Chinese families were never sent to school, and by the time they became adults had to earn their living doing whatever they could. Washing and ironing clothes for not one family but several did ensure they had regular income. I remember we paid our Choo Mei S$6 a month—which was a lot then.

Every other day she would come to wash our clothes and ironed them twice a week. My mother had her hands full taking care of us and cooking the family meals. Bashing clothes on a wooden washboard was quite beyond her feeble frame. Choo Mei also occasionally roped in her mother to help out whenever we needed an extra pair of hands during festive seasons. I once asked her mother why she had not sent Choo Mei to school. She replied: 'What for? She will only become somebody's wife one day.' This was the tenet by which many traditional families lived and their poor daughters had a tough time.

One neighbour had a daughter she was frequently trying to marry off, and when my brothers were in their late teens, they seemed fair game. At that time many girls were married off at fifteen, or even younger. Because they were educated, each of my siblings was a good catch, an excellent meal ticket. Therefore our neighbour would relentlessly press my mother for her consent. We would just laugh.

One day the neighbour had the temerity to bring her daughter to our house, which made us laugh even louder. The only way to describe this poor soul is to say that she was plain, had buck teeth and drooled at the mouth. Incredibly, she didn't even merit a proper name on her birth certificate. Her father, when asked at her birth what he wanted to call her, simply said: 'Char Bor (Girl).' Many a female born in the 1930s and 1940s suffered this deplorable state. Her father wasn't just talking about her gender either. He truly believed girls were worthless and undeserving.

This kind of naming was compounded by the shocking mistakes made by the Registry of Births and Deaths. I had an uncle who had eight children and they all bore his family surname of Quek. However, each child's birth certificate had a different spelling of the surname, from Kwek to Queh to Queck and even Quack! When the old man died intestate, the legal problems of inheritance took a decade to unravel. The reason all the surnames were misspelt was down to dialectal pronunciations and how each one was spelt depended on whoever was the registrar that day.

Kusu Island

While this little coral outcrop, called Turtle or Tortoise Island, is today regarded as little more than a tourist attraction, it was much revered by the Taoists and Muslims up until the 1960s. At one end of the island is a Malay holy shrine, or *keramat*. A Chinese temple at the other. When the tide is high, it is only possible to cross from one end of the island to the other by boat. Legend has it that a Chinese and a Malay sailor were shipwrecked. To save them, a giant sea turtle turned into an island. As an act of thanks, the two men built a Chinese temple, a Malay shrine and a huge turtle sculpture on the island.

Chinese devotees made annual pilgrimages during the ninth lunar month to the temple on Kusu Island to pay homage to Tua

Pek Kong. Muslims visited the *keramat*, which stood at the top of a rugged hillock. You had to climb up 152 steps to get there. Devotees mostly prayed for wealth, good marriage, good health and harmony. Both the shrines were popular with childless couples who would pray for children.

It was a sombre practice among many to hang palm fans and stones on the branches of trees at both shrines. The belief was that if a fan fell, you would be blessed with a daughter. If a stone fell, you would have a boy. When the washerwoman who used to come to my house got married, she visited Kusu Island faithfully during every ninth month. Twelve months after one visit she was blessed with a son. During the August holidays, my schoolmates and I used to picnic there. We were warned not to tamper with the hanging omens, though we were tempted to knock a few down.

Change Alley

In the 1930s Change Alley was hardly the famous tourist place it has morphed into today. Rather it was a meeting place for European buyers and Asian brokers. By the late 1940s and 1950s Change Alley was like a magnet, attracting swarms of tourists who pushed and shoved their way through narrow congested spaces between ubiquitous stalls that had sprung up.

Bargain-hunting servicemen and seafarers docked at the waterfront at Collyer Quay by the shipload, and made a beeline for the commercial centre, Raffles Place, via Change Alley.

It was always stuffed with a mishmash of cramped and dingy shops and stalls offering everything from clothes, to batik cloth, bags, briefcases, watches, toys, fishing accessories, handicrafts and other souvenirs. The alley soon became synonymous with fierce bargaining. Shopkeepers elsewhere became extremely indignant if tourists tried to bargain, shouting, 'You think what? This is not Change Alley!'

The foundations were laid for Change Alley's raucous ambience and the practice of interactive exchange.

Shopkeepers in the alley were multi-lingual, after a fashion, and spoke a smattering of 'broken' French, English, German, Italian and Russian. The moneychangers, many of them Indian Muslims, ran their businesses within their own little retail shops. There were also many illegal moneychangers stationed at both entrances of the alley, touting their currencies at 'bargainable exchange rates'.

Some of the tradespeople were most unfriendly if they knew you were a local. For example, once I took a British visitor there to look for a camera at a bargain price. As my friend was not comfortable with bargaining, I pitched in for him, only to receive abuse for my efforts.

'You local outsider smoke cigar!'

My friend was astonished, not from the derision but the quaintness of the comment.

'What did he mean?' he asked. 'That you should smoke a cigar while I bargained?' Alas, it was too complex to explain one of our favourite dismissive remarks.

At other times, even politeness could not veil this antipathy for local business. We knew we had to knock down prices by a good fifty per cent, just as they still do in Chiang Mai and Penang's night markets. Foreigners find such fleecing incredulous. Many a time I was confronted with comments such as: 'Eh, you, watch your own backside' or the more pithy '*Balik kampung*' (Malay for 'Go back to your village'). All in all it still meant that you had to mind your own damned business.

Sadly on Sunday, 30 April 1989, the shops in Change Alley opened for the last time. Business at the alley, which sat on prime land, had been hit hard by the dwindling number of soldiers and sailors visiting Singapore. On the last day, shopkeepers waved bargains as they attempted to clear their stock before shifting to other stalls provided by the government.

When Singapore Rubber House and Winchester House, between which Change Alley stood, were demolished, this retail strip, that had traded for almost a hundred years, ceased to exist. Change Alley is now a modern, sanitised building complex of shops and offices and really not much fun to visit.

The Brylcreem Years

More than a fragrant unguent, Brylcreem was a fashion statement for every man, and more deserving of being enshrined than you might think. It was created somewhere in Birmingham, England, in 1928, and eighty years on it is still greasing the scalps of millions. Brylcreem has turned sportsmen into pin-ups and actors, from Rudolph Valentino to James Dean, into matinee idols. In 1997 David Beckham saw fit to endorse Brylcreem, until he decided to shave his head.

I found the product's early advertising platform fascinating and the famous 'Brylcreem Bounce' was accompanied by a jaunty jingle that went: 'A little dab'll do ya.' This then mutated into an even more famous phrase when it was uttered by the cartoon character Fred Flintstone. His 'Yabba Dabba Doo' has gone into the annals of cartoon history. This little red jar of slick was in every man's bathroom cabinet, along with Imperial Leather soap and Tancho pomade, a johnny-come-lately really.

I had hair then but it had to be slicked back and only Brylcreem would do, despite the fact that it caused greasy rivulets to stream down my neck on hot days. My pillow was stained brown from the layers of sloughed off hair cream, and it took a lot of shampoo to wash off the grease. This was the golden age of teddy boys and their prominent quiffs that everyone wanted to sport. Then along came Tancho, a Japanese product that promised less grease. It was a godsend but it still made my hair look like the helmet worn by a Roman legionnaire. So it was back to Brylcreem and Yabba Dabba Doo!

One had little choice really as the fashions of the day required men to have slicked hair that never moved, even in strong wind. If you wanted to splurge on a cream with a scent, you went for Vaseline hair cream. That was even greasier. You could go swimming with these hairdos and emerge without a hair out of place.

As for the women, the trend of the day was to have a home perm using a product called Toni. 'Which twin has the Toni?' was one of the brand's famous press and radio slogans.

My sisters were forever perming each other's hair with this product, and the house reeked of peroxide. Before Chinese New Year, streams of women would queue up outside many permanent wave parlours, as hairdressing salons were then called. For something like S$10 you ended up with a head full of curled hair that would last until the next New Year. Some were okay, as perms went, while others were near disasters, as one of my cousins found out. She had gone into a parlour called Kim Novak Beauty Parlour (Miss Novak was the leading actress of the day). After spending more than the requisite amount as she wanted special curls here and there, she came out looking like Medusa.

If women wore any make-up it was usually a layer as thick as a pancake and resembling a mask. Undaunted they would continue to pile it on for special occasions. During days when exhibitions were held at this or that amusement park, they could be seen walking around with what looked like melted cheese on their faces. Air conditioning was still decades away but what a price to pay for beauty.

Eyebrows were plucked within an inch of baldness and then drawn on with eyebrow pencils. The lines were clean, bold sweeps of black without the slightest fuzz that natural eyebrows have. I blame the Hong Kong actresses who appeared on cinema screens looking like that. Everyone wanted to look like Li Li Hua but most ended up looking like Pontianak on a bad hair day!

Pen Pals and Picnics

Pen friendship was a most absorbing means of social interaction with foreigners. Most teenagers had a slew of pen pals, many from Malaya but some from as far afield as Europe and America. I remember the *Weekender*, a rather salacious paper that had endless lists of international pen pals that we would pore over. It was the prose that mattered the most, running the gamut from innocent exchanges of culture and history to quite romantic declarations of undying love! Since it was most unlikely that we would ever meet our pen pals, it seemed safe to pen some passionate passages, a few of which would not only cause alarm bells to ring among parents but could lead to matrimony!

Ah, the delight of sending and receiving photographs of our pen friends from abroad. I spent a small fortune having pictures of myself taken in an alluring light, or so I thought. At the photo studio, the norm was to lean slightly sideways to the camera flashing what would be described today as a geeky smile.

It was considered enigmatic, mysterious and necessary to lure pen pals of the opposite sex from overseas. Hair would be arranged just so, the favourite style being a 'Tony Curtis' which had a flick of a kiss curl on the forehead. Mr Curtis was the epitome of a matinee idol in those days. However, photographs with such poses only elicited rude comments from friends. In one of my photos I was described as a 'cartoon mosibat'. Search me as to what this means, but the term was generously applied to nerds of the 1950s.

The highlight of my week was when the post was delivered. Each of us would wait with hot hands and a thumping heart, for who knew what the next epistle or missive would bring? Epistle and missive were the words we liked to give to the endless pages of poetic declarations. Laugh if you like, but each letter—usually on aerogramme paper (I wonder what happened to those blue sheets that folded and glued neatly for only thirty-five cents)—usually began with phrases such as: 'Dear so-and-so, your epistle was most welcome and I hasten to pen my missive to you ...'

The ways to sign off were of a classic genre, rarely used these days—SMS texts now do not even contain verbs. ITALY meant I Trust and Love You, HOLLAND was Hope Our Love Lasts and Never Dies, and MUYC was an abject apology meaning Mistakes Under Your Care. What this actually conveyed I do not recall, but it was an inevitable ending to every missive!

There was also the inexplicable penchant for knowing each other's vital statistics, height being the be-all and end-all of personal data. Boy, was I obsessed with vertical stature! Since I was all of five feet nothing, I had to embellish my height a little. I gave out the notion that I was a strapping hunk as a few inches made all the difference between getting a reply or silent rebuff. So I added a few inches. Who said size is not important?

One classmate was obsessed with mammary glands and would only reply to his chosen female pen friend if she coughed up her most vital statistics. Since he did not know how to couch his queries in polite language, he sought my help for the necessary and polite prose. Having the reputation for being good in English, I smugly wrote something like this:

Dear Mary (we never met anyone called Abigail or Evangeline as most girls' names were Mary, Jenny and Lily ad infinitum),
I seek to ascertain your most covetous characteristics as it is in my culture to enjoy such Buddha-given comeliness. Would you be blessed with blossoming peaches or melons? If so, my happiness would runneth over!

Jeez, when I think about writing such twaddle today I want to bite my tongue and chop off my hand!

It was the reply that sent my classmate into a near suicidal state. The American girl he had written to was much less prosaic. Her advert in the *Weekender* said she was looking for an 'articulate Oriental' and my classmate must have completely misunderstood the meaning of the word 'articulate'. Anyway, her missive came with a few barbed sentences that read something like this:

> Dear Henry,
> You seem to have an unhealthy obsession with breasts and whether mine are like peaches or melons is none of your business. I will not correspond with someone who has his mind in the gutter, or my cleavage ...'

As much as my classmate was distraught, he nervously looked up the word cleavage in the dictionary. He had thought articulate had something to do with the versatility of his masculine endowment and I hastened to explain that the word applied to a region of his brain rather than his crotch. I don't think Henry was entirely satisfied with my explanation. He had acne and was of an extremely twitchy disposition. I'll leave you to ascertain what his favourite pastime was and I hope that he didn't go blind in the years that followed.

The funny moments of pen friendship came from another quarter. I had a distant cousin who came to Singapore from Taiping during the post-war years and never returned. He was semi-literate, worked in a biscuit factory and desperate to get married as he was pushing thirty. He enlisted my help to scan the *Weekender* for a Malay girl who might be looking for a potential husband. Some advertisements were of this genre, running to such obvious copy like: 'pretty, English-educated Chinese girl from Muar looking for a Singapore pen friend and perhaps more ...'

So without a thought for the can of worms I would be opening, I suggested he write (or rather, I write) to this girl who claimed she was a nurse. On his instruction for syntax, my letters began to fly back and forth, timorous at first and later positively passionate with scarcely veiled promises. He also took to sending her tins of biscuits from his factory and she capitulated by sending him durian cakes and peanuts, which only fuelled his desire for more intimate exchanges. Since my cousin could not even write his own name in English, he urged me to say things like: 'I love your durian cake as it has such fragrant promise, like your good self,' and other similar romantic silliness.

The upshot of it all came when Lily, the Muar nurse, decided to come to Singapore to meet my cousin. In my madness I had given my cousin the name of Rocky after my favourite film star Rock Hudson. When we found out Lily was coming there was almighty panic, but Boon San, as was Rocky's real name, could do nothing but face the music. The meeting was arranged at a restaurant in New World Amusement Park. It turned out that Lily was not Lily at all but someone called Ah Choo who spoke no English and was not a nurse at all but a domestic maid.

As fate would have it, both saw the funny side and there was a happy ending. They dated for a few months and eventually got married. She got a job working in the same biscuit factory as my cousin, and was so grateful to me that she would give me large tins of biscuits as gifts. So Cupid's arrow shot home, bore some fruit—and biscuits.

As for picnics, they were a necessary part of our machinations to meet groups of girls who were not inclined to meet boys singly and unchaperoned. One of my cousins from Siglap was a dab hand at organising these al fresco dos. When word got out that a picnic on Tanah Merah beach was impending, there was no shortage of females, mostly *kampung* girls, wishing to attend.

We would meet at a bus stop somewhere in Siglap to catch the Changi/Tanah Merah bus. There we were, a clutch of nervous pubescent boys and girls all pimply and gawky.

The journey was usually fraught with unspoken desires—mostly from the boys—and the girls spent most of the time 'blinking'. This was the era when females would blink their eyes if they felt that they were receiving unwelcome stares from boys. Blinking was not the same as batting the eyelashes, but more of an indignant gesture of disapproval. If a girl didn't like any untoward attention, she would blink in a haughty manner and the boy would get the message very quickly. Today the girl would probably just say 'Bugger off' accompanied by a gesture of two fingers pointing skywards. Such pungent and graphic dismissals were unthinkable in those days, even if a girl knew her finger work and the meaning of the word.

As for the picnic itself, swimwear was de rigueur. We boys wore assorted shorts, acceptable swimwear in those days, when Speedo only meant fast driving. As for female swimsuits, forget it, let alone bikinis. No self-respecting girl would show so much flesh and most bathed in their *samfoos* and elasticated Banlon slacks, very popular at that time. What these innocent girls did not know was that when wet, these proprietory Banlon slacks showed every curve. Wet T-shirt contests today are nothing compared to this.

Some of us boys, yours truly included, did not have the physique for topless bathing so we would wear cotton singlets. This provoked a few girls to chuckle and call us *pai kwat* (pork ribs). All we had to show were emaciated ribs under wet singlets. Mr Darcy, where were you when you were most needed to be a role model?

Picnic over, we would pile onto a bus for the return journey without having arranged so much as a single assignation. All we could talk about was which girl had not blinked at us. We looked forward to the next picnic when we hoped action would not be restricted to the eyeballs. It was such an innocent time on the surface, despite our throbbing pubescent needs not far below.

Chinese Comics and Other Games

I would be hard pressed to find these Chinese comics today, even in China. They had all but died out by the mid-1950s. Each comic was a thick, eight-inch square with a rough-hewn cover of brown paper. It was bound with string, much like spiral-bound diaries today. What joy these comics brought young children, the stories and mythologies all graphically pictured in black ink. Though I didn't understand a word of the captions and dialogue contained within the balloon outlines, I lapped up the pictures.

Most tales were drawn from the rich store of Chinese folklore: the epic journeys of the Monkey God and Na Cha, a child god who rode on a fiery wheel; the adventures of Dang Chen as he journeyed west with his horse and Mr Pig and many, many more. There were imperial intrigues, some extremely risqué with lurid portrayals of cavorting couples, mostly half hidden among bushes. There must have been some kind of censorship imposed for all I ever saw of these sex scenes were two pairs of legs jutting out of shrubbery. You had to use your imagination about what was going on in the bushes.

There was never any overt nudity as such, but judging from the rapt attention and occasional chuckles from boys reading in the comic shop, the comics must have been salacious. We could not buy them as they were only for rent at ten cents each, with a deposit of thirty cents. If we didn't return them, it was thirty cents down the chute for every comic. If we tore any pages out—and many did—it was a stiff fine of twenty cents. Girls were never the customers for the contents were not exactly suitable reading material for females.

Mother didn't condone us reading them and we took great pains to hide them from her. Once, Father caught us reading in the alleyway by the side of our house and amid my protests confiscated my comic—I could only afford to hire one at any one time. However, he gave it back to me later with a sly grin on his face. He must have relished it but made no further comment.

In later years, English comics such as *The Beano* and *The Dandy* came on the scene. These were entertaining, if not squeaky clean. Iconic characters were Dennis the Menace, Minnie the Minx and The Bash Street Kids, led by toffee-nosed Lord Snooty. For a few years I steeped myself in the lives of Biffo the Bear, Desperate Dan, who was fond of eating enormous cow pies with horns sticking out, Tin Lizzie, who was a robot maid, and the cute couple of Nancy and Sluggo. Dennis the Menace was the eternal wild boy and he even starred in Hollywood cartoon feature films in the 1980s. He was always pictured wearing a red and black striped jersey. Minnie the Minx wore the exact same coloured top, while Roger the Dodger had one with a chessboard design.

A copy of the first issue of *The Beano* was auctioned in 2004 for a massive £12,100 (S$35,300). To think I could easily have been the recipient of such riches if I had kept mine. In the same year, an original copy of Dandy fetched £20,350 (S$59,500)! Both comics are still in print today, and on about the 3,000th issue. There were also collectable items like *The Beano Annual* and *The Dandy Annual,* and specials in hard cover. These were beyond our pockets then but I spent fifteen cents on every weekly copy.

By the mid-1950s, I was a member of Raffles Library. It didn't stock any comics, only a steady stream of Enid Blyton books, such as *The Famous Five* and *The Secret Seven*. These became a treasure trove of armchair adventures. Few in Singapore who went to English schools could resist *The Famous Five* and their endless adventures set entirely in England. It mattered little to us that the books' plots were set in a faraway land, for Enid Blyton knew how to stoke a child's imagination. She churned out hundreds of books before her death in 1968.

Like my schoolmates, I was transported to a world far different from the one I lived in. I was immersed in the adventures of George (a girl called Georgina who insisted on being called George), and her cousins Dick, Julian and Anne. Their escapades and outings came to life through Blyton's deft writing and we could not get enough of her books.

I loved the picnics the characters always had, and for some reason they would always eat sardines and tinned pineapple—food that I could relate to and almost taste. And then there was Timmy, their intelligent mongrel and archetypal loyal mutt. And Jo, the gypsy girl who had the hots for Dick. Sadly, some of Blyton's characters were criticised for being too stereotypical and encouraging sexist attitudes. At one point the books were even banned.

I loved her Five Find-Outers series in which the children regularly outwitted the local policeman, but this was seen as politically incorrect as Blyton portrayed the policeman as a dim-witted oaf. Either way, my early immersion in such children's classics did my command of the language the world of good.

Five Stones

Every self-respecting little girl knew how to play Five Stones, a game that was wholly reserved for the female gender. Woe betide any boy caught playing it as he would be forever tarnished a sissy. On rainy days—in fact on any day that homework didn't beckon—groups of pre-pubescent girls would sit either in a forecourt or anywhere that was shaded from the sun, and endlessly play this game.

Its history is a little unclear but the general belief is that it was derived from an earlier game, variously called Knucklebones, Dibs, Dibstones, Jackstones or Chuckstones, that came from the Middle East or Greece. It was apparently brought to Singapore by early Jewish migrants and Five Stones became its Singapore moniker.

The game is played with five small objects, which were originally the knucklebones of a sheep. These objects are thrown in the air and caught in various ways. Since a sheep's knucklebones were not exactly two a penny, smooth pebbles or stones were used instead. The winner is the first player to successfully complete a prescribed series of throws which, while similar, differ widely in detail. The simplest throw consists of tossing up one stone, the Jack, and picking up one or more from the table while the Jack is in the air. This goes on until all five stones have been picked up.

Another throw consists of tossing up first one stone, then two, then three and so on, and catching them on the back of the hand. Different throws have distinctive names, such as Riding the Elephant, Peas in the Pod and Horses in the Stable. I cannot now recall their local names and given that for a boy, playing the game came with such a damning stigma, I was never privy to the chatter that went with it. Suffice to say that the game was a national pastime for girls that vanished sometime in the late 1960s.

Spinning Tops

The Lord be praised for giving us boys a game with which we could cock a snook at the girls, who felt their Five Stones was the epitome of gamesmanship—or gamesgirlship as the case may be. I loved my *gasing* (spinning top). It was a wooden pear-shaped toy that provided hours of precious entertainment. Each one had a little nail embedded in the pointy end and when the string that was wound around it was rapidly drawn away, it would spin for minutes. The object of the game was to see whose top spun the longest.

The true test was whether you could hit an opponent's spinning top with your own top, then keep your top spinning after the impact. To achieve this was a huge triumph and many a champion top changed hands for money. An uncle once gave me a top that was made of hard, red wood and had intricate carvings along the curved sides. I had it for years and won many a bout with it. I would not part with it for any amount of money. Well, not until a neighbour's son offered to trade in his Mickey Mouse watch for my special *gasing*. Brief though its fame was, it gave me some cachet as the champion top-spinner.

Street Theatre and Medicine Men

Apart from home cures, Mother also had faith in the medicine offered by the many travelling herbalists who came through our neighbourhood. One such peddler came by often, clanging his Chinese gong as he advertised his miracle cures. His chief product, that he claimed was a universal panacea, was his famous *hai kow yew* (seal oil ointment).

The older generation today might remember this medicine man as he was also something of a circus performer. To attract an audience he would perform an extraordinary feat. He would line up a couple of iron balls, each the size of a lime, and with great ceremony and clashing of cymbals proceed to swallow them whole! As the iron balls worked their way into his stomach, he would walk amongst the audience, letting them pat his belly. We could feel the balls all right. The climax came when he regurgitated the balls with furious jerks of his body, and much coughing and spluttering.

What was the point of this incredible ingestion, you might well ask? The medicine man did it to prove that he could control any muscle within his body, forcing his body to eject alien objects that had been accidentally swallowed. He claimed that if we frequently used his many ointments and unguents we would have the same control.

On seeing this, some children would go home to experiment with their own iron balls—only theirs were not balls, as such, but rather copper coins. As you can imagine, this resulted in a few tragedies.

One in particular involved a neighbour's son. He swallowed a number of coins and, in desperation, his mother made him swallow boiled *kangkung* (water convolvulus) and he actually managed to pass the coins. One more triumphant herbal cure!

The medicine man's magic cures did not stop at seal oil ointment; he also sold elixirs for old men. According to him, if you made a brew from dried deer entrails you would enjoy virility well into your seventies and eighties. Of course, the geriatrics in the audience lapped it all up.

Many shysters jumped on this travelling bandwagon and had enough get-well and get-rich schemes to rein in many a gullible person. Don't forget that at that time many people were superstitious and many illnesses were believed to be the result of bad luck and bad-tempered spirits. If a child had a raging fever, the parents would pray for that child's release from the clutches of some demon or other. These quack medicine men preyed on such gullibility and offered a plethora of panaceas, ranging from magic stones that could cure appendicitis, potions that promised to drive away the evil spirits that caused fevers, and so on. There were regular press reports about some unsuspecting person forking out hundred of dollars in exchange for a pebble. These medicine men were convincing with their sales pitches, feeding the unsuspecting customer nonsense about where the pebbles came from—usually some mystical mountain in China. Even up until the 1970s, there were still plenty of stories about Malaysian women being conned into believing this twaddle.

In the late 1940s and early 1950s street scenes were full of wondrous characters. I remember there was a man who would come by every few days trundling a large copper box on wheels. It was as large as a small car, and built into one of its sides were several glass-fronted visors. For ten cents you could press your face onto one of the visors, the vendor would crank a handle, and you'd be able to watch moving pictures. The images were very jerky and much like those in silent movies. The way it worked was that still pictures were mounted on a spindle inside the box. When the spindle was turned by the vendor, the pictures moved, chasing each other around the reel. Primitive the concept may have been, but these early nickelodeons were a source of great wonder for us kids who had never been to a cinema.

Street vending did not stop at food, for many other hawkers also came by on a regular basis. I remember one who we called the Ting Tong Man. He had a kind of metal ring which he would hit to alert households of his arrival. This clanging sound was akin to a ting tong cadence, hence the hawker's name. Supermarkets were several decades away and rural folk had little access to household essentials, such as brooms, pots and pans, woks, earthenware ovens, baskets, feather dusters and every other conceivable container and gadget needed for the home.

The Ting Tong Man's tricycle was laden to the brim, and then some. If you looked at it face on you could not even see the peddler. How he managed to see the road was a constant wonder but there were few cars in those days. From him we would buy all sorts of household wares, and sometimes he would brandish a multi-coloured feather duster as he clanged his metal ring.

Another hawker was extremely popular with kids as his wares were little figurines fashioned from a kind of marzipan in the shape of *wayang* characters and mythological creatures. They were skillfully crafted with fine facial details, grand costumes and weapons. These figurines were about eight inches tall and painted in brilliant colours. They ran the gamut from imperial warriors to fairies, dragons, phoenix and other historical figures. They were purely for decoration. Kids would buy them and use them like puppets to act out costume dramas. It was great fun as we allowed our imaginations to run riot.

There used to be a travelling puppet show conducted in Hainanese. Again, the glove puppets they used were miniature replicas of historical characters from ancient epics. The puppeteer and his wife would set up the show under a shady spot and begin to spin their heraldic tales, replete with clashing cymbals and gongs. We would wait eagerly for them to arrive, clutching our ten cents admission fee. For an hour or so we would watch the show, transfixed despite the fact that we did not understand a word of Hainanese. Sadly, by the early 1950s these kinds of puppet shows had vanished.

Rombongs

Street theatre of another genre was eagerly awaited by Mother and my aunts. A group of Malay women from somewhere in north Peninsular Malaysia would come laden with all sorts of beautiful coloured baskets made from woven palm fronds. These baskets were called *rombong*s in Malay, and would be exchanged for old clothing and other household items. In my home today I still have a little green hexagonal basket of woven pandanus leaves. It has a rustic and ornate design. Even though I inherited it from my mother more than fifty years ago, not one of the fronds has frayed. I still keep my keys and other small items in it.

From the early 1940s, groups of travelling Malay women, believed to come from as far away as Kelantan and Trengganu, would hawk an incredible array of woven basketry, mats and conical food covers in many different colours and sizes. You still see some of these in shops along Arab Street today.

The terms of trade when I was growing up was that we would give these women second-hand clothes and in return they would give us baskets, mats or food covers of the equivalent value. Such baskets were the precursor to wardrobes, as Mother kept all our clothes in them. They came in different sizes. Some could be as large as chests, while others were so small they were only good for my mother's betel nut and *sirih*.

When the group of women arrived, they would set up their wares on our front patio. It was like a mini carnival. Sometimes there would be as many as eight to ten family members. They walked for miles carrying their wares, some on their heads and others packed in sarongs slung around their shoulders. They would come by only a few times a year, but there always seemed to be the need for yet another basket or mat. The large mats of muted greens, reds, yellows and tan were very useful in later years for paktology (dating) sessions on the beach. They could be rolled up and tucked into the boot of a car, and when they got dirty they could simply be scrubbed and dried. The colours never ran and the fine basket weave was of such quality they it lasted for years, even decades, as mine testify.

The Night Soil Man

Night soil is one subject I do not particularly relish dwelling on, but the night soil man was an integral part of Singapore history from day one. I would even go so far as to say that he provided an essential service. Night soil, for the record, is a euphemism for human waste. At that time there were scarcely any flushing systems, especially not in rural areas, and even newer towns had not yet been blessed with plumbing systems. My family home did not have modern plumbing until the early 1950s and if the night soil man missed even one of his twice-weekly visits, it would be hell on earth.

The night soil man was a stocky man who spoke Hokkien. He was completely dedicated to his odorous task. The system in our home was simply a bucket placed under a simple hole-in-the-floor toilet. The night soil man would come and collect the bucket every two or three days, take it away and put a fresh, clean bucket in its place. Even with a lid on, the full bucket would slosh as he carried it through our hallway. He had to go through the hallway as our toilet was situated at the back of the house and this was the only access route. Mother despaired of his visits, and we were made to mop up his footprints after he'd left. What a pungent chore!

Later, the Public Works Department introduced a more updated—if still smelly—system. The night soil man was replaced by a large covered lorry with twenty-four compartments for buckets. It serviced the whole area. We called it the *to sai chia* (waste removing vehicle) as there was no other polite term for this service.

It was always disconcerting to see tins of hot tea and coffee suspended from lengths of vegetable fibre stripped from fried leaves called *opeh*. This was the precursor to today's clinical plastic food wrapper. Each lorry was manned by several men, and the drinks were hung from the handles of each compartment door.

The *to sai chia* was a sight we never forgot but it was certainly a better system than the night soil man. Another improvement was that Father, fed up with the unpleasant aura around the house, built a door leading to a back road behind our kitchen. This gave the lorry direct access to our toilet, ending our weekly suffering.

Several times a year, these PWD workers would go on strike for one reason or another and our bucket wouldn't be collected for up to two weeks. I shall not go into graphic details of the problems this caused.

House Beautiful

Interior design in the late 1940s and early 1950s was a truly eclectic mix of traditional Chinese, Nonya and loads of plastic. In Grandfather's cavernous front hall, that passed for what would be the sitting room today, there was a complete set of Chinese ebony furniture inlaid with mother-of-pearl. The set consisted of a long sofa, two armchairs, a massive altar table and several occasional tables, all similarly decorated. Beautiful they were, but comfortable they were not. On one occasional table sat either a bowl of artificial plastic flowers, or trees made from ceramic with leaves of jade. On another was a stuffed mouse deer with beady eyes that I swear followed you as you passed.

In one corner of the room was a teak lounge chair that had an arm that swiveled to the front so you could rest a cup on it. Grandfather would often snooze in this chair when he was not otherwise smoking opium; most of my memories of Grandfather are of him either in an opium-induced haze or asleep. The altar table must have weighed a ton, had been shipped from China in the 1920s and contained all the paraphernalia required for ancestor worship and Taoist prayer rituals. I remember that this room always smelt of incense as joss sticks would be burnt every day.

As the years passed and Granny grew tired of these uncomfortable chairs, she decided one day to give them all to the rag and bone man! Had we known their value then, we would have put a stop to this. If you could find similar items today, they would be worth tens of thousands of dollars. Granny traded them in for furniture all topped with Formica. This tatty plastic alloy promised easy maintenance and was prettily designed—everyone had to have it.

Bedrooms were never carpeted or even had rugs. Every bedroom floor was covered with wall-to-wall linoleum, the 'new' interior design material that became so pervasive it even ended up on beds, dining tables and every surface that needed a table cloth. For years afterwards, our town home was a linoleum fest. The large platform that I shared with my two brothers—beds were a luxury that didn't exist until the mid-1950s—was covered with linoleum in a pink and green design. On warm days it would stick to your flesh as you slept.

Dining tables in every home were lino-covered and replaced before every Chinese New Year. I grant that they were easy to clean, saved on laundry bills and were scratch proof. When they became grimy, you simply changed them for a new roll. Then plastic came along and our dining table became the recipient of a really kitsch table cloth. Mother would not hear of us using a proper table cloth and she took great care in securing the sides the plastic sheet under the table with thumb tacks.

Malay homes were considered very stylish as the community was extremely house-proud. In every rural home, however humble, the living room was always immaculately decked out with rattan or bamboo furniture, velvet cushions and pretty plastic lace mats which sat on coffee tables. But it was the bedrooms that deserved a place in décor magazines. Each bed was covered with a pink or yellow satin bedspread, fat satin cushions with frills and not a crease in sight. Did they sleep on them? No, their cats did.

We had an old Malay neighbour we called Mak Jun who could have been a hundred years old. She was a war widow, lived alone in a small attap hut and lived off the earnings from her rag and bone business. Her bedroom—it was a studio-type hut with a bed, sitting and dining room all rolled into one—was as pretty as a picture, spotless and featured a small bed covered with immaculate linen bedclothes. Given that she was usually so unkempt, this was a real surprise. An even bigger surprise was the sight of four cats sleeping on the bed. Apparently, she always slept on her (linoleum-lined) floor while the cats slept in luxury. They were her only family and lapped it up.

The Plastic Era

This plastic/linoleum/Formica era raged on and pretty much set a universal trend, augmented by plastic flowers. These were everywhere; tulips, chrysanthemums, roses, lilies and other exotic blooms never needed watering, never faded and only needed washing every so often when they collected a patina of dust. Fresh flowers were rare and expensive, reserved for weddings and funerals—except for one family I knew. Their daughter walked down the aisle carrying a spray of white lilies and orchids—made of plastic!

Plastic flowers were even in evidence when couples went to a photo studio to have commemorative wedding pictures taken. The proprietor would go into overdrive, urging couples to pose against picturesque screens, heart-shaped gateways or moon-shaped doorways all strewn with branches of plastic flowers. They would even make a bride pose with a coquettish smile as she held a spray of plastic flowers. This was common until the 1960s. I know this because I almost became the victim of the same awful experience.

Plastic covers pervaded every corner of my life. School books were wrapped in plastic, wardrobe shelves were similarly treated and women carried handbags covered with the transparent stuff on the premise that their bags would last longer if protected. Mother usually carried a woven palm-frond basket—her faithful handbag in which she kept her betel nut and *sirih* leaf accoutrements—and this was also completely covered in plastic. When our first set of rattan furniture and cushion covers arrived wrapped in plastic, she wouldn't allow us to remove it for years. Well, the cushions did last much longer but sitting on them was a squishy, squelchy experience on hot days.

When it came to making things last longer, many parents even rationed the use of items such as spectacles and watches. They believed that if their children used these items less they would last longer, especially if they were wrapped in, you guessed it, plastic! Watches may indeed have lasted longer if used less, but spectacles? I have suffered from myopia since the age of six and my first pair of windows was very much doled out to me only when I needed to see things in perspective. Even in later years Mother would sternly chide: 'Everything new must use. Keep with me and they will last longer!' So I groped about for some years.

Adult Education and the Civil Service

The subject of education brings to mind the year 1959. I had just finished my secondary education but was too young to take on a civil service job, for which the requisite age was eighteen. I was a few months short of this age and instead earned an income teaching in a local school for adult education. It was a Ministry of Education scheme that encouraged illiterate people, like my mother and her equally untutored neighbours, to educate themselves. The school was Rangoon Road Primary School, my alma mater, and the average age of my students was between fifty and sixty.

A few could just about write the letters A, B and C. The rest could not even count to ten, let alone read simple texts. We had text books that ran the gamut of 'This is a dog, that is a cat' and so on. One Cantonese lady was reduced to tears trying to curl her tongue around certain words like 'people, pepper and paper'. Once, wailing with despair, she moaned me, 'Pipper, peeper, papper, all the same what!'—at least that is what I remember. Needless to say she did not last long in my class.

In other lessons I was driven to despair by the older pupils, who would sit chatting at the back of the classroom and share food while I was trying in vain to interest them in the alphabet. My teaching experience lasted all of six months. That was as long as I could take it. Certain phrases still ring in my head: 'A for *ah pek*, B for *bola*, C for *ngiaow*!' Three o'clock became 'teelee o crock', orange juice sounded like 'ong joo' and teacher (what they had to address me as) was mangled to *cicak*, the creature that lives on our ceilings. You work it out. I had had enough of nicknames in my youth. Mother refused to attend my classes but she did educate me in the mysteries of her own interpretation of the English language.

So I had little choice but to scan the daily papers for jobs with the civil service. Frankly I had few other options, plus Mother was adamant that I should work for the government, earn my pension and live in government quarters. The number of times I had my ears filled with 'garmen', 'penchen' and 'quatar' I cannot tell you. Her brothers had gone this route, ended up in the postal service or PUB and did live in government quarters.

Mother also often referred to something called *sap ping kia* when talking about a court case that a neighbour was involved in. And there was frequent mention of *jar min*. These were her garbled phonetic pronunciations of the words 'supoena' and 'examine' in the Teochew (Swatow) dialect. At least she knew what they meant for I didn't, even with all my education.

Despite her educational handicap, Mother was as sharp as a tack when it came to monitoring our education. With Father gone she was the only adult privy to our term report cards. She knew only one thing about these report cards: if there was anything written in red ink we would earn a thwack from her trusty cane. If any of our marks were below fifty, it would be written in red. Fortunately it didn't happen that often with me but did for my second brother, who had problems with his arithmetic. He had weals on his upper arm for years afterward. Mother was a disciplinarian of the old school variety and did not spare the rod, but we did benefit from this.

When I reached my final year at secondary school and scored highly on my Cambridge Overseas Certificate, she was proud indeed and showed it audibly. If we were on a bus—which was rare for her—or in the wet market where I often helped out, she would brag about my results to the vegetable man, the noodle seller and the butcher—as if they were remotely interested. Most of these tradesmen had children who rarely finished school. One pork seller chided his fourteen-year-old son for *wanting* to finish his schooling.

'What for?' he cried. 'Better you help me sell pork and make quick money!' The poor boy ended up acting out the role of a soldier in a Chinese *wayang* troupe.

In those days there was also an obvious divide between students who were Chinese educated and those who were English educated. Those of us who were sent to English schools received the blunt end of many strident remarks from Chinese students. They alluded to us being 'traitors and turncoats' for denying our culture. I found it ridiculous as we were just getting on with what was expedient and did not see it as anything more. In our defence, all we could do was retort that they should go back to China, if indeed that was where they had come from. No, they were Singapore-born and simply misguided about the importance of education, any education. It was a battleground I steered clear of. Many years later, during Mao Tse-tung's Cultural Revolution, these would-be nationalist students went en masse to join the Great Leader. Many were never heard from again.

1960s

Radio Daze

The 1960s was a memorable era for me. I had finished my final Cambridge Exams (O Levels today) and just started my second job. At that time, Radio Singapore was part of the Ministry of Culture and we were civil servants, as such. If there was any glamour about being a radio announcer I certainly did not feel it.

Sure, it was far more exciting than my previous job as a post-primary schoolteacher, a job I was most unsuited for. For one thing, I'm of small stature so my pre-teen students would tower over me. One afternoon I threw in the towel when I took my class for a swimming lesson at Farrer Park. The attendant would not let me sign the register to admit us, saying: 'How can you be teacher? You so short!' I silently prayed that he would drown in the pool, returned to school and quit the next day.

So the radio job saved my life and self-respect as on the radio no one could see me, only hear me. I thought it was ideal; listeners could fantasise about me. I was a gauche eighteen-year old, very much from the wrong side of the tracks compared to the swinging DJs such as Tan Hock Lai, Tan Swee Leong, Larry Lai and Vernon Martinus—all idolised by swooning teenagers. While each had a sonorous voice with a rich timbre and on-air charisma to match, I must have sounded like an adolescent schoolboy. The only reason I passed my voice test must have been because of my good diction, courtesy of my English teachers.

For me, being a radio announcer was a job that paid more than a schoolteacher—all of S$279 per month compared to the S$190 a trainee teacher earned. We were trained by BBC overseas personnel, and I went on to present classical programmes and the odd news bulletin. For some reason I never did get the glamour bug. I did not have the finances to swan around in a sports car like my colleagues did. I could only afford a Vespa scooter. On the odd occasion when there was an audience participation show at the radio auditorium, I was never asked for my autograph. Worse still, when I helped to usher in the public they took me for an office boy! It was mortifying, to say the least, but I stuck with the job as there were other compensations.

For example, I would meet the stars of the day when they came by for concerts. At least I could bask in the reflected glory of luminaries such as Cliff Richard, Lulu, Ann Margaret and Lloyd Bridges, whose two sons Beau and Jeff went to become stars in their own right. I remember attending a lunch and a press conference with the two boys when they were ten and twelve respectively. I also had the pleasure of taking tea with Shirley Bassey, lunch with Sophia Loren and dinner with Dick Van Dyke.

My job also allowed me to cover the Asian Games in Bangkok in the mid-1960s, commentate on the Grand Prix in Thomson Road, and interview Pat Boone, Frankie Avalon et al. But more than anything else, I was able to hide behind the anonymity of a radio microphone, act in radio plays and generally enjoy being no more than a voice. Years later, my mother asked me why she never saw me singing on television. She never understood my job and often chided me for giving up teaching.

It was a distinct pleasure doing the odd request programme. One I remember was to draw the public's attention to funds needed to build Singapore's first National Theatre near River Valley Road. The scheme was such that every listener who wanted to make a request had to buy a card costing S$1, write their preferred choice of song on it and send it in. Little did I know that there was some sort of syndicate whereby those listeners who had their names mentioned the most often were elevated to a special status within their fraternity. They didn't give a toss which song was played but they were very concerned that I got their names right. There was a slew of names such as Elvis Aaron Lim, Frankie Avalon Wong, Cliff Ang, Lulu Goh and so on. Talk about hero worshipping, but it was a serious affair and rumour had it that fights would break out among these teenagers when they felt hard done by. Usually they would be annoyed because one listener was mentioned more than another and so on.

Even my mother got roped into the National Theatre Card scheme. She used to go the local wet market in Cambridge Road most mornings. Some of the radio fans had got wind of who I was and that she was my mother. One morning she came back with her shopping basket stuffed with cards that had been surreptitiously slipped inside without her knowledge. She never understood my explanation and was worried that I was the target of some triad activities. I could only tell her to be careful about not leaving her open basket unattended.

Occasionally, when there was a live show either at National Theatre or some other public venue, hordes of youngsters would turn up dressed like teddy boys and rockers, the groupies that London was stuffed with. They were the Ah Bengs of the 1960s with impossibly quiffed, curry-puff hairdos and skin-tight trousers. Their stance was menacing and they would swagger a lot. Of course I basked in the limelight of being not an office boy this time, but one of the radio production team.

There were hilarious moments within the studios too. I remember once one of the more seasoned newsreaders, a man of indeterminate age and who had been broadcasting for ages, was about to read the news. In order to switch on his microphone he had to flick a switch. This would turn on a little red light in the studio, indicating that he was on air and silence should prevail. What he did not know was that a devious colleague, who I shall not name, had replaced the fifteen-watt bulb for a one-hundred-watt monster. When the newsreader flicked the switch, an almighty blinding light filled the room and he nearly fainted from fright. Still, being the professional he was he read the news and only collapsed afterwards when he was outside the studio. It was a cruel trick and the perpetrator was warned that if he ever did it again, he would lose his job.

There were moments of pure comedy too. One colleague, a Malayalee who did not understand Chinese, was hosting a request programme which involved the same National Theatre cards. In his BBC-tinged plummiest tones, he read out the request to brothers Wan Hung Hi and Wan Hung Lo who had asked for the song 'Cocktails for Two'. Not long after, our supervisor hauled him over the coals for being obscene.

'What do you mean "obscene"?' he asked.

'Think about the names of the two brothers and their choice of song for a moment,' replied the supervisor. The host did and cottoned on to this sneaky bit of lascivious trickery. Thereafter the programme was handled by someone else, wise to such double entendres. In retrospect it was funny, if now somewhat below the belt.

As for me, I had high moments of a different nature. Once, I was asked to interview an important VIP from an international airline. I sat him down and we engaged in preliminary chit chat. The gentleman asked me what type of education I had, probably seeing me like a young upstart. Innocently, I said that I had a Cambridge Certificate—well, in those days this was enough to get you anywhere in the job sphere. He went on to ask which hall I had attended. Again, without guile I asked what he meant by hall. In my mind I had taken my tests in the usual examination hall at my school. It turned out he had thought I had graduated from Cambridge University, a university which has various academic halls such as Trinity and Magdalen. When I set him right, he refused to be interviewed by someone with mere O Levels. At least my supervisor saw the funny side and tamed the gentleman's ruffled feathers somewhat. The interview went OK, although he remained most bumptious.

There was also near tragedy and irony. One day one of the

studios in Caldecott Hill, where the radio station was located, caught fire. Firemen came and put the blaze out. Many tapes and recordings had been burnt to a cinder, but when the firemen tried to pull a smouldering box from the rubble they found a stack of 45 rpm discs still intact. It was pure irony when the first disc was examined and found to be a recording of *Fire Down Below* by Shirley Bassey. The story made headline news. It also boosted the sales of her recording as it was played on the air over and over.

My radio career was a rich experience steeped in our multi-lingual and multi-cultural milieu. There were four main radio channels: English, Malay, Tamil and Mandarin. The Mandarin channel also fielded dialect programmes and news in Cantonese, Hainanese, Hokkien and Teochew. There was a lot of social interaction among the staff of the different language streams, and I was privy to programmes about the culture and history of all our main racial groups.

Radio also enabled me to hone my craft of communication and float in a romantic realm of soft music and dream-like imagery. I was and still am an incurable romantic. One of my radio programmes was called Sunset Serenade in which I would compile and play a selection of dreamy music for dusk. The script I had to read is still fresh in my memory and I paraphrase it here after nearly fifty years of intoning it every evening.

'On wings of melody come sweet caressing sounds to soothe away the troubles of the day. This is Sunset Serenade with Mantovani and his Magic Strings.'

Radio was a wonderful world of escapism and allowed my imagination free reign. Programming and writing scripts are crafts that use up all your creative juices. It also led to many a confrontation with my immediate superior, a lady who did not mince words.

I had to script and present another programme called Lunchtime

Listening. Each episode had to have a theme. I began with the songs 'Sophisticated Lady', with 'A String of Pearls' as the attendant narrative and went on, ever so smugly, with 'I've Got Rings on My Fingers', 'Golden Earrings' and 'Silk Stockings'. These were random songs meant to portray my chosen theme of a lady at the height of fashion in a romantic setting. I ended the programme with 'Two Cigarettes in the Dark' and sat back to wait for the appreciative phone calls to roll in.

There was only one—from my superior.

'Oy, do you realise that your sophisticated lady is naked? Could you have not at least given her a dress like "Alice Blue Gown" or something? We might get complaints that we are broadcasting porno!'

My supervisor really pricked my ego but it was a learning curve about syntax and standards. As for addressing me as 'Oy', I might let the proverbial cat out of the bag and add that as broadcasters away from the microphone, we tended to lapse into colloquial English. When on air it was like stage acting, with every vowel and consonant in place.

Newer staff who had not received the BBC training we had also made faux pas. One of these chaps was presenting a programme about artists and painters and was heard talking about someone called Dee Gas. I couldn't believe my ears. As broadcasters we were people not only trained in the fine nuances of language, but also had to have at least basic knowledge of the arts and music. This chap was obviously referring to the French painter Degas, pronounced Day Gah.

From time to time auditions would be held to find new announcers. We would sit and observe more out of curiosity than executive function. Some of the voice tests were real howlers. Each candidate would be given a script peppered, deliberately, with names of great composers such as Tchaikovsky, Chopin, Shostakovich and Rachmaninoff. Other difficult-to-pronounce words they were tested on included Marseilles, Chevrolet, Moulin Rouge and Rendezvous. We had to go through these tests to determine our level of knowledge and our ability to pronounce them correctly. It was broadcasting, after all.

These sessions would have us in fits of laughter, but it wasn't out of smug derision. If you aspired to being a radio announcer, you should know how to pronounce these words, or at least do your homework before applying for the job. Anyway, our ears were assailed by mispronunciations such as Itchy Koski, Chopping, Soda Kopi, Ramen Enough and Nutcracker Sweetie. As for the rest, the mutations were priceless. Imagine Marsilling, Chek Bodek, Moulmein Route and Reindeer Mouse. Thank heavens I had learnt my lessons well.

Hantu, Hantu!

Radio studios were for public use and the Radio Orchestra, headed by Ahmad Jaffar, was a shining beacon of music presentations. Classical and pop musicians of the day would be in and out of the studios and it was like being part of a big family.

There were a few scare stories, for Caldecott Hill was apparently the site of many Japanese war victims and rumour had it that a few studios were haunted. It got so bad that broadcasters on the late-night shift could not bear being alone in any of the studios. One day, in the early evening, one of the Malay announcers was seen running from one of the studios at the rear of the building screaming at the top of her lungs. She ran to the canteen panting and gasping, '*Hantu, hantu.*' ('Devil, devil.') It took a while for her to calm down and explain exactly what she had seen.

'I was editing one of my tapes in Studio D (the one most reputed to be haunted) when I heard a noise in the big room.' Each recording studio had a small room where the control panel was and this led to a larger room where radio plays and other entertainment programmes would be taped. The 'noise' she had heard was of someone grunting and making guttural noises. When she saw what looked like a disembodied spectre covered in a sheet, she fled. Rumours like these always gave me goosebumps whenever I used the studio alone.

As it turned out, the ghost had not been a ghost at all. One of the studio cleaners, a middle-aged lady, had decided to take forty winks after a hard day's toil cleaning studios. She'd laid down on one of the couches in the large studio and covered herself with a large white towel—the studios were air-conditioned to an arctic degree. Rumours of ghosts continued and some people swore they heard typewriters clattering on their own, lights going on and off and many other stories fuelled by lurid imagination.

It didn't help that dotted here and there around the studio compound were frangipani trees. Anyone who has attended a Singapore funeral in the three decades between the 1950s and 1970s will know that the distinctive perfume of the beautiful white frangipani flowers is associated with death. The blossoms are used for wreaths and other funeral bouquets. The frangipani is very much a part of Singapore's horticultural palette and you can still see these trees around the island. Some have pink and yellow flowers but the white flowers symbolise death. Actually the perfume is very heady and the belief is that if you can smell it, that means a spirit is lurking nearby.

I Was (Not) a TV Star

The arrival of television to Singapore in the mid-1960s caused much excitement. This idiot box was a technical marvel as it meant that we did not have to leave the home to seek entertainment. The picture was still black and white but it was mesmerising. I had already been trained to do a little television work after my radio stint, still had all my hair and every vowel and consonant in the right place. However, my TV debut did not set the world on fire. I fronted an early morning programme at a time when the government was exhorting the public to keep fit. It was called *Daily Dozen* and I had to comment while a fitness demonstrator went though his routine. What I objected to was the hideous T-shirt I was made to wear by the producer. You remember the range of imported shirts with the brand name Montagut? Well, the one I had to wear was a made-in-China version, a total copy of the original French range and called Monakut. It was a bilious shade of green with mustard stripes and it was supposed to make me look sporty and in tune with the essence of the programme. I looked awful and what made it worse was the thick make-up and that my body was the antithesis of fitness. Any hopes I had of becoming a high-flying anchorman ended with that series.

My only saviour was a colleague who was producing a series of TV programmes about life among the people. It was called *Down Your Way* and we had to conduct live interviews on the spot with people on the streets. Trying to elicit comments from members of the public about current affairs, music, politics and other lifestyle elements was like squeezing water from a stone. Nonetheless, we had to capture the thoughts of the public.

One passer-by was asked what he thought of urban transport, flower power and psychedelic music—highlights of the day. His answer was most cryptic.

'What transport? Cannot get taxi at four o'clock! Flour where got power, only good for making cakes. How can bicycle got music?'

At least he was right on one count: four o'clock was the time that taxis changed their shifts and one had to wait till kingdom come for a cab.

My producer tried another tack by going into a shopping centre in the hope that we might encounter a more enlightened public. I stopped a young lady who seemed to be fairly savvy and asked her a few questions about things close to a woman's heart.

'Do you think wearing high heels is healthy?'

'Eh, why not healthy? I can reach high shelves in my supermarket, what!'

'What do you think of the new London fashions, the miniskirt and Vidal Sassoon hairstyles?'

'Where got money to go to London? Miniskirt save money because my tailor use less cloth. Vidal Sassoon? Who dat? I perm my hair in Katong beauty salon!'

We retreated to the drawing board and decided to change the rationale for the programmes. One programme we did was about how the clock at the Victoria Memorial Hall was maintained and serviced. We managed to gain access to the clock tower and I was to interview the man in charge of maintenance. While waiting for the sound engineer to set up his gear, I poked my nose into the mechanics of the clock. Being rather nosy, I touched a lever and suddenly there was a loud 'Bong!' I had accidentally pressed the gadget that rang the hour bell. I was terrified that someone had heard our equivalent of Big Ben chiming an unnecessary gong! No one heard, apparently, for my producer was not hauled over the coals.

Two More Cheeks to Powder

Ah, those were the days. The world was enchanted by the spell cast by Swinging London and The Beatles, although their sensational sound did not sweep Asia until 1963. Mary Quant's miniskirts preceded them and ruled every woman's wardrobe. This fashion item gave birth to a really funny saying: 'If miniskirts get any shorter, there will be two more cheeks to powder!' I do not have to explain the allusion, surely. Every young girl, and not so young woman, began to show legs and thighs that until then had been modestly covered.

This short skirt looked fine and even sexy on a nubile young girl. On a stout middle-aged lady, it was a different matter. Never had Singapore's fashion scene been subjected to so much human flesh and cellulite. There were no rules and fat or thin, young or old, miniskirts were the order of the day and night.

Getting onto buses and into taxis resulted in what we cheeky young men termed as 'free shows'! Knickers had never had so much airing, and tailors moaned about the loss of business. It took very little fabric to make a short skirt and tailors in Chinatown were often heard to moan that they could not wait for the length of skirts to drop. They weren't being salacious, just hopeful that they would sell more fabric. This mini fad was to last a few years and represented a kind of liberation from the rather straight-laced 1950s.

Everyone who was anyone had to have a Morris Mini Minor. Its sister was the Austin Seven. By 1962 other models such as the Austin 850 and Morris 850 hit our roads. Each car would cost some S$3,000 but it was a snip given the cachet it offered. Some years later, after I had graduated from my trusty Vespa scooter, I could finally afford an Austin 850. The numerals 850 meant it had 850 cc horsepower. One of my favourite jaunts was to drive up to Mount Faber, but on occasions when my little mini was loaded with five people made up of cousins and friends, it wouldn't climb up the blessed hill! My passengers had to get out and walk as the combined weight was too heavy for the steep gradient. One of my cousins was to remark:

'Ayoh, worse than Lau Pok Car!'

The late 1960s wasn't just about fashions and frippery, although it marked a kind of radical change in people's lives. International luxuries were more readily available, the British had departed and there was a new hope and faith in our ability to forge a cohesive society in the future. Although the Indonesia–Malaysia confrontation was over by 1966, caution and alertness were key.

Our radio station, as a vulnerable communications centre,

was still guarded by soldiers who would patrol the buildings. Our office was a one-storey wooden building with large windows—air conditioning was confined to the studios. Our office windows were essential for letting in cool breezes. One of my female colleagues, a rather uptight lady, repeatedly complained to our supervisor that the soldiers would ogle her as she sat by one of the windows. She claimed one of them had even stuck his head in and leered at her cleavage. The supervisor did not entertain her paranoia and simply said, 'Well, you will wear low-cut blouses, won't you?'

We used to chortle behind her back as she did have the habit of wearing dresses with plunging necklines and very short skirts. What did she expect? The soldiers must have been bored to their helmeted skulls patrolling and she was a welcome distraction. In time the soldiers stopped patrolling. When complimented on her titillating mode of dress she was heard to moan, 'What's the point of my looking sexy when there are no randy soldiers around?'

I silently wished she would make up her mind.

Platform Shoes and Bell Bottoms

The rest of the 1960s were memorable mostly for the quirky trends and many fashion disasters. It was the era when fashion was everything, style took a back seat and comfort was the least of our worries. We all succumbed to the faithful T-shirt, an example of casual wear that has gone from strength to strength and long may it last. However this fit-all, says-all cotton garment was yet to find its global niche as a message board, with slogans scribbled large across the chest and back.

The mid-1960s featured some of the most ludicrous fashions, and this was just for guys. The skin-tight trousers of the 1950s had billowed into flares, Winklepicker shoes reached great heights and some falls. Elvis the King had stamped his trademark quiff on the fashion scene, a quiff that was able to reach even greater bouffant heights. The colloquial term 'curry pop', in reference to the bouncy quiff, became a veritable puff ball. The women had big hair with so much lacquer it must have made the first hole in the ozone layer. There must have been enough chlorofluorocarbons (CFC to you) in the air to pollute Mars.

All along North Bridge Road, especially in the shops selling watches, salesmen looked like they had stepped straight out of London's Carnaby Street, the mecca for 1960s style. The only problem was that the way they mixed and matched their clothing did not quite gel. One guy was often seen with a bouffant hairdo, and wearing a purple shirt over a yellow vest. When he stood up, he was wearing a pair of lime green bell bottoms and platform shoes that must have added five inches to his height. Once, he removed his shoes to climb on a stool so he could reach watches on a high shelf. His bells fell around his calves and he showed his true diminutive stature of being inches short of the five feet four inches he claimed to be. He looked like Henri de Toulouse-Lautrec.

Against my better judgement, I too succumbed to London fashions on my first trip to Carnaby Street. I cringe with embarrassment today when I think about my jade green velvet bell bottoms, yellow stacked platform shoes and body-constricting pink voile shirt. At the time I thought that I was the bees knees but now, having seen pictures of myself taken forty years ago, I think not.

Among the guys who sported these fashions were those who had a fondness for permanent waves, as in permed hair. If you wanted to fit in with this crowd, you had to go to a female beauty parlour and fork out S$50 or more to have your crowning glory curled to within an inch of an Afro. For the bolder ones amongst us—especially those in the entertainment industry or those who wanted to be seen as such—Afros were de rigueur. Some styles were a yard wide and blocked out the sun.

Because of such fashions, sometimes it was difficult to tell if someone was male or female. People wore clothes of acid green, purple and yellow, beads and necklaces adorned every other neck, and the message was one of peace and love. Thank goodness I didn't go this far else my mother would have fainted with fright.

Snobbing It

Perhaps it was because we had become a British colony after the Japanese surrender that there existed an incipient snobbery among Singaporeans. It was not an overt attitude, as such, but a reflection of what it meant to be able to afford imported products. Thus the made-in-England tag became a catchphrase with some people, and many were caught up in the spiral of keeping up with the Jones's.

There weren't that many imports from the mid-1950s, certainly not in the form of consumer durables or luxury items. Middle-class families probably had a better hand in the import barrel and as the years went by, name dropping began to catch on. When it came to sweets only Callard and Bowser Nougat would do; hair cream and soaps had to be Yardley of London; shoes had to be Clarks; noses were turned up if biscuits were not Gem or Marie; women hunted for material from Tootal Fabrics for their dresses; and men smoked Players Navy Cut cigarettes which came in tins. First Mother managed to get hold of some once and I started smoking again after having given up on Granny's rolled cigarettes. Evidently, she too was seduced by the made-in-England cachet! It was inside these empty cigarette tins that we put fire crackers. When they exploded, we pretended they were war missiles.

In the meantime, poorer folk had to make do with biscuits from Thye Hong Biscuit factory, shoes from the Lee Rubber Factory and Monakut shorts. While the haves could enjoy Lyle's Golden Churn butter, the have-nots had only Malayan margarine. The well-to-do sniffed Pyramid Egyptian cotton handkerchiefs of very fine denier, others simply cut up squares of flour sacks and recycled them into rustic napkins. These napkins, however, lasted years after Pyramid Egyptian handkerchiefs had become useless rags. Middle-class homes wafted in the scent of imported English aerosols but my home reeked of mosquito repellent. We had coils of a brown substance fixed in sand which we lit to deter the pesky insects.

One friend got so caught up with this sense of superiority from using imported products, that he would give us a tour of his home, pointing out various objects with the puffed-up aplomb of an art critique.

'You see my toilet, it's Shanks, made in England. And this kitchen pail is also English plastic. I make my sandwiches with Shippams Fish Paste and I only use Parker pens or Croxley paper.' Jeez, I was very tempted to counter by saying I could not live without my night soil made-in-Malaya tin pail and my favourite sandwich spread of mashed Ayam sardines. He went on and on and pulled his wife into his spiel. She was ironing and he pointed out the iron was a top quality Morphy Richards and their radio was a Philips.

I refer to this because a certain class of Singaporeans—the number is growing—cannot resist anything with a label, be it a bar of soap, a pair of shoes or a can opener. I guess we all suffer this syndrome at one time or another, but when it becomes pervasive you really want to tell them to shut up. Especially when you hear comments such as 'You like this English Axminster carpet? S$1,000,' or 'You like my cushion covers? Sanderson fabric, made in England.'

Soap Operas

Television brought a new joy to many a housewife, especially those in the Cantonese-speaking community. TV was now in colour and Hong Kong studios churned out endless episodes of soaps with story lines and plots right out of domestic situations everyone could relate to. First there was *Chameleon* starring Carol Cheng and Chow Yun Fatt who has since gone on to become a Hollywood superstar. He also starred in *Man in the Net*.

Each series ran for an incredible fifty-two episodes, a year to be precise. On screening days, many a business and household in Singapore ground to a halt. Everyone was glued to their TV sets and nothing, not even World War III, could prise them away. Maids abandoned their duties, shop assistants took sick leave and housewives popped dinners into microwaves because they did want not to miss a single minute of the gripping shows. The next day conversation among these soap addicts was devoted entirely to who did what to whom and why. The public critiqued every episode, bringing new meaning to many lives.

False Fronts

As I've already mentioned, the 1960s woman, if she was aware of London's influences, would not be seen dead without her miniskirt. Her more *kampung* sisters who had never heard of Mary Quant pretty much had their own equivalent—mostly to the chest area. Even our family washerwoman suddenly had a more well-endowed bust. Padded bras were on sale everywhere, especially at the Chinese Emporium shopping mall. Perhaps it was a pointed gesture against the notion that Chinese women were all flat-chested. But no more!

We used to frequent a famous fish head noodle stall on Nanking Street and, according to my sister-in-law, the waitress there had blossomed from a B cup to a Z cup. The stall was on one side of the road and the customers' tables spread across to the other side. The poor dear had to lope across the road every so often to serve customers on the other side and on one occasion my sister-in-law noticed that something was amiss. She nudged me and whispered that one side of the waitress's blouse was indented. She must have noticed it too because she nonchalantly popped her hand under her blouse to adjust the imbalance. After that we ate our meal amid choking laughter.

Stone Me!

The region went through a most unpleasant time when Singapore and Kuala Lumpur erupted with racial riots. I will not go into the whys and wherefores of this best-forgotten episode of Sino-Malay unrest in our otherwise peaceful history. Working as a broadcaster, I had moments of pure terror. The 13 May 1964 is not a date most Singaporeans care to remember. The statistics tell a grim enough story when hundreds were needlessly slaughtered.

I had to report for duty despite the imposed curfew. One evening, on my way to work, I was riding my scooter towards Caldecott Hill, near Kampong Java Road. The streets seemed quiet enough but suddenly, out of nowhere, a stone the size of a baseball came whizzing towards me. It missed me by inches and I revved my scooter in a fit of terror. Luckily I arrived at work without further mishap but did not leave the radio station for two days, sleeping on the floor of my supervisor's office.

I felt my job was my duty to promote peace as I had to do hourly bulletins about the state of civil unrest. Early on the last morning, when the curfew was over and the violence had been contained, my supervisor arrived to find me in a dishevelled state, having had no change of clothes for forty-eight hours. Was she sympathetic? Probably, but she didn't show it.

'My word, Terry, you look like a riot victim!' she stated.

Whether she was trying to be topically witty or was just plain tactless, I did not wait to find out. I had not shaved for two days, had suffered from the discomfort of sleeping on a hard floor and was dying of hunger. I was just thankful that the trouble had ended sooner rather than later. However, when I reached home I discovered that First Mother had had a much more traumatic time.

She had been helping my aunt who ran a dry goods stall at MacPherson Market on Upper Serangoon Road when the curfew was announced. There were still a few buses running and people were scattering in terror. Outside the market there was a monsoon drain and when the police began to clear the area, she did the only sensible thing: she slid into the drain which fortunately was dry—she was already in her sixties—and stayed there for nearly four hours.

A friendly policeman found her cowering in the drain and escorted her home. When we asked her how she'd coped, she grinned and said she'd had a little nap in the drain. This was typical of First Mother, God bless her soul, who was as feisty as they come. Once, I took her to Penang and instead of riding with me in a trishaw she saw fit to hire a bicycle and do her own sightseeing.

A Dental Circus

As a child I was fond of the circus but the few that did set up their tents were abysmal, to say the least. However, one from India was better than most. It was billed as the Great Indian Circus and promised much. It did deliver, after a fashion. Among the acts was Jehan the Juggler who tossed not oranges or even juggling pins but stainless-steel Indian cooking pots! He wasn't very good as one or two fell on his head. Had he not been wearing a turban, he probably would have suffered concussion.

It was the Dental Act that had me in stitches. The ringmaster announced it with much fanfare but it was his running commentary that really entertained us.

'Ladies and gentlemen, now for our famous Dental Act. You see

Ariokam is biting a piece of wire.' We all turned and Ariokam was indeed hanging by his teeth from the end of a length of suspended wire. On went the ringmaster, reeling off rhetorical questions that had our gums bleeding with tension.

'Will his teeth fall out? Will he fall down and break his head open? No, he will not as he is India's best dental aerialist and he will twirl for a long time to entertain you!' He did, and for a long time afterwards we could not stop talking about it.

The circus also featured the progeny of an unlikely match. They were called 'ligers', the offspring of a tiger and a lion, or so it seemed. I did not think this was biologically possible but apparently it was true. Each liger had stripes only on the rump and a little mane. However, I don't think genetic engineering agreed with them as they had the strangest disposition. Despite the ringmaster's commands to sit up, stand on a stool or otherwise trot around the ring, they simply sat down on the sawdust-covered floor and scratched themselves out of boredom.

Realising he was getting nowhere, the ringmaster gave up and moved on to the finale, which was a real howler. A cyclist was positioned on a tight rope with another acrobat balanced on his head, turban to turban. The cyclist began to cycle. They were about half way across when one of the turbans began to unravel.

'Ayoh!' cried the ringmaster. 'Hurry and cycle across or you will crash and hang by your bladdy turban. Faster, faster or you will fall!' They didn't, by some miracle. To cover up the mistake, a couple of clowns started throwing pots of yoghurt at each other. I have never been so entertained in all my life, and all for S$2.

House Parties

In Singapore in the 1960s there weren't many nightclubs. Instead, people threw house parties for entertainment. I was good at organising these and would often be able to entice my colleagues and friends to part with S$4 per head for an evening of dancing and finger food. Mother was pleased as it meant she could keep an eye on us while showing off her culinary skills. I would organise the music, which was mostly long-playing instrumentals such as the waltz, foxtrot, quickstep and loads of Latin American numbers.

I loved decorating our spacious hall with balloons, bunting and twinkling lights. Mother did her usual *sambal* sandwiches, jellies and curry puffs and the drinks were almost always Green Spot, F&N Ice Cream Soda or sarsaparilla—drinks now mostly forgotten. Our hall could accommodate at least fifty people and I usually ended up making a little profit. Everyone had a grand time and after seeing the fun and profit to be had, some people began to organise their own house parties. After deducting the cost of food and decorations, I still came away with about S$50, which was a lot of money then.

Before I was old enough to work, I had the pleasure of wearing my first pair of long trousers. Throughout my school days I wore nothing but shorts. But with the money I made from throwing parties, I could afford to buy a pair of long trousers made of seersucker, the popular fabric of the day. This was shiny and slippery and my trousers were held up by a pair of metal buckles on either side of the waistband. Belts were not yet in fashion and these buckles had the disconcerting habit of becoming undone when pulled at vigorously.

As a dance enthusiast, I was more than vigorous with my rumba and one evening, as I danced on, my trouser buckles decided to do the inevitable. My trousers slid to my ankles amidst the roar of the gathered crowd. It was embarrassing but luckily I had on clean underwear. The few dances I did after that were more sedate waltzes and foxtrots. However, it was a most mortifying introduction to the adult world of fashion.

For those people who didn't have spacious homes, throwing a party at home just wasn't possible. Instead they would hire the hall of the St John Ambulance headquarters near to Merdeka Bridge (Merdeka means 'freedom' in Malay). It was here that I had some of my best times. The hall could accommodate more than a hundred people. The cost of renting it was redeemed by the cover charge of S$15 per head—a lot of money in the early 1960s when you consider a schoolteacher earned just S$190 a month. In today's terms it was probably about S$150 per couple.

But it was the spectre of Merdeka Bridge that bothered my mother the most. She, along with many of her generation, believed that this concrete structure that linked the city with the east coast had been built at the gruesome cost of many lives. Some scaremonger had created the gossip that in order for the bridge to be stable, human heads had been sacrificed and mixed with mortar. When Mother found out I was going to attend a party near the bridge, she became hysterical. Never mind that it was already built. She firmly believed that the surrounding area was haunted by the headless ghosts of many a young man who had been sacrificed.

During the time when the bridge was being built, rumours were so rife that we weren't allowed to go anywhere near the area bounded by Beach Road. So I had to lie in order to attend the parties at the St John Ambulance headquarters. There are many old people today who still believe this horror story about how Merdeka Bridge was built.

Much Bravado About Nothing

The 1960s were all about swaggering and male chauvinism. This didn't sit well with me. The truth was that behind every macho male, who claimed to be a whole lot of things, there lay a baby's bottle. That is if he were married. But in those days you wouldn't catch a man admitting to preparing a baby's milk, much less wash a nappy. I guess I was also caught up in the notion of having to be a briefcase-toting, swaggering executive.

I would brag about making money, driving a top-of-the-range BMW and, with a wink and a nudge, boast about my frequent trips to Hat Yai for you know what. Except my false front was just that—a false front. It was tiresome trading tales of carnal conquests in locker rooms. One had to read *Playboy Magazine*—banned in Singapore but available across the causeway!—and never admit to suffering from humiliating syndromes such as dysfunctional erections.

If men were married they preferred to downplay their paternal roles. Fatherhood and all that went with it simply did not fit with the much-vaunted image of an international playboy who could sow his wild oats till the cows (or could they have been bulls?) came home.

If a guy earned S$1,000 a month, he would up this amount several times to prove his market value. I had a journalist friend who related this story to me. He once interviewed a car salesman who got himself into rather a mess because of his snide bragging. When asked how much his income was, he replied with a rather astonishing figure. The salesman then went on to say that he did not declare this to Inland Revenue. When asked how and where he liked to go on holiday, he cheekily winked and replied, 'You know, where men like to go when they have time—Hat Yai. The women there are fantastic!'

So my friend published his feature, warts and all and, surprise surprise, all hell broke loose. The Inland Revenue came after him demanding an audit and his wife slapped him with threats of divorce. I don't know what happened after that but it illustrated a point I have never forgotten: If you are not macho, don't try to be, for your boasting could cost you dearly.

Being macho also meant that you had to invest heavily in your wardrobe. My tailor in Geylang stitched for me the meanest pair of drainpipe trousers but Mother thought I looked like a gangster. By wearing tight T-shirts and drainpipes you could really stand out from the crowd.

Pasar Malam and Other Night Markets

In the early 1960s the advent of night markets sent a frisson of excitement through most Singaporeans. A night market was a travelling retail business. Traders would set up makeshift stands, some directly on the kerb, from which they would sell all manner of goods. Most sold cheap household wares and prices were competitive because the traders had no overheads. So virtually every evening at the weekend there would be a *pasar malam* somewhere on the island, and it was great fun picking up things at bargain prices.

Some night markets stretched the entire length of a street or a car park, and as time went on they became more colourful and theatrical. Soon food stalls became part of these travelling markets but it was when they began using signs that we really found it hysterical. One fabric salesman had written on a broad length of cloth in bold black lettering: SOPHIA LOREN SAID, 'I WANT TWENTY YARDS OF COTTON.' Whether he knew that Sophia Loren was an Italian film goddess did not really matter. What was hilarious was the fact that this gave him the edge as some customers believed La Loren actually did buy from him. From then on traders began competing over who could come up with the most enticing sign. Soon another fabric salesman did one better with: BRIGITTE BARDOT SAID, 'I WANT THIRTY YARDS OF SEERSUCKER.' It brought back memories of my unfortunate trouser fiasco years before. However, more importantly this fabric salesman understood the importance of a sales pitch and thirty yards represented a good sale.

Of course, then the food hawkers joined in this signage war. One of my favourite supper dishes was *kai choke* (chicken porridge). I don't know why but the hawker of this stall put up a sign saying: VERY NICE, THIRTY CENTS FOR COCK PORRIDGE. I don't think he was being salacious as roosters have been cooked for centuries, especially among the Cantonese. Perhaps he knew something we didn't, but his stall was always crowded.

As *pasar malam*s spilled across the island, many began to take on more permanent sites. The makeshift stand of an itinerant food hawker evolved into a more permanent coffee shop but the signage war continued unabated. One stall owner selling *char siew paus* saw fit to encapsulate his wares with a sign that read: COME AGAIN CHAR SIEW PAUS. This resulted in a similar stall across the road putting up a sign that read: COME EVERY DAY CHAR SIEW PAUS. If you understand the phonetic significance of these words that purport to good luck, you'll understand the need for such flyers. It was the hope for repeat business.

As this signage war spread it gave rise to many similar hoardings that had nothing to do with food or hawkers. In one area where there was a cluster of ironmongers, one shop front had a sign that read: WEE KIAN FATT IRONMONGERS, Wee being a widespread surname. Whether out of pure cussedness or sheer coincidence, the ironmonger's across the road soon put up their own sign saying: SOH KIAN WEE. I don't think I need to elaborate further on the phonetic humour of these names.

Other Junk Stores

I bought many items from the CCC junk store, a veritable Aladdin's cave near Newton that sold, yes, junk. But if you browsed with a keen eye, you could pick up some good stuff, such as old British Army collapsible beds, irons, butter knives, commemorative QE2 china and even the odd antique or two that could turn out to be an auction winner. No such luck for me though, but I still loved going through heaps of rusting World War II canteens, Swiss Army knives, cracked milk jugs and other items.

There was another junk place we all made a beeline for from time to time. This was called Sungei Road and was on the eponymous street.

It was where I made many discoveries. It was my father's favourite haunt during the early 1950s. The site ran between Serangoon Road and Jalan Besar, and there used to be many affluent homes belonging to Europeans and Chinese there. Locals sometimes called it Kek Sng Kio (the bridge where ice is made) but I'll explain more about that later. Sungei Road is situated opposite the former Kandang Kerbau police station, hence it was known to the Chinese as *tek kah ma ta chu* meaning 'tek kah police station'. It was more commonly known as Thief's Market, alluding to the dodgy trade practices that have been going on there since the 1930s.

The people drawn to this flea market were in search of bric-a-brac, used clothing, motor parts, bicycles, electrical appliances, counterfeit watches and World War relics. In later years it was overrun with pirated VCDs, mobile phones and other IT detritus. Father used to go there to hunt for discarded parachute materials and Japanese weaponry, the former to augment our wardrobes and the latter simply because he was a collector. By the late 1960s and into the 1970s, it was a very busy place where one could find just about anything.

On nearby Lavender Street there stood the attap house of Cho Ah Chee, who'd been the carpenter of the SS *Indiana*, the boat in which Raffles travelled to Singapore in 1819. The house was demolished in the 1970s and a small public park built in its place. During the Japanese Occupation, a street market known as Robinson Petang (meaning 'Evening Robinsons') was set up along the banks of the Rochor Canal. Here, the poor could buy cheap household wares and other merchandise in short supply, akin to what the upmarket department store Robinsons sold. A peddler came to be known locally as the *karung guni* man (Malay for rag and bone man). He wouldn't give a receipt, so a refund was impossible.

Until the British army withdrew in the late 1960s, this was also the place to buy army merchandise such as uniforms, army gear and other army surplus, possibly looted from British military stores. In the early 1970s, opium dens were common in the Sungei Road area. The drugs were popular with workers looking for a cheap way to ease the hardship of the day's toil.

I know of a rags-to-riches story about Pang Lim, who was a fruit hawker in Sungei Road in the 1970s. His big break came when he saved enough money to rent a coffee shop in 1990 with his younger brother and uncle. They rented the stalls out to other hawkers and managed the drinks stall themselves. The business took off and from one coffee shop, Pang is now the managing director of Koufu, a company which operates twenty food courts, five coffee shops and five cafes across the island.

Despite its long history and tenacity, the days of this flea market are numbered because the site, which sits on a huge chunk of state land about the size of a football field, is slated for redevelopment.

Do you remember I mentioned Kek Sng Kio, the bridge where the ice is made? Well, it began operating in the 1930s. The factory was the first ice-making plant and a popular establishment that brought refrigeration and air conditioning to Singapore. In 1958, it was renamed the New Singapore Ice Works. In later years the factory was bought over by Cold Storage. However, in 1984, the Housing Development Board redeveloped the site. The factory was demolished and the plant operations re-located to Auric Pacific at Fishery Port Road. This facility has since closed down after being in use for over twenty years. Many referred to the whole place simply as Kek Sng Kio.

Stamp Pad or Tampax?

The opening of capacious stores that sold made-in-China merchandise was a milestone for Singapore's retail trade. Suddenly you could buy a whole host of goods at a fraction of the prices charged by upmarket department stores such as Robinsons and John Little. Before, these department stores monopolised the retail industry and we hadn't really had much choice, especially if we wanted to buy winter clothing; international travel to temperate climes was beginning to take off.

These new emporiums that opened were eclectic, if nothing else. They sold everything, from violins to ginseng, stationery to kitchen appliances—everything the heart desired, in fact. One day I was looking for a stamp pad, a little box with a red ink pad. I spied a bored-looking salesgirl and asked if she had a stamp pad. I had to repeat my query twice before she disappeared saying, 'Wait, ah, I check with my manager.' Much to my irritation, it was common for the sales staff in emporiums to know very little about their goods, unless you asked for something perfectly ordinary. Even then a simple request could still floor a few. After a few minutes she came back with a product that I was very unlikely to need or ever ask for: Tampax. Stamp pad, Tampax, I guess it was all the same to her.

On another occasion I asked for a stapler and was handed a pair of slippers! And so the mirth went on. Soon other department stores were employing staff without offering basic training first. Even at such a hallowed store as CK Tang I experienced some howlers you wouldn't believe. As was the practice in many department stores, young ladies were employed to sell perfume on commission. These enthusiastic scent purveyors would waylay customers and without even asking would spray some scent or other into you face as you passed by. Their accompanying spiel was more offensive than the scents they sprayed.

Imagine being ear-bashed by, 'Hello, madam, try our Gwee Ah Leng perfume. Very nice, special offer!'

I think what she was trying to say was Guerlain, the French perfume manufacturer. However, she'd obviously got the name confused with Dr Gwee Ah Leng, a highly respected founder member

187

of the Academy of Medicine—hardly likely to lend his name to a bottle of pong! Everywhere you went there was this abuse of brand names, especially when it came to exotic French products with names few locals could pronounce with any panache. Lanvin became Lanveen, Pierre Cardin was Peeree Cardeen, L'air du Temps was transmuted to Lar Tee Tamp and worst of all, lingerie became lingeree. Until today this word is garbled beyond recognition. An American lady was once heard to ask a salesgirl where their lingerie department was. The salesgirl replied that there was no laundry department and she would have to go somewhere else.

Chinatown, My Chinatown

The words from the song 'Chinatown, my Chinatown' have many resonances for me, for Chinatown remains a beloved place in my heart. In the late 1970s I chronicled the evolution of this place in series of articles for the *Sunday Nation,* but my memories of this enclave go way back to the late 1950s and early 1960s. It was a atmosphere of human activity that you can't evoke from looking at museum exhibits. Everywhere you turned in Chinatown there was much to be had by way of food, ancient crafts and traditional Chinese products.

The area bounded by Mosque Street, Pagoda Street, Temple Street and South Bridge Road was solidly Cantonese, made up of a clutch of goldsmiths, tailors and tea houses. It was here that you could feel the real pulse of Chinatown, although there were vague demarcations between enclaves of different dialects. The migrant Hokkien carpenters made their homes along Amoy Street and Telok Ayer Street, while the Teochews, mostly vegetable wholesalers and hawkers, rarely strayed far from North Canal Road, Merchant Road and River Valley Road. The Hakkas dispensed their herbal brews along Upper Chin Chew Street, Upper Hokkien Street and Upper

Cross Street and were also expert shoemakers.

The small Fuzhou community made coffee history with their iconic *kopi tiam*s. They were also the first trishaw pullers and concentrated along Victoria Street, Ophir Road and Johore Road. The latter became a beacon of the flesh trade. There would not be chicken rice today if the Hainanese had not made their homes in Middle Road, Purvis Street—the very name of this street brings back drooling memories of our beloved national dish—Seah Street and Beach Road. And when they were not boiling chickens, they turned their hand to making waxy paper umbrellas.

The later arrivals, the Shanghainese, concentrated in Havelock Road and Killiney Road and were masters at making and carving intricate rosewood, ebony and teak furniture. I still own a treasured coffee table made by a Shanghainese.

Chinatown's covered food court was as special then as it is now. One of its main attractions was an itinerant fiddler, a grizzled old man who used to saw at his Chinese string instrument without any thought for musical cadences. He would wander amongst tables while customers ate. His ploy was to place a little paper boat—in which were two pickled green or black olives—on the edge of a customer's table. He wouldn't say a word. If the unsuspecting victim ate the olives thinking they were for free, he would start to play his fiddle and you would be forced to pay the mendicant some money. It was kind of pathetic and you paid because you felt sorry for him. I could have done without his nerve-inducing music though. After a while we got wise and simply ignored the olives. He would go away and try the same stunt at another table. My sister-in-law said he probably spent all his money on opium anyway, given his emaciated physical state.

Still, Chinatown was and still is my favourite haunt when it comes to evoking a rich sense of history. After all, it was where our forefathers tramped and laboured so that we could have a future. For this reason alone it has a special place in my heart, though much of the old Chinatown has now been replaced and modernised within an inch of being soulless. We have only to look beneath the surface of the labyrinth of slushy side lanes and incessant noise, or up at the still-handsome Palladian, Chinese Baroque and Doric architectural styles to feel a palpable sense of migrant history. May all these live on forever.

Beauty Queens and Pageants

During the years when I was with the broadcasting service, we were often called upon to be judges at one beauty contest or another. There were plenty of these events, from Miss Singapore to Miss Tourism and even rural pageants such as Miss Keropok (Miss Prawn Cracker). Contestants for Miss Singapore, the ultimate title in the beauty world, came from all walks of life. Most didn't have the slightest idea of what winning the title entailed or indeed what constituted beauty.

At a preliminary session for the Miss Tourism pageant, girls had to pass an intelligence test. It was astounding to discover how low their IQ levels really were. Questions were simple enough, but it was the answers that gave us the hiccups. One girl, pretty enough, was asked by the panel whom her favourite pop star was. She vibrantly shook her body and answered, 'I tink so Elvis Presley!' When asked why, she said, 'Because his body got magnet, what!' She must have meant Elvis had a magnetic personality but it certainly did not come out right.

Another contestant was asked if there was any difference between a female and a male ambassador—given that the eventual Miss Tourism had to represent Singapore as an ambassador for tourism. Her reply sent shock waves through the panel of judges.

With a coquettish nod of her pretty head she said, 'I tink so. Mans and womans all the same, what!' Not only did she come across as an airhead but she could hardly grasp English grammar too. She lost on IQ points alone.

As for the Miss Keropok pageant, I was among the panel of judges selected to choose a winner among those contestants who had generated the most sales of prawn crackers, I kid you not. One of the set pieces of the pageant required each girl to perform a dance or song on stage. One young lady—I'll call her Aminah—decided she would sing a song. Standing on a makeshift stage and backed by a three-piece pop band, she began to sing the then popular Malay song 'Singapura'. Now this would have taxed even Whitney Houston as it has cadences of very high Cs. Aminah could not reach the middle register, much less the top notes, and part way through began sobbing, 'I can't breed, I can't breed!' I think she meant she couldn't breathe. Needless to say, I quickly lost interest in beauty contests.

Paktology at MacRitchie Reservoir

Paktology is a curious word, a Singlish amalgamation of the Cantonese word *pak tor* (courtship) and the suffix -ology. The term referred to a couple who were courting, or dating. However, dating then was not the same as it is today. Parents had to give their consent. Then there was a period where the couples got to know each other. If this was a success, a formal engagement and the exchange of engagement rings followed. These days this prelude to a civil ceremony seems to be rather passé.

In my opinion, there was a rather devious reason for a couple to court: it gave people time to think about, save for and even buy the wedding gift. The 1960s were still fairly hard times for many and wedding guests were expected to give the couple a red packet of the going rate of S$20. If the guest was accompanied, a little more money was expected. And woe betide the couple if their subsequent wedding banquet did not come up to scratch. Disgruntled guests would sometimes be heard to petulantly cry, 'We gave S$20 and the food not worth it!' Giving cash as a wedding gift was practical because a dinner table for ten people usually cost in the region of S$100. Therefore a red packet of S$20 per person neatly covered the cost of the dinner. However, on many occasions the red packets would fall short and couples had to resort to pawning jewellery just to pay their banquet bills.

If a guest was really short of cash, he would give an item rather than a red packet. I can't tell you how many sets of his and hers towels, cheap alarm clocks, Chinese Emporium tea sets, irons and other tat I received at my wedding. It was a convenient way for guests to get out of giving cash. One gift I received still had the price tag on it—S$5.95! It was impossible to know which guest had given which gift and it was rarely the practice to enclose a card; only colleagues and literate guests did this. Still, we had fun fathoming it all out. Unwrapping the presents would elicit comments such as, 'Wah, damn *lokek* (stingy), donno who gave this cheap alarm clock,' and other ungracious remarks.

The good thing was that these gifts could be recycled and given at the next wedding of a friend or relative. It was all par for the course, if not rather mean. We all had to recoup some costs. The practice of throwing lavish wedding dinners still goes on today but I am not privy to the workings of recouping the cost of cash gifts. I believe the going rate for a red packet is now S$100 per couple as these days a table for ten guests can cost more than S$1,000. Even if you do find a hotel that charges less than this, you would need to book more than a year in advance. However, this tradition of a wedding dinner is very much embedded in our culture. It's a nice tradition, if not a little painful on the purse.

Back to paktology. As well as being Singapore's first reservoir, MacRitchie Reservoir was also a popular haunt for lovers during the 1960s. It became the place to be if you wanted privacy from prying eyes. However, these swains and their girlfriends should have thought twice, for MacRitchie also spawned the evil practice of voyeurism. Yours truly was among the perpetrators. In my defence, we did not have much else to do of an evening and the prospect of tormenting lovers was irresistible. There was no malicious intent, I have to add. We were just restless youths with few outlets.

Couples would normally stay in their cars, the windows plastered with newspaper to shut out prying eyes. These amorous couples were wise to our deviant ways but it must have been stiflingly hot inside the car. Still, what was a little more heat when the body was generating enough to steam up the windows anyway? We would hunker down behind rocks and when we spied a car that seemed to rock from the activity within, we would go up close and shout, 'Oy, slow down, steep hill ahead!' It was a wicked thing to do but we really meant no harm, probably because among my crowd we were mostly post-pubescent or plain 'frus', as the saying went. Given our frustrations of not having romance in our lives, much less illicit copulation, it seemed only fair. Psychologists would have had a field day getting our heads straight.

Mount Faber was another romantic idyll and it was the same scenario all over again. When I look back on those days, I am mortified to think I was party to such heinous hobbies. Today, we would be labelled sexual predators and clapped in irons. But we were not looking for sex for ourselves, just hoping to see if others were doing it.

Matchmaker, Matchmaker

By the time my brothers and I reached our young adulthood, many busybody aunts and neighbours went into overdrive trying to marry us off. This was not out of concern for our nuptial needs, but more for the promise of a fat red packet they would receive if their matchmaking endeavour proved successful. If you were eighteen or above for a boy, or sixteen and above for girl, traditionalists deemed that it was time for you to have a spouse. The parents of daughters who were perhaps not particularly pretty or intelligent would tirelessly scour the neighbour for a good catch.

My aunts started to urge Mother to think about who our potential brides could be and drew up a list of suitable candidates. One aunt would endlessly harangue Mother.

'I tell you, this young girl from a very good family will make your eldest son (he was not even twenty-one yet) an excellent wife. She can cook, sew and has child-bearing hips.'

We'd seen the girl in question many times before. She was the seventeen-year-old daughter of a charcoal merchant in the neighbourhood. I used to wonder why charcoal shops also sold blocks of ice until a wise old neighbour proposed a theory. Chinese culture is based on the ancient tenet of yin and yang; of opposites that strike a universal balance; of day and night, hot and cold. Since charcoal—traditionally used as cooking fuel in those days—gives off heat and ice is cold, it bodes well for businesses to have this balance. It puzzles me why the electricity and water boards do not share the same office!

Anyway, the charcoal merchant's daughter only received a few years of primary education before being yanked out of school. This was quite common as many traditional parents, especially first generation migrants from China, subscribed to the notion that education was wasted on girls. What was the point when they would just end up being someone's wife? It wasn't like they would earn a living to support the parents. Peranakan women today can thank their lucky stars their parents, probably being very pro-British and shrewd, made sure their daughters were well educated.

This young charcoal merchant's daughter was put to work hoisting large blocks of ice and shovelling black charcoal for customers. Her face always seemed to be smudged with charcoal, which didn't help her plain countenance one bit. My aunt ignored this fact—promising hips counted for more than facial beauty!

Mother, bemused, was entirely against the idea. She shot my aunt a lot of questions. Once, she asked, 'Was she born in the year of the tiger or ox? My son is a rabbit and if he marries her, she will eat him up if she is a tiger. If she is an ox, she will trample him!'

In those days many of the older generation still believed that decisions concerning marriage should be based on the Chinese zodiac.

'No, no,' my aunt replied. 'She is a pig (her zodiac sign, not her habits) and will give you many children. You want I talk to her father.'

Brother joined in the fray and teased Aunty. He wound her up with comments such as, 'She got Senior Cambridge or not?' Senior Cambridge was the ultimate educational certificate, the springboard to greater things. 'And can she do the cha-cha?' Of course, Aunty's efforts bore no fruit and she rounded on Mother once again to ask if my second brother would consider marrying this fertile girl. I beat a hasty retreat before she could turn her beady eyes on me.

Actually, matchmaking was very much a vaunted task among other ethnic communities such as South Indian Tamils and Malays. Like the Chinese, many of their daughters never went to school and, like the female characters of Jane Austen's books, finding a husband was the be-all and end-all. How else were parents going to support so many mouths if the girls did not bring in any money?

Among Tamils, the question of a dowry was another challenge to overcome when their daughters did find a prospective husband. This system broke many an Indian family's bank. In Chinese tradition, the dowry comes from the man's family, a fair exchange for taking away a daughter who has cost plenty to bring up. However, it was the reverse for traditional Indians. One of my neighbours, a first generation Indian Muslim from Bangladesh called Zakir Hussein, had four daughters ranging from twelve to sixteen. None of them had more than a few years of cursory education in Tamil schools. The eldest was deemed of marriage material—many in the community married their daughters off as young as thirteen, right after their first menstruation, for it meant the girl was ripe for child bearing.

A matchmaker found a suitable man, a twenty-four-year old newly arrived from the same province as the family. He had been a goatherd. He was keen to find a wife as he planned to start his own goat-herding business. Transactions complete, the wedding date was set. But instead of being happy, Mr Hussein came to us wringing his hands in despair. He was a labourer and could just about support his family.

'Ayoh, how am I to pay for her dowry?' he said.

We asked him how much the man was expecting and if we could help in any way. Zakir was a good man, a very helpful neighbour who often did odd jobs around our sprawling house such as chopping up firewood and doing heavy chores.

'No, no,' Zakir replied. 'He only wants a little money and that I have already saved. But where am I to get six goats?' My heart went out to him for it was a real dilemma. Fortunately, it was soon settled as Zakir was able to contact a friend who sold him not six but four goats, which the suitor accepted.

The dowry system was a heinous tradition that began in ancient times. It originated in the Vaishya Hindu community and subsequently crept into other Hindu and Muslim communities. It affected the entire fabric of Indian society, especially the poor, backward and middle-class families whose economic and financial resources were limited. It also explains why so many Indian Chettiars were in clover.

It was based on a rigid mind-set. The Hindu religion regards boys as superior to girls and more worthy of rights than girls. Traditions such as *sati* and the dowry custom were rooted in discrimination and prejudice. In respect of *sati*, a widow was denied social status and remarrying was taboo. So her only choice was to torch herself on her dead husband's funeral pyre and avoid being ostracised and discriminated against. Girls whose fathers or family members died were also denied any share of the family's property or wealth. As soon as they reached womanhood, a female would be disposed of through marriage and the payment of a dowry. This was their only inheritance. In 1961 the Indian Government prohibited the payment of a dowry, although the custom still goes on in some parts of rural India.

Among Singapore Muslim Malays there was less of an onus. Their traditions were of a different order and the custom of *nikah* (marriage) was fairly straightforward. Their unions were solemnised by an Imam in a mosque with two witnesses. No dowry was needed and all costs were paid for by the groom or his family. Some Muslims, probably influenced by their Bangladeshi counterparts, did subscribe to this practice of paying for the wedding, but more as a token gesture.

However, among many early Chinese men, paying for the wedding was still a heavy burden, and some new husbands resorted to borrowing from loan sharks and ending up in debt. At my sister's wedding there was still a hint of this custom but my family made light of it.

I found the whole wedding ritual fascinating. The matchmaker would hide the bride's face with a fan and would only allow the groom to see his bride when he'd agreed to pay the amount demanded. The fact that the couple had been courting for a year had nothing to do with it. In early days the amount was conveniently pegged to the amount of a dowry. In my day, however, it was just a bit of fun. As this mock bargaining session went on at my sister's wedding, we shouted from the sidelines, 'Higher, higher, not enough, not enough!' We had to be silenced by Mother. I once asked my two mothers what their dowries had been and they replied in unison, 'We never saw it as our mothers took it all!'

Pontianak and Other Spirits

Sometimes when we stayed at Grandfather's house we would spend our evenings sitting by the beach listening to ghost stories told by the many local fishermen. Their favourite tale was of a *pontianak* but another scary story involved Oily Man. The tale went that some randy chap smeared his whole body with black oil and attempted to molest young women out on their own at night in deserted areas. He was no ghoul, but a real man with raging hormones. He was finally caught and incarcerated.

We were also acquainted with the spirit of the banana tree. It seemed that if you tied a red string around the trunk of a banana tree and asked for the winning numbers of the lottery, you would be amply rewarded. The story went that one superstitious woman had done this, won the lottery but forgotten to remove the red string she had tied round the banana tree in her backyard.

As a result the banana spirit was incensed and one night, while she was sleeping, it stuffed several bananas down her throat. She died an agonising death. Whether this was true or not we never found out, but Granny had a few banana trees and we were absolutely forbidden to ever try this stunt. Around the *kampung* where Grandmother lived were many *kapuk* (cotton) trees that yielded soft cotton balls like pom poms. These were harvested as stuffing for pillows by the local Malay folk.

These cotton trees were also believed to be the home of a particularly evil spirit called the Kapuk Spirit. If you wanted to harvest the cotton balls, you first had to say a prayer and offer food and other tokens to appease the spirit. If you didn't you would suffer the terrible fate of having cotton balls stuffed in every orifice and you'd die an agonising death.

As the fishermen told us these stories, the hair on the back of our necks stood on end, and we would scurry back to Granny's house clinging to each other. Every breath of wind that shook the leaves on trees seemed to foretell the appearance of some spirit or other. The worse thing was that the only toilet in the house was outside under one of these cotton trees. I cannot tell you the number of times I chose to be constipated rather than use this facility at night.

The sea was also believed to be home to many spirits, principally the Sea Devil. We were never allowed to swim at night for this was the time when the Sea Devil would be lurking in the shadows, waiting to drown anyone foolish enough to sully her watery kingdom. One story we were told was about an old lady who had been found dead on the beach one morning. She must have been ill and probably died from drowning, but the gossip spread like wildfire—she must have offended the She Devil who then suffocated the lady with mud and seaweed. So naturally we never swam at night. With such gruesome possibilities, no one would have dared to tempt fate.

The Eleventh Gong Festival

Before I begin my anecdote about Chinese New Year, our most joyous festival, I cannot resist sharing a story about the Mandarin greeting 'Gong Xi Fa Cai'. For a long time my family would use the greeting 'Kiong Hee Huat Chai' ('Happy and Prosperous New Year' in Hokkien) or 'Sin Nee Tua Tan' ('May the New Year Bring You Wealth' in Teochew). When the Speak Mandarin Campaign was launched in 1979, the non-Chinese educated amongst us had to curl our tongues around the newspeak. One American friend came to Singapore for the first time and guilelessly asked, 'Are you celebrating the Eleventh Gong Festival?' I'll leave you to deduce how he came about this interpretation.

I have to say with candour and some regret that Chinese New Year ceased to be fun for me—and many others, I'm sure—when firecrackers were banned in 1972. Oh, the joy of these pyrotechnics. They really made the festival and it was never the same again. To some it might be difficult to understand why such a din and mess should be an integral part of New Year celebrations, but we loved it. Noise has always been the crux of a Chinese celebration, be it a happy or sad occasion. Perhaps the noise bonds the community, or heralds the arrival of good fortune. Quiet reflection about the good things in life is not really the way. In ancient China bamboo stems were burnt to create small explosions and drive away evil spirits. This concept was transferred to Lunar New Year celebrations in Southeast Asia and noise has become an integral part of these celebrations.

Explosions were most evident on the eve of Chinese New Year and the story from China goes as such. A certain Mr Li Tien had a neighbour named Chung Sou who was of feeble health. Every time he fell ill, which was frequent, it was blamed on evil spirits that had possessed his soul. Mr Li suggested that when bamboo stems were hung from dozens of poles and ignited, the scorching would cause the stems to explode. The ensuing racket would chase away the evil spirits. So on New Year's Eve stems were burnt, and thenceforth creating a terrific noise became a ritual observed every Chinese New Year. This also filtered into other Chinese festivals. As its purpose was originally to drive away evil spirits, it also became integral to funerals.

When my father died in the early 1950s, his cortege included a Chinese orchestra and a brass band—on his orders, I might add. The brass band was a motley group of geriatric musicians who seemed to know only two songs: 'In the Sweet Bye and Bye' and 'When the Saints Come Marching In'. The group wasn't really in tune to begin with but it must have been the clashing cadences of Chinese traditional music and off-key brass oompah pah that made Father smile in his coffin and the neighbours reach for their earplugs.

However, over time firecrackers took on a more positive connotation and came to be used to commemorate joyous events such as wedding processions, rituals during festivals and auspicious occasions. During Qing Ming, or All Soul's Day, firecrackers were let off to chase away the hungry spirits that were believed to lurk around, trying to eat the food offered to ancestors.

Many traditional Chinese people also believed that the incessant firing of crackers would bring prosperity. On the first day of Chinese New Year practically every road and street would be carpeted with bright-red broken wrappers from crackers. For everyone, young or old, firing crackers epitomised the joy of the season and we would spend a lot of money on them. Our fingers and clothes would be constantly stained bright vermillion from handling them.

I loved the single tubular type of firecracker that had a short detonation fuse. We would light the fuse and hurl it, preferably towards a passer-by! It was all part of the festive fun and the passer-by was just as likely to hurl one back at us. The second type of firecracker I enjoyed was a streamer. This was usually hung from the top of a building and ignited from below. When let go, it would create the spectacular effect of moving blasts as the streamer lit up in a brilliant flash.

Firecrackers proved to be popular with other races and religions too. They would be lit at festivities such as Christmas Eve, Deepavali and Hari Raya. Sadly firecrackers were banned after an unfortunate incident. Two unarmed policemen were attacked on New Year's Eve as they attempted to prevent celebrants on Upper Serangoon Road from letting off firecrackers without a permit.

The permit system, a precursor to the Dangerous Fireworks Act of 1972, was enforced after a terrible episode one Chinese New Year in 1970. Celebrations caused the deaths of six people, injured sixty-eight more and caused at least S$400,000 worth of damage. Today, the Dangerous Fireworks Act has the power to fine anyone possessing or discharging fireworks up to S$5,000 and/or imprison them for up to two years. These days the only sign of firecrackers during Chinese New Year is long streamers hung as decorations over doorways.

Sometime in the mid-1960s some bright spark decided to invent simulated firecrackers. These plastic things were godawful and nothing like the real thing. As a journalist I was assigned to test them out for a story. I needed only one line to describe them: 'These plastic firecrackers sounded no better than someone breaking wind.'

When we young lads had the chance, firing crackers meant we could really let off steam in many devious ways. We would buy the fattest single cracker, a double whammy that exploded not once but twice. We called it *pong piak* in reference to the ensuing explosions. But this was not all. We would light one then hurriedly place an empty cigarette tin over it. When the firecracker exploded it would send the tin flying sky high. It was a marvellous high, but is also caused a few accidents. Sometimes the tin would split from the impact, spraying shrapnel with lethal results. Mother banned us playing with these before the government could.

Sparklers—sticks that burned with a bright flare—were also popular but caused many accidents. You would light one, bend the thin wire handle and hurl it up a tree to get the maximum sparkle effect. One Chinese New Year someone inadvertently hurled one onto the roof of an attap hut somewhere in Siglap. My brothers and I were on our way to pay our respects to Granny and instead spent the morning helping to fight a conflagration. The sparkler had set fire to the roof of the hut, then spread to the entire *kampung*.

Vanishing Foods

I know, I know, I go on about food but is it not the most important element in life? Besides, I want to tell you about the foods that are now hard to find in Singapore.

During the heyday of Chinese *wayang*, many hawkers sold sweet snacks and one, *tang hu lu* (rock sugar bottle gourd), has really vanished. Small, brown-skinned fruit called Chinese haw, similar to a crab apple, were dipped in a syrup of melted rock sugar then skewered five or six to one stick. If anyone out there can find this sweet today, I will be your friend for life. Another snack called *keropok ubi* (tapioca crisps) was sold by Malay hawkers. It was made from small pieces of tapioca deep fried, coated with powdered sugar and sold in a paper cone. I have not seen it for decades now.

Crab apples pickled in salt and chilli were another treat. With one bag of this I could sit through hours of Chinese opera. I was also inordinately fond of a tar-like fudge called *san cha* (haw paste) that was full of small pips. You bought it from a large urn and got really sticky fingers eating it. I have no doubt somewhere in some shop in Chinatown it is still available but I have never seen children eating it.

Obviously, many foods assumed to have vanished are actually somewhere in Singapore but it is hard to find them. In the early 1950s a hawker used to come by with his tricycle cart selling dried bean curd stuffed with a mixture of stewed duck, chilli sauce and other condiments. It was called *tau kwa pau*. I have not had this for the past thirty years and hope that it is still available.

Other snacks were Nonya specialities, and there was one in particular I loved. It was a little rice flour cake called *apom balik*, which was often perfumed with pandan leaf essence and tinged green or red. I can make it myself but I do miss the little old lady who hawked it in our area. *Jemput jemput* was a Malay curry puff filled with no more than cooked bean sprouts and doused with fiery hot chilli sauce. Another Malay favourite was *kueh lopis*, a triangle of compressed glutinous rice smothered with steamed desiccated coconut and drenched in palm sugar syrup. I still remember the bottle the hawker used to dribble the syrup onto the *lopis* as she unwrapped them from their banana leaves. The bottle had a spout shaped like a twirled banana leaf that dispensed just the right amount of syrup.

During Chinese New Year, Mother would make a delicious treat called *sargon*. It was made of desiccated coconut fried with chopped nuts and sugar. She would fill paper straws with the mix and we would hold the straw over our upturned mouths and tap the contents down our throats. Such fun it was. Other snacks were snacks per se but rather invented by us. Who can forget the delicious way of dunking love letters into orange squash, drinking the squash through the love letters and finally consuming the lot in a messy gulp. Love letters, de rigueur during this festival, were wafer-thin, crispy, hollow rolls that looked like short, fat straws made from eggs, sugar and coconut milk. We loved to float dollops of vanilla ice cream in ice cream soda, making a sort of soda float; dunking into coffee little gem biscuits and their swirls of pink, yellow and green solid sugar; and dipping fried bananas in melted palm sugar.

There used to be an Indian ice seller who sold the most divine syrups of banana, mango and rose essence. He also sold ice balls—no longer around today, ice *kacang* notwithstanding—and it was a daily treat to suck at these lumps of shaved ice, the size of a tennis ball, doused in pink, green and brown sugar syrup and condensed milk. The hawker, however, was something of a dirty old man. If he had a female customer, he would wink and say that she could have the ice ball for free if she came round to the back of his stall and groped him. I never actually saw this happen but one of our neighbour's daughters once ran crying to her mother saying he had propositioned her. Needless to say, my sisters were forbidden to go near this lech.

Cosy Corner

I have no doubt anyone who lunched along Orchard Road during the 1960s would know about the fabulous Cosy Corner. As the name suggests, it was cosy and tucked away in a little corner near the old CK Tang. It was the place to go for a set lunch that cost all of S$3. This included a soup to start, a main course (usually cold meat salad or a steak), jelly with cream and coffee. It was a fair distance to travel for me and my radio colleagues during our lunch hour, but lunching here was considered the epitome of chic—eating a Western meal gave you a mark of sophistication. We would pile into one colleague's car and make a beeline for this place, even though it would always be packed.

Oh, the joy of eating off real china plates on snow-white tablecloths; most of the time it would be *char kway teow* or chicken rice while seated at greasy *kopi tiam* tables. Each table had a little posy of fresh flowers and a little table lamp. The ambience was really cosy with very dim lighting and unobtrusive waiting staff—hence the name Cosy Corner. Once, I was in the mood for even softer lighting and switched the lamp off. A waitress promptly clicked it back on again, remarking, 'So dark, how can you see your food?' She completely missed the concept of mood lighting.

Cosy Corner was the all-time favourite lunchtime haunt for many and if it was full, we would go round the corner to Batik Inn that had the best satay in town. Forking out an average of S$3 for a meal might not seem much today, but when you consider my pay packet was S$300 a month, it works out to the equivalent of S$40 for a set lunch for an executive earning S$4,000 a month. 'Dam siong' as we say in Singlish. By the early 1970s, these places had gone the way of urban redevelopment. I was most saddened.

Gamblers Anonymous

If there had been a Gamblers Anonymous organisation, its counsellors would have had their register permanently full. Gambling probably dates back to the pioneering days when it was the only absorbing distraction for migrant workers otherwise deprived of every other leisurely pursuit. Regardless, in my day everyone was at it, enjoying games such as mahjong, Chinese playing cards and a Nonya game called *cherki*. Chinese playing cards were slim, each an inch wide and three inches long. Each card had a black back and colourful face with Chinese characters depicting earth, elephant, horse and other cultural elements.

The Nonya cards were of similar size and shape and each one had a pink back and a white face depicting much the same but in a more stylised form. Playing cards took place every evening after dinner and at weekends, mahjong ruled. It was as much a social gathering as the need to assuage the gambling instinct. To call it an addiction would have been too severe as stakes were generally small and no one became neurotic or freaked out over it.

As a young lad it was invariably my chore to go to my neighbours' houses and invite them to play cards with my mother and aunts. It wasn't a thankless chore, though, for after a game the player or players who came out trumps would usually tip me handsomely— say, fifty cents.

There was also a lot of superstition involved that led to many a hilarious situation. One Nonya neighbour called Aunty Nya Chik was a true victim of gambling superstitions. Whenever she lost, she would flounce out of the room, head to the bathroom and scrub her hands like a compulsive obsessive person. She said this was to *buang sial*, cleanse the bad luck. Thus anointed, she would resume play. If she again lost, she would look around the room to see if she could spot a broom. Then I would get an earful.

'*Celaka*! (this was a favourite Nonya swear word) Why you not remove that broom? Sweep away all my luck. Next time don't come and call me!' As it had been my unfortunate task of inviting her to play in the first place, the onus was laid squarely on me. Of course, if she was asked again the next evening, all would be forgotten and the scenario would unfold all over again. I got wise to this and when it came to inviting Aunty Nya Chik, I made my younger adopted sister do it.

Chinese New Year was when gambling reached its zenith. Even if parents frowned on it, the festive mores prevented them from complaining. So throughout the season we would gather in the house, under trees, anywhere in fact, and someone would fish out a red or blue pack of playing cards. These were the common Western-style playing cards typically used for poker and other games.

My favourite game was called Twenty-one, or Buang Lak. Each player was dealt two cards. Both cards had to add up to a minimum of sixteen and if the banker had seventeen, you lost your bet. It was exciting hoping and praying for the ultimate hand of a pair of aces, for this meant the banker had to pay you double. Five cards was the maximum you could draw from the stack and the maximum score was twenty-one, hence the name of the game. To take a fifth card and still not go bust meant you had a *ngor leng* (five dragon) and this would trump every other hand. Each player could take turns being banker until he was bankrupt or decided not to push his luck.

Another game was Number Nine, or Pak Kau. Each player had three cards. The maximum score was ten and anything above this meant you lost. This was a fast game as you didn't draw cards from a stack but were dealt them. Your luck fell with the cards drawn, and you staked your bets on the cards not having a combined total of more than ten. It was a fast game and many a Chinese New Year's Day saw me robbed of my *ang pau* money.

Chap Ji Ki

Chap Ji Ki was an illegal syndicate that announced two numbers each day. It was so secretive and underground that, to this day, no one has ever found out who ran it or from where. To play, you would write your two chosen numbers on a slip of paper and hand it to a collector. The collector could be someone who worked for the sundry store owner and would cycle past to collect the slips on behalf of the syndicate. Even on pain of death he would not reveal where the syndicate's headquarters were.

Many believed it was run by triads and very probably too. Mother, my aunts and myself took part in this syndicate almost daily. For a S$1 stake could win you S$100—it was that high a return. How the number was announced was even more cloak and dagger. We never found out how, but the syndicate would inform someone in the street or neighbourhood who would walk by and shout, 'The time is now three minutes past twelve!' Of course it wasn't that time at all but by the sinister machinations of the syndicate, we all knew it meant that the day's winning numbers were three and twelve. *Chap ji ki* actually means twelve numbers.

There were some hairy moments as the authorities were ever assiduous in tracking down the syndicate members. The sundry goods store owner was a large, feisty woman. Whenever she got wind of the police coming to raid her premises, she would tuck the betting slips down her capacious bra and simply stand nonchalantly while the police searched her shop.

The reason why her bra was so capacious was that she had sewn secret compartments in it just for the slips! She lived a dangerous life because if she had been caught, it would have meant a hefty fine or jail. As for the collector on a bike, he had a clever ploy too. He would roll up all the slips he'd collected, secure it with a rubber band and tuck them into his front lamp. He too was never caught. Chap Ji Ki was Mother's Achilles heel but it did give her much joy and hope, especially if her numbers came up trumps. It brought me and my brothers joy too as if she won, we had better food such as chicken, duck or prawns.

4-D

Haven't we all, at one time or another, hoped to strike it rich with this form of gambling that is still the rage after many decades? I would have become a successful bookie had I not had notions about middle-class morality serving me better in later life. Not that I set much store by morality but we are talking about money, the raison d'etre for life.

After all, a stake of S$1 could win you S$1,000. This is not something one frowns on, whatever the moral stance. Actually the machinations about getting the right numbers gave me more than a few laughs.

Driven by the desire to strike it rich, some very sane people have done some very insane things. One relative had this weird notion that you should place ten numbered slips into a new pair of shoes and shake the shoe. The first four slips that drop out would be the winning numbers. Every time a friend came visiting she would lunge at his or her feet to see if the shoes were new. Or she would actually go out and buy a pair of cheap but new shoes. As well as doing this with the shoes, she also went through some mumbo jumbo ritual, waving a lit joss stick about and chanting, 'Please, Tua Pek Kong, give me the right numbers!' Then she'd go down to the betting shop and place her numbers. Usually they didn't come up and she would then hurl her new shoes on the floor and stomp on them.

I had any number of aunts who would visit and narrate this dream or that dream they had had the night before. The dreams were always numerical and the women folk would gather round to analyse the significance of their numbers. One tale from my mother's elder sister was particularly rich. I paraphrase here as best as I can remember.

'Ayoh,' she said. 'Last night I dreamt that a handsome young man came to me to comb my *kondek* (chignon) and when he'd finished, he asked me if I wanted him to clean my ears.' Ear cleaning was a task that First Mother often performed on me using a little gold pin with a tiny scooped end. It was delicious lying down on her lap as she gently cleaned me of my ear wax on a regular basis.

My aunt continued. 'When I said yes, he did so and when he took his ear cleaner out to put the ear wax on a piece of paper, the wax became four numbers!' The gathered throng urged her to tell what these numbers were but she was reluctant at first. She wanted the winnings all for herself. Later, however, she relented and they bet quite a few dollars for numbers that did not come up roses, or was it ear wax?

Even food came into play with this kind of superstition. Another aunt would deliberately overeat and consequently she suffered from dyspeptic nightmares that she hoped would result in good numbers. She had an interpretation all her own. She asked my younger sister to stand guard while she napped in the afternoon. If she was heard to belch or moan, my sister was to write down how many times. She took the sum of these audio emissions, worked out some strange formula and came up with four numbers—what else?—and proceeded to place her bets.

One time a cortege passed by our road. She peered closely at the vehicle number of the passing hearse and promptly placed her bet based on three numbers on the number plate. All 4-D bets had to be made up of four numbers, so for the fourth number she rationalised that since it was a funeral, the last number must be the number four (the word for four and death are the same).

Unfortunately she copied down the numbers in the reverse order and was beside herself with annoyance. I chipped in to say: 'Aunty, I saw the hearse turn around later on. Maybe you should have placed a bet with the numbers in the reverse order!' This only resulted in a stream of curses, this time directed at me.

'Why you so *bodoh* (stupid)? Never tell me the hearse had

turned around. I could have won a few thousand dollars but for your stupidity!' All this was spat at me in a curdle of Malay, Teochew and fractured English and I fled to my room in terror.

Today, playing this numbers game is still fraught with superstition, incantations and assorted mumbo jumbo. Just a few years ago I actually placed a bet using the four numbers of my new apartment in Penang, a combination of floor and house numbers, and I won a few thousand dollars. Mumbo jumbo! I don't believe it.

Tontine Funds

My mother's generation did not believe in banks, even though they were around to a certain extent, but only downtown. Ever since she had been a young girl, her only recourse to saving money was through a tontine—either this or putting it under her mattress. A tontine was a rotating savings and credit system. In essence it was a simplified form of banking for simple folk who did not understand or trust conventional banks.

It was named after an Italian financier called Lorenzo de Tonti but we always referred to it as a *pio huey* (meaning 'to bid'). Whatever it was called it worked much the same way as a modern annuity. On our patch there would be a Huey leader, who was usually a savvy woman of impeccable credibility and reputation. In fact during the nineteenth century in Europe, it was largely women who organised savings clubs between themselves. However, if the leader was less than kosher it became a risky business, giving rise to tontines being dubbed Diddly or Diddlum clubs.

From the early years in the developing Asian countries, tontines were widespread and called Cheetus in Sri Lanka, Chit funds in India (which explains why Indian money lenders were called Chettiars), Huey in Hong Kong, Pio Huey in Singapore and Malaya, Paluwangan in the Philippines and so on.

People from Southeast Asia have used tontines as an alternative means to finance their business or personal needs since the early 1930s. In Kampuchea (Cambodia) it was known as Roscas and coexisted alongside the formal financial system. This was because various ethnic minority communities found Roscas a convenient stepping stone for financial freedom and a vehicle for capital accumulation and investment.

In Singapore whether they were legal or illegal was a moot point. Tontines were simply outside the normal banking practices of the mainstream or dominant society. In our community they were practised within a closed socio-cultural system which was well understood by participants. How it worked in simple terms was thus. The leader would suggest a monthly savings amount of say S$10. Every member—and these were mainly up to twenty or thirty women living in the immediate area—would deposit this amount with the leader. Once a month there would be a bidding date set. If you needed money desperately, you would bid as high you dared. If the amount bid was say S$1, you would then be given S$9 multiplied by the number of members. The S$1 was a kind of interest payable to the Huey. You then had to continue to pay in S$10 per month that would be worth S$9. Like buying on the never never, really. The higher you bid, the less total amount you would get in return for high interest. It was simple for women, especially the illiterate, to understand. The bidding, by mutual agreement, would take place in any of the members' homes and ours was selected once in while.

Only the members who wanted to bid turned up and it was quite a sombre ambience; six or seven women sitting around a table with the leader as she collected the bidding slips. Some of these women could not write but had their children or friends scribble down the amount either in English or in Chinese characters. When all the slips were opened, the highest bid would be announced and the bidder would be given the cash on the spot. Sometimes, if another bidder had lost even mere cents, she would sulk and try to persuade the leader to do it again.

But the leader's answer was always the same: 'You want money quickly, why did you not make a higher bid? Sorry but it is the law.' It was her law but it was sacrosanct.

There was one Huey syndicate run by a former singer who subsequently ran away with thousands of dollars of hard-earned cash. She was never found. Still, it was the only way that women could lay their hands on ready cash without too much fuss and for a much lower interest rate than that money lenders charged. Tontines were based on common practices without any collateral and conducted entirely on the basis of trust and goodwill.

Indonesia–Malaysia Confrontation

This unfortunate episode in Singapore's history, known as Konfrontasi in the Indonesian language, is still sharp in my mind. This unpleasant state of political affairs began in 1961 when the island of Borneo was divided into four separate states. These were Kalimantan, Brunei, Sarawak and British North Borneo. The latter was later renamed Sabah. When the UK prepared to withdraw from Southeast Asia, the British authorities mooted to combine their colonies in Borneo to form Malaysia. This was vehemently opposed by the Indonesian government that was then under the rule of President Sukarno.

He claimed that Malaysia would become a British puppet state and that the suggested consolidation would only increase British control in the region. His claim was that this would threaten his country's independence. Meanwhile, in Brunei, the Indonesian-backed North Kalimantan National Army (TNKU) revolted in December 1962, tried to capture the Sultan of Brunei, seize the rich oil fields and take European hostages. The rebellion was quelled on 17 April 1963 and the Sultan escaped.

At a later meeting of the would-be member states of Malaysia, the Philippines and Indonesia—the Philippines had continually made claims for Sabah on the premise that it had historic links through Sulu—formalised an agreement to recognise Malaysia. This would come about if a majority in the disputed region voted for it in a referendum organised by the United Nations.

However, North Borneo and Sarawak, anticipating a pro-Malaysia result, declared their independence on 13 August 1963, even before the results of the vote were announced. The Indonesian government interpreted this as a broken promise and further evidence of British imperialism. They unleashed their Confrontation on 20 January 1963 and Indonesian soldiers began infiltrating Sarawak and Sabah. They would engage in raids and acts of sabotage while at the same time spreading propaganda for their cause.

Malaysia had been formally established on 16 September 1963; Brunei voted against joining the new federation and Singapore would leave it in 1965 to become an independent republic. Tensions rose and a mob of rioters ransacked the Singapore embassy and the homes of Singaporean diplomats in Jakarta. Some Indonesian agents were captured in Malaysia and in retaliation, Malaysian rioters attacked the Indonesian embassy in Kuala Lumpur.

By 1964 Indonesian troops began to raid areas in Peninsular Malaysia and on 16 August armed Indonesian agents were captured in Johore. Singapore was on full alert when Indonesian paratroopers landed on the southwest coast of Johore and attempted to establish guerilla groups in early March. On 10 March 1965 Indonesian saboteurs planted a bomb in MacDonald House along Orchard Road, killing three people and injuring thirty-three. I had been doing some freelance work with an advertising agency housed in the building. Fortunately I was not there that day.

In the late 1960s General Suharto came to power and Indonesian interests in pursuing the war declined. On 26 May 1966 the Malaysian and Indonesian governments declared that the conflict was over at a conference in Bangkok. Violence ended in June, and a peace treaty was signed on 11 August and ratified two days later. It had been a scary period during which soldiers were everywhere, a period that, thank goodness, did not escalate into full-scale war.

1970s

Mass Confusion

The 1970s were most memorable for me as many things in my life changed. I left my broadcasting job to venture into the new world of public relations, advertising and then to become a newsman. I also became a father amid boundless joy, and whilst the years following were full of onerous responsibility, they were also full of laughter, tears, celebration and crises.

I was enticed to join a British company called Sime Darby that had huge stakes in the Malaysian rubber and palm oil industries. It was a swish job: Public Relations and Advertising Executive for the Holdings division. The company had offices in Kuala Lumpur and London and had just built a massive complex, the present day Orchard Towers. I was ensconced in an office on the ninth floor, had a private secretary and my job was to market the new shopping complex and residential block at the rear podium.

It was the first time I was in the public sector and my salary far exceeded that of my radio job. The job wasn't too taxing as it was mostly corporate work but when it came to my duty as centre manager for the shopping complex, it was a daily nightmare. By then retailers had moved in. Boutique owners, jewellers and camera shops occupied the front block and smaller traders rented the upper floors and the rear block. In the three years that I spent dealing with disgruntled merchants, I encountered a litany of problems that would have driven anyone up the wall.

In association with an appointed agency, I organised events such as fashion shows, art exhibitions, a Peranakan festival and even a Miss World pageant to bring shoppers to the complex. The agency came up with a bright idea to give Orchard Towers the name

Shopper's City. This ploy did bring in the crowds but the retailers felt it wasn't enough. I received daily complaints such as: 'So, my business still slow. Last week I only sold two dresses!' Another would say that no one had visited her shop for days. Some threatened to not pay their rent; others were simply aggressive, believing that their loss of business was the holding company's fault.

I could never repeat those years. Retailers had the most horrendous attitudes, expecting the landlord to bring in the customers while they sat back. Worse still, I would get calls about the toilet not having toilet paper, light bulbs that had blown and other such trivial complaints that were really the maintenance department's responsibilities. One trader barked at me: 'What do you call yourself? Public Relations Executive! Where is the public? You should reduce my rent,' and so forth till it came out of my ears. Years later, after the company moved their headquarters back to Kuala Lumpur, Orchard Towers deteriorated into a sleazy joint full of pimps and transvestites. It was sad but life went on.

The years I enjoyed even less and remember sparingly were those when I slaved away as a copywriter in the advertising industry. It was a world peppered with pretentious claims, irritating hang-ups and fake gestures, even some unethical practices. Advertising people, especially the creative group, were constantly air kissing, wrote copy to delude the public into believing the promises of luxury products and generally behaved as if they were God's gift to humanity.

For me advertising was an attempt to cause mass confusion on the back of mass communication, hoodwinking the unwary public into spending money on things they didn't need. It was a crafty thing to convince people that without this or that product their life would have been so much less complete. I guess I was as guilty as most and with the wisdom of hindsight I realise it was a way to earn a living, even if integrity took a back seat.

In all honesty when I was offered the job of copywriter, I did not know what the hollow world of advertising would be like. I can only hope it has changed for the better and developed a more social conscience.

Sparring with indignant retailers and unreasonable traders in Orchard Towers was something I was glad to leave behind. I suppose it was flattering then, as private sector employers paid far better than the civil service, a situation that irked many but did not change until the 1980s. As a copywriter it was fun and absorbing crafting clever words, writing slogans and sparkling jingles to sell everything from aerosols to airlines, but it was tinged with false promises. As I wrote I knew how damaging aerosols were to the environment, a blight we are still trying to rectify today.

If you had a good client who had principles it was okay. If not you had to really lay it on thick about this or that product that promised everything from curing cancer to banishing varicose veins, but rarely delivered. It didn't sit comfortably with me to learn that the production cost of a lipstick was no more than fifty cents yet it retailed at twenty times this. I admit I took some glee in pointing out to my female friends that the expensive designer lipstick they'd paid a lot of money for was worth the price of a bowl of laksa!

Slimming products were the worst. You would take a picture of a fat woman and display it next to the same photo but that had been airbrushed to death, then claim that anyone could lose ten pounds in one week. This is not physically impossible but it was the message that had me doubting my own integrity. I was not comfortable earning a fat pay packet for doing it. The worst of it all was when I had to attend award ceremonies. At these events there was more air kissing, fake accents and pats on the back, everybody thinking they had done the world a great big favour.

One client from Johore Bahru eventually caused me to throw in the towel. Enche Hassan (not his real name) ran a small factory producing some embrocation products and sundry ointments. He wanted to promote his products via the Singapore media. The spiel he gave my account executive must have been convincing enough for our creative director to set up a meeting at his premises in Johore. When we arrived, we were shown to the factory itself and expected to sit on plastic chairs around a trestle table.

Nearby was a longer table around which sat several women filling little bottles by hand. This was the owner's product, for which he did not have a name as yet. He claimed he had a lot of money to spend but little did we know that his idea of a lot did not tally with what a media budget was. Anyway, we heard him out and at the end of the meeting he told us his proposed name. This was the final straw that floored our advertising team.

He wanted, or rather demanded, that I write copy for his main product called Minyak Can Sir, and that I pitch it as an ointment for cancer. I could not believe my ears and nor could my Australian creative director. Mr Hassan had about S$2,000 to spend on the entire campaign. Not only would the production cost alone have been five times that, but our agency was not about to be made a laughing stock by promoting something so spurious.

There was another pesky thorn in my side during my advertising years. Most firms were foreign owned, either Australian or American. Singapore was a good base from which they could reach an ever-growing market. As such all the jobs were filled by expatriates, even though some had scant knowledge of Asian culture and all the idiosyncrasies of consumer demands and spending habits. In the creative field one had to at least be aware of certain sensitivities. But no, the expatriate boss's word was law.

I was in charge of a campaign to market a certain food product with an advertising platform in two main languages, English and Mandarin, and sometimes in dialect as well, depending on the market it was aimed at. The product was Cerebos Salt and the name had to be translated phonetically in all media. Cerebos became See Lau Boo in Hokkien, which means Dead Mother. I pointed this out to my creative director who simply brushed aside my cautionary advice. As a result, sales for the product slumped dramatically. There were many similar incidents where a lack of local knowledge led to some very tricky situations.

The other irksome thing was that expatriate salaries exceeded local ones by fourfold and this grated on my nerves. However, they were the pay masters and you either liked it or lumped it. I decided to lump it and left the business in the mid-1970s.

Fatherhood

For me, the early 1970s were most marked by the arrival of our pride and joy, a boy we named Chris. His mother Dorothy ruled the television era as a newscaster for many years. Fatherhood was to give me a totally different sense of values, as well as many traumas that every parent must go through. There were moments that touched our very souls, those that provoked much merriment and a few that had me exploding with apoplexy and indignation. My wife and I amicably divorced in the late 1980s but we are still in touch, for nothing can change the fact that we are the parents of our son. I count my blessings that I have a close personal and professional bond with Chris and we have co-written several cookbooks.

We all still laugh over many things, especially when Dorothy regales us with her tales of what went on in the maternity ward. At that time she was a division two civil servant and entitled to a private ward. Unfortunately when she went into labour this was under refurbishment and she had to deliver Chris in a class three ward among some half a dozen mothers-to-be.

'My God, I wasn't suffering because of the contractions and birth pains but rather from the other women caterwauling. They screamed and cursed in Hokkien, Malay, Cantonese and language that would make a sailor blush!' The ward sister, who became Chris's godmother, augmented these tales of maternal woe.

'I tell you, I have worked in this ward (it was the Kandang Kerbau Maternity Hospital) for many years and I see the same women here year in and year out. One woman complained that it was her sixth child and was sick of her husband. I asked her why she did not use contraception and her reply was hilarious. "No, my husband does not like condoms. He says it is like playing mahjong wearing gloves!"'

These women belonged to a community of hard-core traditionalists that completely ignored advice about various methods of contraception. It was an uphill battle that still goes on, apparently. Even with the government campaign of Stop at Two it didn't help. One mother said her husband interpreted it as 'Stop at Two Dozen'. So the maternity ward at the KK Hospital continued to echo with the howls of these baby machines.

After the birth of Chris, I was driving to the hospital with his maternal grandmother. She was in seventh heaven over the birth of her second grandson, but I remember her saying something to me which nearly made me drive my car into a monsoon drain.

'We are so lucky it is a boy!' What did she mean? I could not resist asking that if it had been a girl, would she have strangled her at birth? I did not catch her drift, nor she mine, but it was too joyous a moment to get into a protracted argument about her skewed beliefs. Instead I made a closing remark about the fact that she herself had been born a girl. She was about to say something when we arrived at the hospital gates. She was of the old school, the poor dear, the very old school. It was to be the first of many moments of indignation. The fits of apoplexy were yet to come.

We had hoped that Chris would come home with his mother after a few days but it was not to be. He had been born with a condition called G6PD which meant that his immune system was short of an enzyme. This caused severe jaundice that required an immediate blood exchange. For the rest of his life he would not be able to take certain drugs and, most of all, any potentially haemolytic foods like fava beans. If he was to do so, his red blood cells would break down causing anaemia and even brain damage if unchecked.

He came home when he was one month old and for the first few weeks of his young life we rid the house of every mothball, a product that can be lethal to babies with G6PD. Unfortunately at that time just about every Singaporean was in the habit of loading their wardrobes with these white balls. We used them to deter cockroaches but did not know that they could also be killers. During several visits to the paediatrics ward at the hospital we saw babies that had severe brain damage. I said a silent prayer that Chris would come through okay.

Before he was brought home I had gone to the hospital to collect his first set of soiled nappies and brought them home to wash. I was about to rinse one of the nappies when I noticed it was coated with a shiny, black lump—I later learnt that this was the baby's first bowel movement. I was about to wash it out when his grandmother gave an almighty shriek and snatched it out my hands. Was this going to be another episode steeped in tradition that I did not know anything about? It was, for she truly believed a father, meaning a male, should not soil his hands with such faecal matter. What would happen if I did?

'You won't strike lottery for the rest of your life, what!' was her terse reply. What a fate, but again it was too complex to enter into an argument, given the silliness of it all. It was far easier to let her do the washing, much to my relief. There was so much to be learned about folklore and superstition but this was nothing compared to the traumas to come.

Maid agencies did not exist then and you could only find a maid through referrals, such as someone knowing someone else who knows someone looking for a job. As it turned out we did find a sixteen-year-old girl from Malacca called Ah Lian, I kid you not. But not before we had gone through a slew of child minders who drove us bananas. In the first three years, I am not proud to say that we went through at least four or five of these nannies, not to mention several confinement carers who, if anything, were even more aggravating.

One was caught smoking while carrying Chris in her arms. Another quit when asked to make me a drink, the ensuing retort being, 'I am a child minder not a servant!' It was a fine line, I tell you. Yet another would not let us into the room where she slept with Chris after 8 pm. The litany went on but other horror stories we heard would make your blood curdle. It seemed some child minders doped the formulas of the babies in their care with a tincture of opium so they slept through the night.

One story had me in fits of incredulity and a little mirth. The nanny, a black and white *amah cheh*, used to stick her toe into her baby's mouth because she couldn't be bothered to look for a dummy! In the 1950s and 1960s *amah cheh*s ruled the child-minding realm like latter day Florence Nightingales, only more fearsome. They were expensive, haughty and had total control over their employers for one reason: they were dedicated and professional—when they weren't up to their outrageous practices.

We went through a few but in the end it was humble Ah Lian from Malacca who stuck it out until Chris was ten and we left for the UK. She was hard-working, if not a bit slow and myopic. We did not know she had trouble with her eyesight until one day when instead of putting sugar into my coffee she put MSG! We also noticed that she would sit barely two feet away from the TV set in the evening when her chores were done. We took her to the optician and it turned out she was severely short-sighted. Bless her soul, but she left us to return to Malacca, probably to get married as she was past twenty by then.

Anyone who is a first-time father or parent can understand what this entails. It is a job that lasts for years, decades even. It is a world filled with wet, soiled nappies, sterilising equipment and enough baby gear to outfit a department store. You worry, fret and ring for a doctor if your child so much as sneezes. Travelling with a toddler can also be traumatic, as we found out once when we took Chris to Disneyland. He was six or thereabouts and we wandered into the MGM Complex after a day of rides in the Magic Kingdom. Unbeknownst to us a lion was chained to a metal gate in the basement as an attraction. This beast represented the roaring MGM lion, a symbol that exists to this day. While we were wandering around, Chris somehow got lost and we really panicked. We went berserk, fearing most that he would be mauled by the lion. Actually it was a mangy lion way past its prime and only interested in sleeping. Anyhow, we searched the whole place in desperation and were just about to call the police when we saw Chris sitting on a stone lion at the entrance. After I'd given him a tongue lashing, he replied sweetly: 'Dad, you always told me to wait at the entrance should I ever get lost.' Cheeky fella, but I love him all the more for his innate common sense.

This wasn't the last of our nerve-racking experiences. Later, in San Francisco, Chris went down with a spell of severe vomiting and could not even keep water down. We had little choice but to ring for the hotel doctor whose diagnosis was startling to say the least. Upon examining Chris, he told us to give him a drink of coke and charged us the incredible sum of US$100 (S$175)!

'You have dragged this child all over the place. He's exhausted and his body has shut down. The sugar in the coke will settle his tummy.' It did and it was the most expensive bottle of coke ever. We also learnt more about childcare than several volumes of Doctor Spock could impart.

My Press Days

After I left the advertising industry, I was offered a job with the then *Sunday Nation* as a features writer. I had earned some credibility as a humour columnist with *Her World,* and the magazine belonged to the same press group as *Sunday Nation.* Actually, my step into the print media world came about in a funny way. Chafed by the fact that children were being spoilt by a plethora of commercial toys, I wrote a feature about the joys of making our own toys. As children, my brothers and I had few toys. So we would scan the grounds of Farrer Park looking for shiny red seeds, sew them into cotton bags and play with them as toys. We made our own kites from old issues of the *Nanyang Siang Pau* newspaper and had much fun flying them at the park. The feature I wrote for the *Sunday Nation* was entitled 'Why my son will never really own a beanbag'. It was about how children are missing out on natural and rustic playthings that cost nothing but give much pleasure.

Anyway, I sent the story to *Female* magazine—I knew the editor socially. A while later, we met at a party. We began to chat and she mentioned that she had received a poignant story about a father who made beanbags for his son.

'And you know the silly chap did not give me his name or address as I want to pay him for the story,' she said. Talk about coincidences. With a meek smile I said I was the silly chap and did not give my name or address as I entertained little hope of it being published. It was the only time I was thrilled about being called a silly twit!

It turned out that I had some promise as a writer. The first three months of lectures at the school of journalism were fraught with tension, especially when I discovered I had to pass a Teeline shorthand test. I did pass, but not without a little surreptitious peek over the shoulder of another would-be journalist who seemed to know Teeline inside out.

I graduated and went on to work at the *Sunday Nation* as a features writer. The five years that I spent crafting stories were some of my most satisfying and memorable. I had the privilege of working for a formidable female editor who pulled no punches when it came to editing my stories. Actually, editing is putting it mildly, for my early stories were literally ripped to shreds for a host of reasons which I will not go into. Suffice to say that I learnt more from her than any mass communications university course could have taught me.

Some of my assignments were heartbreaking, even more so for a rookie writer. I was not, and never did, develop into a hard-nosed newsman. Once, my boss sent me to interview the parents of victims of a catastrophic oil tanker explosion, a job that required not just writing skill but also nerves of steel. I returned without a story as it was extremely painful trying to get comments from people whose sons had just been incinerated. One sobbing retort from a parent sent me reeling.

'What you want me to say? My son is like satay now. Go away!'

How did newsmen cope? On another occasion I was to write a story about life on an oil rig moored far out in the South China Sea. It was then that I realised I suffered from severe vertigo. When I arrived at the rig I was then hoisted onto a metal platform with no sides. The platform must have been at least ten storeys high. By the time I arrived at the wind-buffeted main production area I was nearly on my knees with terror. How I managed to file the story later I'll never know.

Thereafter I pleaded with my editor to let me do 'safe' stories about human endeavours. I was in my element doing this and over the next five years enjoyed writing stories that covered topics which touched the lives of many.

One story I remember involved Bee Cheng Hiang *bak kwa*. In the mid-1970s the old man himself would man his Chinatown stall dressed in his regulation 'Good Morning' singlet and striped shorts, barbecuing his now globally famous barbecued pork. Some sixth sense told me that he was sitting on a fortune for he already owned several outlets manned by his sons. Writing the story was fun and most enlightening as I was invited to visit the factory where the pork was sliced and prepared before being barbecued. To cut the story short, I believed that my feature would catapult his business into the stratosphere. Today the name is truly international, making millions for the original family.

More to the point, only a few years ago I happened to visit the same shop in Chinatown looking to buy what is my all-time favourite snack. There, on one of the walls and framed, was my *Sunday Nation* feature for all to see as the prelude to Bee Cheng Hiang's phenomenal success. I introduced myself and boldly asked if I could have a discount. The chap running the outlet was most unimpressed that I had the nerve to suggest that their business had succeeded because of my story. I had to pay the full price, sigh!

How many young men remember the first Sri Dewa barbers? These young Malay men were the first to form a mini chain of stalls along the pavements outside shophouses and became popular with people who wanted style at low cost. It was only S$2 for a cut and no blow dry. Sri Dewa went on to became a real retail chain with something like seventeen outlets all over Singapore. And no, I didn't dare ask for a discount, despite writing a story that must have made some difference to their burgeoning business. Such injustice, but no matter, I feel I have done my part to help lay the foundations for entrepreneurial enterprises.

I had also planned to do a series on the early history of Chinatown and this almost resulted in the loss of my life, or at least a finger or two. Late one afternoon I went to Pagoda Street with a photographer hoping to catch some of the vegetable sellers after the morning rush. One grizzled old lady was sitting near her heap of vegetables cutting her toenails with a small paring knife that I swear she had earlier used to trim her *kai lan*. When the photographer pointed his camera at her, the feisty lady shot up and hurled her knife at us, missing us by a few inches. I learnt that you simply do not take pictures of old Chinese women as they believe the camera will trap their souls forever. This would happen to me again years later in Shanghai when I tried to do the same to a dumpling seller on the Bund. I earned the indignity of having a hard dumpling make contact with my face, and I did not even get to taste it.

In the process of writing my features I managed to gain access to a room in which lived eight young men. They were all from Malaysia working at a construction site nearby and could only afford to share one room. It was squalid to say the least, all eight sleeping on the floor and each only able to hang his clothes from a nail hammered into the wall. They seemed cheerful and forthcoming despite their living conditions but it was sobering to know what our migrant workers had to cope with.

Rasa Singapura

Well do I remember Singapore's first attempt at corralling hawkers together at what is now Tudor Court. The street food scene then was in its infancy and the Singapore Tourist Promotion Board initiated the move. Myself and a few other food writers were involved (Did I say that apart from writing human-interest features, I also dabbled in food writing?) We were approached to set up an eating committee which would then select twenty-five to thirty of the best Singapore hawkers.

Everyone was agog and the scheme was successful for a few years. However, when I returned some time later to check up on culinary standards, I was amazed. With success had come inertia and inevitably complacency. My sugar cane juice contained seventy per cent ice and very little else, the *nasi beryani* chicken was days old and the chicken rice stall was pathetic. I wrote about it in a column that evidently got up the nose of the chicken rice seller. Through the grapevine I learnt that he had threatened to chop off my fingers if

I dared to patronise his stall. Thank goodness my earlier visits had been incognito. Who said writing about food was safe?

I must just mention an earlier food venue called Glutton's Square. It was a car park in Orchard Road that became an al fresco food court after sunset. Once, however, there was one pesky problem. Every car had to clear the car park after 6 pm but one chap evidently forgot for some reason. Having no other choice, the stalls set up around him, completely encircling his vehicle!

Budget Travel

Now this was a time that enabled many budget-conscious people to take advantage of cheap coach, train and air travel. The Cameron Highlands was a favourite destination and one company charged the incredible sum of S$45 for a weekend trip, inclusive of accommodation. So my family and some friends decided to take them up on their offer. We were told that the coach that was to take us there was parked near the old New World Amusement Park. As there were several coaches there, we were given coloured slips which corresponded to a specific coach.

The management of this travel company was either colour blind or stupid; we were given dark pink slips and the other group were given red slips. The problem was that both colours were almost identical and there was utter confusion, to say the least. After a while we sorted out the problem and set off on the long journey. There were no toilets on the coach so the coach stopped off at intervals along the Malaysian highway. These stops were punishing to the bladder and our dignity. At one stop we were simply told to get off and look for the nearest bush. Some lady wailed and said she could not possibly expose herself in such an undignified way and would wait until we found a coffee shop. Unfortunately others, myself included, were already crossing their legs in discomfort. The lady had to ask one of her travelling companions to hold up an umbrella so she could do her business in private. Well, at least semi-private.

And so we trundled on for hours until we arrived at Brinchang, or was it Tanah Rata? The driver had lost his way and now there was the additional problem of locating our guest house. By then it was nearly dark and we could not find where we were supposed to be staying. Instead we turned to a Buddhist nunnery. The tour leader begged the head nun to let our group stay for the night. She took pity on us bedraggled lot, who were by then hungry and angry.

We were assigned large rooms that slept six, but before we could settle down there came a loud knock on the door. It was the head nun. She could not allow males and females to sleep in the same room and would we kindly separate. As it was a mixed crowd with couples, this was irksome. She was insistent and we ended up sharing quarters with total strangers of the same sex. We left early the next morning, having had no dinner the previous evening and receiving no breakfast that morning. I soon learned why it was so cheap and vowed never again.

Breakfart and Woo from Seep

I hasten to explain the above heading, else you might think I am being coarse. One of the first budget airlines was called Saber Air. It offered the lowest fares to Europe. At a time when international travel was way beyond the pockets of most salaried people, the airline was a godsend. Suddenly I had enough money to buy return tickets to London for myself, Dorothy and my sister-in-law.

I was so excited that on the day of departure I fell into a monsoon drain as I lugged my humungous suitcase. We were really *sua ku*, trying to be sophisticated and packing enough for an exodus to the Promised Land. Only my pride was hurt, though. Once we'd checked in at the airport and the formalities completed, we settled down for the long flight. There would be a stopover in Bombay and Bahrain before touching down in London sixteen hours later. Little did we know it, but we were to find out why it was a budget airline.

Once on the plane, the stewardess came around to serve us. I noticed she was wearing a rather attractive uniform of a peach-coloured jacket, a skirt and a hat. She looked quite smart and I said so, asking her what material her uniform was made out of. Her reply had Dorothy and her sister choking on their pasta.

'This one made of woo, you know, from the seep.' Of course, wool from the sheep, silly me not to know. I checked my chuckle and turned my attention to Dorothy, who was the world's worst traveller. She was dressed to the nines, as was the style then, wearing a chic tunic, a pair of trousers and a long scarf. Long before we arrived in Bombay, let alone London, her outfit was covered in a regurgitated mess of pasta, cream sauce and tomato ketchup.

Somehow during the flight we managed to sleep a little, despite the fact that our seat gave us barely enough room to stretch our legs— being a budget airline they'd crammed as many seats into the plane as possible. Towards dawn, en route to London, an announcement came over the Tannoy system that woke us all up.

'Laddies and jungleman, in a few moments breakfart will be served.' I wondered from where Saber Air recruited their crew but Singapore Girls they were not. Today's fractured Singlish is nothing compared to the English of this lot. The airline did not last more than a year, probably due to passengers suffering from extreme fright. At one point I asked a stewardess if the turbulence was dangerous. At that time strong turbulence was common as planes were not fitted with good stabilisers so when they hit an air pocket, everything went flying. Her reply was far from comforting to someone like me who, despite decades of flying, is still terrified by every jerk and roll.

'Yes, ah, sometime you can knock your head on the ceiling!' She then proceeded to place a breakfast roll on each table, whilst dragging a black bin bag full of rolls!

The only other time I had a worse flying experience was on a Greek Olympic Airlines flight a few years later. The stewardess serving me had a cigarette hanging from her lips. The chief steward was doing the same. Smoking was still allowed on planes but by the crew? It was too much and I never flew that airline again.

Discomania

This was the beginning of a craze that would take Singapore by storm. The Beatles had unleashed their rocking sounds on the world and everybody who could twitch a little would spend weekends at some discotheque or other. The term discotheque was shortened to disco because when it was pronounced by Singaporeans it sounded very similar to a rude word in Malay.

As I was fond of dancing, I was in seventh heaven when this craze came around. But it was not always a pleasure to see middle-aged men and women twitching as if they were having fits on miniscule dance floors. It mattered little what rhythm was being played; everyone did their own thing and some even performed grand solos. The age of formal dancing was over. You could cut the rug all night long by yourself and no one would pay the slightest bit of notice. Discomania wasn't really about dancing, but more an act of liberation, to let the body move every which way without the slightest regard for tempo or style. When I threw a party at our family home, Mother commented that my friends seem to be suffering from epilepsy. She was not far wrong, you know, given the dancing skills of some of them.

High Teas and Tupperware

My memories of the 1970s are mostly within the realm of food: coffee houses, ice cream parlours and hawker centres, to be precise. In the mid-1970s posh hotels and supermarket chains suddenly began to spring up. Singaporeans focused their attention very firmly on where one could find the best *an pan* (red bean paste puffs), chiffon pandan cakes, *kueh lapis*, *nasi padang*, Hokkien noodle soup with pig's tail, fish head curry—the list was endless.

Weekends saw shoppers crowd into Yaohan, a new Japanese supermarket chain with outlets in Plaza Singapura and Bukit Timah Plaza. When Japanese bakers introduced their delicious *an pan*, queues stretched for miles. People also seemed to have a penchant for the toilet rolls from this supermarket and every trolley would be laden with them.

The new Hotel Malaysia opened a swank coffee house and it became infamous for its Knickerbocker Glory, a humungous ice cream dessert that could cause a cholesterol meltdown. My mother-in-law had the most peculiar philosophy when ordering her favourite banana split. She would order two scoops of vanilla and strawberry ice cream and tell the waiter she didn't want any banana! I asked her why, stating that it would make more sense to simply order a double scoop of ice cream from the menu, which was cheaper, instead of paying for a banana split.

'I want cannot, ah!' was her indignant reply. I gave up trying to understand her logic.

Everyone wanted pandan chiffon cake made by a certain Mrs Kwan, who went on to become wealthy from her iconic bakes. At every party, the cake would invariably be from her patisserie in Bukit Timah. If one wanted *kueh lapis*, a clove-scented Indonesian speciality, one went to Bengawan Solo. Whether these ideas were due to hype or the Singapore syndrome of wanting to be there first, it was hard to tell.

No sooner was a particular item talked about than swoosh!—it would disappear from shelves at the speed of greased lightning. It was the same with chicken rice. The first hotspot was in Toa Payoh and then somewhere else. The chic crowd would pay over the odds for their chicken rice at the Chatterbox coffee houses in Mandarin Hotel.

The best *char kway teow* came from a man based somewhere in Newton (not the circus) and his stall was so hugely popular, he even installed a phone to take orders.

Conversation centred around food most of the time and Rasa Singapura was, by then, a waning venue. Independent hawker stalls ruled the day, and many went on to make a fortune. I remember at Liat Towers, across the road from CK Tang, there was a Danish restaurant where smorgasbord became the in thing to eat.

Polar Café was for chicken pie, the Troika Russian restaurant for *shashlik*, GH Cafe for cream puffs, Rendezvous restaurant for *nasi padang*, Muthu's for fish head curry and Koek Road for pork satay. Everyone had his or her say about which restaurant served the best food and no two people ever agreed. And it wasn't just related to food. If someone so much as mentioned that umbrellas were going cheap at Chinese Emporium, a crowd would soon gather. Perhaps it was out of sense of ennui, but there was an incessant need to own things or eat foods that were deemed, by general opinion, to be the best.

Thus I often had to drive the family hither and thither in search of this viand or other. When Kheng Luck opened its first chilli crab stall, we were there like a shot. When a humble sandwich stand in Tanah Merah received the highest accolade for its bacon sandwiches, the poor lady was swamped every Saturday evening. Well do I remember seeking out the best *ang ku kuah* in Blair Plain, *yew chia kuay* in Tong Bahru market and *rojak* in Chomp Chomp, Serangoon Gardens.

This feeding frenzy was not confined to Singapore, for it came blowing like a straw in the wind that a seafood stall in Kukup, Johore, served the best chilli prawns and off we would go in our cars, on our motorcycles and scooters. No place was ever a secret or exclusive, for Singaporeans not only loved to eat, but they loved to talk about it. Paradoxically they would moan when prices were hiked up as a result of intense patronage.

Ah, High Tea! This was when you could have a blowout. For the nominal price of S$20, you could stuff your face for several hours at a hotel coffee house. It was a culinary shift towards obesity, as I soon discovered. Human beings are the only mammals who do not know when to stop eating. These international banquets were a gourmand's Aladdin's cave. I had friends and a few family members who felt that since they could gorge an unlimited amount of choice viands, why not go the whole hog? And hogs they were, for it was an orgy of feasting that did not end when the face and stomach were full.

People would go to the coffee house with Tupperware containers in their cavernous bags. When they could eat no more, they simply sneaked food into these takeaway boxes to feast on back home. The sheer avarice of it all was so widespread that hotels imposed a condition: any unfinished food had to be weighed and the customer had to pay for the excess according to the weight. It must have been an embarrassment for those caught stealing food.

Boutiques and Other Bijou Places

When Swinging London fashions took the world by storm, a dozen boutiques sprang up in Singapore aping those in Carnaby Street and with names to match. Suddenly fashion-conscious girls could buy their imported gear from shops with cute names like Rooftop, Hunky Dory, Etam (Mates of London spelt backwards), Biba (a brand of Mary Quant cosmetics) and Oggi and Leather Plus for leather goods. Money seemed no object and the priority for most working girls was the fashion items they bought had to take up half their salaries or more.

There was one boutique called Poor Little Rich Girl in Liat Towers. It was where the mothers and daughters of the upper middle class would shop and screamed class and money. You would see these women, mutton dressed as lamb, parading around wearing clothes quite unsuitable for their age.

Fashion also spilled into the dozens of coffee houses. Most weekends they would stage fashion shows for free. One could linger for hours nursing an ice cream and be treated to a parade of sashaying models wearing the latest togs.

However, not everyone in the rag trade managed to pull off London chic. A few seamstresses of the *swa teng* (countrified, rural, unchic) genre decided to jump on this new bandwagon. They usually operated from shop houses, whether in Geylang, Katong, Hougang or wherever they had clientele. Not really understanding the fashion trend of the day, they proceeded to ape their Orchard Road cousins and renamed their dressmaking shops 'boutiques'. Unfortunately, whether from sheer ignorance or simply bad spelling, the names of their boutiques would be rather strange: Ah Noi Bootik, Swee Lian Butik and Rosminah's Batik Butik. Some went on to do roaring business, others simply faded into oblivion when department stores slowly but surely put paid to small dressmaking businesses.

National Service

Yes, I had to do National Service despite not being of the age of enlistment. It was because in the early 1970s I had, in a moment of madness, rejoined the civil service. At that time all new civil servants were drafted and what followed was two years of marching, toilet cleaning, frustration, deprivation and much laughter. The Singapore Army was in its infancy, I have to say, and the template far different from what it is today.

As for laughter, you had to look on the bright side of things if you didn't want training sessions to drive you mad. I had the bad luck of sharing a common wardrobe with another national serviceman who did not seem to have the slightest idea about basic hygiene. He would wear his underclothes for a few days, turn them inside out and wear them for another few days. He was too lazy to wash them and I bore the brunt of it, enduring the pong every time I opened the wardrobe doors.

I tried sprays, perfumes and even TCP to diffuse the rank odour but none of it worked. He was a nice enough chap but I did not have the heart or the nerve to tell him his lack of hygiene was giving me throbbing migraines. Training in SAFTI was tough but my biggest gripe was the food. I was already something of a foodie and facing hard-boiled eggs at 5.30 am was painful. So was the prospect of rubbery mutton, bread that looked and tasted like a mortarboard and other culinary delights.

On the other side of the training camp fence was a man selling *char kway teow* who knew of our need for decent sustenance. He did a roaring trade every night. It was a bit awkward buying from him as we had to slide money under the fence and wait for his packet of noodles to be returned the same way. Some soldiers were caught and had their supper confiscated by the trainers who, I suspect, ate it themselves!

I made a lot of friends during the basic training period of three months and went on to become a typist. Such were the unfathomable machinations of the army that their computers deemed me to be only good for clerical work. I was a fully trained broadcaster then, but I guess there was no service within the Ministry of Defence that called for a disc jockey! When my son reached the age to enlist for national service, I told him that it would do him the world of good. When we exchanged views later, his description of training conditions seemed worlds away from mine—a holiday camp, to be precise.

In retrospect they were the best two years of my life as I learnt about teamwork, became fighting fit, could rapidly change from pyjamas to full battle gear in two minutes and strip an AR15 rifle down in one minute. I achieved many other things that I think make me worthy of entering the *Guinness Book of Records*: doing thirty push-ups on blazing hot tarmac; cleaning a toilet with a toothbrush; or cutting a whole lawn with a razor blade. I leave you to deduce the circumstances that led to such challenging pursuits. Suffice to say they were not rewards for sterling behaviour.

My Stage Debut

In the late 1970s I was still working as a magazine editor and doing charity work for The Spastics Society. Some of my colleagues had the great idea to stage a musical based on our multi-lingual and multi-cultural society to raise funds for the charity. We didn't know what we were getting ourselves into, except that it was going to be fun. Apart from such luminaries as Jacintha Abishegenaden and former Asian Games gold medalist swimmer Pat Chan, both of whom were wonderful singers, the rest of us were totally without either singing or dancing talent. At least I was.

So we began rehearsals under the baton of Jacintha and Pat and in the six months that they whipped our vocal chords up to standard, I realised I was never going to make it to the Top Ten. Neither could any of us dance, *Her World* editor Betty Khoo being the original clunk with three left feet! Still we persisted and the upshot of it all was a glorious musical called *Broadway Kopi Tiam*. It was made up of Chinese *wayang*, Indian dance, Taiwanese singers and Broadway elements, all in an eclectic ensemble that brought the house down and raised thousands of dollars for charity.

I'm proud to say it really was the forerunner to *Beauty World* and other productions in later years. Ours was the original template, the script a motley collection of Teochew slang, Tamil jokes, Cantonese curses and enough one-liners to fill a Las Vegas comic standup show. The finale was a glorious tableau of Broadway songs culminating in a show-stopping rendition of 'New York, New York'. I still have my sequined tuxedo and sometimes I take it out and shake off the mothballs, recalling those wonderful memories. I had sung and danced on stage and was happy to have had my fifteen minutes of fame, even if my performance had been a bit dubious.

Canto Pops and A Go-Go

When the New World Amusement Park's popularity waned, it became the setting for a new sound: Chinese pop songs and A Go-Go music. A Go-Go was a sub-genre of funky music that originated in Washington in the mid-1970s. It had an alluring toe-tapping beat characterised by the syncopated rhythms of bongos, snare drums and percussion instruments. A Go-Go took Singapore by storm, and A Go-Go fashion soon followed. It followed the trend of colourful miniskirts, large hoop earrings and lots of sequins. At least that was how an emerging crop of Chinese pop singers interpreted it.

A Go-Go was to spawn a whole new language of its own, such as if you dressed in what looked like dancing gear, you were an A Go-Go girl. At discos everywhere, the raison d'etre was to do the A Go-Go, which actually had people making very jerky and rhythmic movements while arms flailed wildly and faces were rapt with concentration.

The dance featured in many American films, mostly depicting girls dancing solo in suspended cages. They wore the regulation A Go-Go outfits of kinky boots, short skirts, knitted vests and hooped earrings. It was almost a throwback to the fashions of the 1960s, with pale lips and lashes of mascara, but this time the music had a new, exciting sound.

Many will remember the diminutive Sakura Teng, a Hainanese girl from Muar who made her debut at New World with her sensational voice and ability to yodel. She was no more than seventeen then but had a voice that belied her stature. She had begun singing in the 1960s but really made it big in the 1970s. She went on to become the queen of A Go-Go. She recorded more than fifty singles and popped up regularly in television musicals devoted to Chinese pop music.

Television in the 1970s was the platform for many other Chinese entertainers who went on to become virtual icons. The stand-up comic pair of Wang Sa and Ye Fong had a huge following, entertaining audiences with their brand of multi-dialect turns both on television and with live shows at New World and other theatres. Wang Sa spoke resounding Teochew and Ye Fong, an eclectic mix of Mandarin, Cantonese and Hakka. They were billed as the Laurel and Hardy of Singapore, colloquially nicknamed Fat and Thin (Ah Pui and Ah San).

Other 1970s music icons have all but faded, many going overseas or settling into domestic life. I shall always remember Lena Lim, Lara, Rita Chao, the Chopstick Sisters and the Ming Choo Sisters. All were home-grown and made Singapore proud, though many were born in Malaysia. This mattered little, for Singapore was their entertainment platform.

There were few local singers who made the grade in the English genre despite the annual Television Talentime Competition that hoped to find unknown talent. A few found regional fame, such as Naomi Suriya and Alban De Souza who was entertaining at Zouk as late as the 1990s. However, the most popular were still Chinese pop stars. In the Malay-language stream there were a few who made it big and hosted their own pop shows. Lavish musicals included Kalong Senandong and Dendang Ria which almost always featured luminaries such as Kartina Dahari, Anita Sarawak, Alinah Rahman and Julie Sudiro.

These shows were entertaining enough in their own way. They always followed the predictable format of background dancers, gorgeous costumes, and the singer doing his or own thing with a microphone without much thought for choreography. They would just sing one number after another to canned applause, blatantly miming to pre-recorded music. The show was static all round. Of the male singers, the most high profile were Sugiman Jahuri and Ahmad Daud. The former was billed as the Matt Monro of Singapore and had a fabulous baritone but he has not been heard of since the late 1970s. The latter earned a place in the *Guinness Book of Records* for recording 30,000 songs.

Anita Sarawak has never really stopped entertaining, having burst onto the pop scene in the 1960s. She went on to successfully wow two generations of Singaporeans, Malaysians and Indonesians. Undoubtedly one of the most talented entertainers in the region, she was the first born-of-the-soil singer to break local boundaries. A real live wire, although standing at no more than five foot nothing, her choreographed moves, whether on television or in sophisticated nightclubs like the Kasbah in the Mandarin Hotel, were dazzling. She had a repertoire of pop, rock & roll, soul and disco. Despite being Indonesian, she even dared to sing in non-native tongues such as Mandarin and wowed the crowds even more. Her dance moves were widely copied and her costumes, while outlandish, sat this side of sassy originality. Some nights she would be a sinuous version of the Queen of Sheba, on others she was pure Las Vegas showgirl. Always, however, she would be unique and stunning. Indeed, she was the only local singer to make it big in Las Vegas—and that's saying something.

As popular entertainment goes, most singers seemed to be stuck in a time warp and did little to polish their talent to fit an international market. When imported American and British shows came on the scene, local singers were eclipsed. Perhaps it was a change in tastes, or that there was little universal appeal, but this kind of predictable entertainment—one song after another, outlandish costumes and rather feeble sets—did not endear itself to the public. People were travelling more and returned to Singapore spoilt by more sophisticated entertainment in London, New York and Tokyo. Nonetheless, local singers were iconic in their time, and worth remembering almost thirty-five years later.

Bring Come and Take Go

As the 1970s drew to a close, I was becoming a little disenchanted with a few things that would prompt me to make some radical changes in my life. I was ever more disgruntled with the education system and the fact that ten-year-olds were streamed into vocational studies if their Mandarin was abysmal. My son was only eight and his struggles with Mandarin were nothing compared to what was to come. His teacher had sent us a note with some unpleasant news so we went to the school to speak to her. It seemed that Chris had been classified as ESN (educationally sub-normal). We found it hard to believe as Chris was more precocious than most ten-year-olds, had read most of Agatha Christie's novels and was otherwise very bright. It must be a mistake, I thought.

To cut a long story short his teacher had noticed that Chris could not pay attention during English lessons. Her deduction was that he was unable to take in information and therefore must suffer from ESN. We spoke to the headmistress who, fortunately, knew about our son's above average IQ and told us to go home. But not before I heard the same teacher uttering words that struck terror in my heart:

'You there, bring come your book and take go this ruler!'

This from someone who deemed one of her students to be educationally sub-normal.

As for myself, I was beginning to feel dragged down by

journalism; my ideas had dried up and I lacked motivation. I had also become increasingly more interested in food and cooking and had written two cookbooks that resulted in a job offer in London. It seemed providence had taken a hand and Chris would have the chance to get a decent, quality education.

By the end of this era, I was also becoming more and more confused by the local patois. Words such as kiasu, wah leow and dam siong were tripping off everyone's tongues. Street language was mostly Mandarin, a language I never quite mastered, and English, if spoken at all, seemed to have morphed into a language from another planet. Once when I visited Lucky Plaza I thought I was in Manila, having to push my way through hundreds of Filipina ladies who seemed to have made their home on the steps of the shopping centre.

My colleague and I decided to go into a clothing shop and were immediately accosted by a salesgirl who kept addressing us both as 'uncle'. I told her we were not related but my sarcasm was completely lost on her.

'Yes, good morning, Uncle, what can I offer you, Uncle?' she rattled on.

My friend replied that he only wanted to browse, to which the salesgirl replied: 'Oh, we got plenty brouses. Small, medium, any colour you want!'

This episode has since become my friend's party piece.

Eat What Where?

While deciding where to go for lunch with a few friends, I asked in my best English, 'Where shall we go for lunch?' A simple enough question I thought. I might as well have said, 'Whither shall we goeth for our sustenance?' I was met by a minute's silence so I repeated my question.

'Oh, you mean eat what where?' This was my first introduction to the literal translation of Mandarin or dialect into spoken English.

Once, I was walking down Orchard Road with a former press colleague when I stopped a woman and asked her how frequently the airport shuttle bus departed. I got the same puzzled look. I repeated my question and it must have rung home as she replied, 'Oh, you mean how many times one hour?'

My colleague severely admonished me by saying, 'My dear Terry, you cannot use words of more than two syllables any more!'

It seemed that suddenly less was more. I had to decipher what was being said by applying the thought process first in Chinese then mouth the words in Singlish.

The late 1970s was also my favourite time to shop at Giordano. I remember one time I bought a pair of chinos that were too long, and asked someone at the shop if they could take the hem up by a few inches. There followed a few seconds of befuddlement before the salesgirl replied, 'Sorry, sir, we cannot do this but we can cut short for you.'

I was learning day by day and even got the opportunity to throw out the occasional 'wah leow!' but without the requisite body language that seemed to be a kind of semaphore code. There was a certain toss of the arm and head and the words were spat out with vigour.

I was also introduced to the emergence of Ah Beng and Ah Lian. As I recall the only Ah Lian I'd known many years earlier had been our maid but this new breed was an entirely different sub-culture. I asked my niece exactly what or who these new people were. She was most enlightening.

'You see, Uncle Terry, an Ah Beng is one who wears tight trousers, speaks only Mandarin, always has a comb in his back pocket and makes himself as ugly as possible! Ah Lian has chalk-white skin, wears dresses that expose too much flesh and has a hand phone glued to her ear.'

Food names did not fare any better as hotels along Orchard Road and in the city now housed a proliferation of European eateries. Try asking for and pronouncing words such as Ratatouille and you would be faced with blank stares. More than likely you would be asked if you wanted rat stew. Once, we went into a brasserie and ordered steak. I told the waitress I wanted mine medium and she said they only did steaks one size!

Telephonitis

Telephonitis was a new disease. Once, I rang a local supermarket asking for escargot and quite correctly pronounced it with a silent 't'. I was told in no uncertain terms that if I wanted air cargo I should ring the airport! Another time I was staying at a local hotel and some British friends tried to reach me. The receptionist later told me to call Mr Orang Utan (it should have been Mr Owen Houghton). Another message was to call a Mr Devil Curry—his name was Neville Guthrie.

Telephone operators and receptionists had a language all of their own. If you rang a company wanting information, you were likely to be met with the standard reply: 'Excuse, what is it regarding concerning about?' Talk about redundant language. Where did it all come from? I guess as language is dynamic, it mutates all the time and it was no use trying to be eloquent when dealing with this lot. All my years of elocution classed with the BBC were thrown out of the window. I mustn't be unkind though, as the only thing that matters is getting the message across.

When I returned to Singapore in the 1980s, I found the MRT to be amazing. I queued up for a ticket and asked the girl behind the desk if I could buy a weekly season ticket. She stared blankly at me and replied, 'No, sir, we don't have season ticket.'

When I asked her why not and how I could get a ticket to cover a week's travel, her reply was, 'We have stored value ticket but no season ticket, sir.'

She had learnt her job well, sticking to the book. So I bought a stored value ticket, which is no different to a season ticket.

PUB, CPF, PIE et al

Even before I left Singapore in 1983, our lives were suffused with acronyms that are still used in perplexing signage all over the island. Yes, there was HDB, CPF and PUB when I left. But there were even more when I returned on business trips. I thought PIE was a sign indicating pie stalls along the highway. Or MRT that Singaporeans persist in pronouncing incoherently. An English friend on his first visit to the country asked a Singaporean lady what was the public transport system called and was told it was 'Mert Lor'! He subsequently asked me if this was indeed the name, like the London Tube. I extracted the vowels for him and explained it was not a word but an acronym. The same gentleman thought the PUB was a chain of his beloved brown ale and stout. When he visited my brother's home he was utterly confounded by our conversations peppered with CPF, NTUC, CBD and others that he is still trying to come with grips with. I am also still trying to come to grips with them.

The media didn't help either, assuming every reader could decipher the likes of POSB, SBS, SBC, HUDC and CYC. The latter was a brand of shirt that went on to become iconic but I do not know what the letters stand for. Probably Chan Yong Choon or some such Chinese name.

Local residents may well be totally familiar with what SAFRA, PWD and PDF stand for, but visitors and those who have been away for a long time can suffer 'acronymitis' from so much abbreviation. Acronyms save space but not sanity. When coupled with Singlish, it can be a real trial for the uninitiated to understand what is going on.

I paraphrase below a few conversational gems I heard in the 1970s. They are worthy of a place in the National Archives.

'Wah leow, my fudder complain his CPF was so little and he cannot invest in NTUC. I must take the MRT to talk to him as today the traffic is very bad on the PIE. I tell him better to save in POSB so he can upgrade from HDB to HUDC.'

'Don't talk cock, man, he KLKK spend so much money at SIC playing mahjong and on SPG. My friend who work for PWD only buy from CCC junkstore man! I dam SBS and dam NATO!'

The Birth of Singlish

When chronicling the history of Singapore, one cannot possibly avoid the cultural and linguistic phenomenon that is Singlish, the constantly evolving patois that has become an integral part of people's everyday lives. Whether you subscribe to using proper English or not is not the point. Like life itself, language is dynamic and Singlish is something we cannot ignore and should not discourage. It is an ingenious form of word play, not merely fractured English much more than the sum of its parts.

It is a language born not of a specific time as such, but since the mid-1960s it has slowly evolved alongside many other changes in Singapore.

Members of my extended family still use it, often entirely excluding proper Queen's English. Even Chris, my son, who spent most of his formative years in England, has decamped from our London home to work in Singapore. He can switch from public-school English to Singlish at a rate that is absolutely mind-boggling.

Singlish, as the name implies, is when someone mentally phrases a comment in one of the several Singapore dialects where grammar is completely different, but then speaks it in English. It is extremely difficult to standardise Singlish spelling as there is no existing translation from, say, Hokkien or Teochew, the two main Singapore dialects that are bound up with Singaporespeak.

Many of the words are an amalgam of different dialects and even languages. The words I find the most fascinating are those that are straightforward English words tweaked at will.

The glossary below is by no means comprehensive. For a much more learned treatise of Singlish, look for the *Coxford Singlish Dictionary*.

Agaration—from the Malay word *agak*, meaning 'to estimate' or 'guess'.

Ah then?/arbuthen—meaning 'of course' tinged with sarcasm and a retort to blindingly obvious statements. Arbuthen could be a mutation of 'ah' and 'but then'.

Akasai—a pejorative description to mean someone or something is girly. Could come from the phrase 'act cute until like sai' (act cute like shit)

Atas—literally meaning 'up' in Malay but alluding to people of a snobbish disposition or simply the rich.

Bludder or Blarder—meaning brother. Mudder means mother and fudder means father.

Blur like sotong—used to describe a person not altogether there, the reference to *sotong* (squid) being rather obscure. As squid are known to have a much higher intelligence than fish, they might object to this comparison.

Can die one—an expression of extreme frustration or despair, usually in response to a question such as, 'How's life?'

Chiak or Cheat my money—an accusation of trickery, not overt fraud, usually referring to a less than honest transaction.

Cheebilised—a crude form of the word 'civilised'. The first two syllables in Hokkien and Teochew refer to the word for a female's private parts.

China or cheena gherk—another pejorative term for new arrivals from China. The gherk reference is no more than an expletive, such as nerd or jerk.

Dam siong—literally meaning something is very heartfelt.

Do' wan done—an expression of indignation, such as 'that's just too bad' or 'go to hell' in less polite terms.

Exkew or Exkew me—'excuse me'

Hock or Co?—a question used to ask someone if they want their drink to be hot or cold.

Occifer—a mis-pronunciation (usually rudely deliberate in the army) of 'officer', as in 'Occifer think he so grand, KKLK all over the place.'

Pumchek—derived from the English word 'puncture' and the default term for a flat tyre.

Reddy oreddy—a redundant phrase indicating impatience, as in, 'I have been reddy oreddy long time waiting for you.'

Talk 3 Talk 4—from the ancient Hokkien phrase '*kong sar kong si*' meaning idle chat.

What you talking?—a terse form of 'What on earth are you talking about?', the abbreviated form no less succinct in meaning.

Singlish Acronyms
BGR—boy–girl relationship
CMI—cannot make it, resignation and despair
CAB—not referring to a taxi but meaning 'Chao Ah Beng' or 'Bad Ah Beng'.
KLK—*kwai lan kia* in Hokkien, meaning a troublesome child
KLKK—*kia lai kia ker* in Hokkien meaning to wander about aimlessly
NATO—definitely not the North Atlantic Treaty Organisation but meaning 'No Action, Talk Only', a derisive comment.
OCBC—not the bank but Overseas Chinese, Bukan Cheena, another derisive snort about not someone not being Chinese enough.
SBS—*si beh sian*, meaning extreme ennui in Hokkien
SPG—Sarong Party Girl, used to describe local girls, usually skimpily dressed, who only date Caucasians

Stir-fried and Not Shaken into the Future

I decamped to London in 1983 and only witnessed the incredible urban development and social and cultural evolution that Singapore underwent in fleeting bites when I returned for brief visits over the next two and half decades. Since then I have also got to grips with more Singlish and am now fairly proficient. I have also learnt to ask for a stored value ticket when I want a season ticket. I also ask, 'Go where?' instead of 'Where shall we go?'; 'Like that can die,' instead of 'I'd be better off dead.' When I left Singapore I spoke one language but when I returned I found I had to speak another just to be understood. In the time that I had been away, Singlish had really taken hold; English syntax became blurred by the government exhortation to learn Mandarin, and there was an entirely new sub-language forming. My return, while filled with excitement, was also fraught and full of confusion.

As a final note I bring closure to my historical memories from the 1940s up until the time I left Singapore in 1983. It is not, however, a closed door and I hope that I will continue to be robust enough to observe and record the passage of time and events for more publishable recollections. Perhaps in the year 2022, when I am 80, I might bring to light my memoirs of life in Britain over forty years. I should be so lucky to reach my eighth decade without arthritis. Perhaps computers will then operate on voice command. Until then, stay cool and don't be *kiasu*, man!